NEW YORK

AN ILLUSTRATED ANTHOLOGY

NEW YORK
AN ILLUSTRATED ANTHOLOGY

Compiled by Michael Marqusee

Introduction by
Jay McInerney

SALEM HOUSE PUBLISHERS
TOPSFIELD, MASSACHUSETTS

CONTENTS

First published in the United States by
Salem House Publishers, 1988,
462 Boston Street,
Topsfield, Massachusetts, 01983.

Project Editor: Emma Callery
Text Editor: Mary Davies
Picture Research: Nadine Bazar
Art Director: Mary Evans
Art Editor: Trevor Vincent
Editorial Assistant: Simon Willis

LC number 88-61184

ISBN 0 88162 349 0

Jacket Photograph: Zefa Picture Library
Typeset by SX Composing Limited
Printed and bound in Hong Kong

COMPILER'S NOTE

From the beginning, writers have seen New York as a city of contrasts and extremes. Rich and poor, sophisticated and naive, eccentric and conformist, awesomely magnificent and brutally squalid. One after another, they line up to speak of New York as the most, the least, the best, the worst, the first, the last ... For Walt Whitman, the city was an inexhaustible poetic subject simply because it contained everything. In its sheer scale and diversity was concentrated the whole human experience.

In New York, Whitman found unlikely things to love – 'numberless crowded streets, high growths of iron' – and poets like Hart Crane and Frank O'Hara have followed suit. Adoptive New Yorkers O. Henry, F. Scott Fitzgerald, and Thomas Wolfe set their scenes in Maxim Gorki's 'city of the yellow devil' and showed their characters enmeshed in its greed-fueled machinery.

New York is and always has been self-absorbed. Nearly every New Yorker has an opinion about the city, and visitors may have been overwhelmed by it but rarely silenced. As a result, dozens of anthologies could be compiled from all that has been said and written on the subject. I have tried in this one to include not only samples of the best writing about the city but also some representation of the diverse types of life lived within its confines.

In this book, loyal natives (Whitman, Lewis Mumford) rub shoulders with passing strangers (Mark Twain, G. K. Chesterton). Here New York is not merely Manhattan (and usually reduced to a mid-town patch at that) but all five boroughs and countless ever-shifting neighbourhoods. Here the reader will find the world-renowned glamour and celebrity, but also the struggle for survival, for dignity, for democracy that has gone on uninterrupted since the Dutch seized the place from Native Americans three hundred and fifty years ago.

I have tried to respect the original form of the writings included here, which is why the reader will find both English and American spellings in the text. The main aim has been to help people look afresh at the 'supreme metropolis of the present,' to remind them of its familiar attractions and introduce them to some of its forgotten history.

MICHAEL MARQUSEE

INTRODUCTION

BY JAY McINERNEY

Last night I had dinner in a Manhattan restaurant with five New Yorkers – a novelist from Los Angeles, two editors from Nashville, Tennessee and Salem, Oregon respectively, an entertainment lawyer from London, England and a fashion model from Independence, Missouri. If asked, on holiday, where they come from, I have no doubt they would all answer New York. I too am an adoptive New Yorker. I spent the first twenty two years of my life elsewhere but I consider the island of Manhattan my hometown and I would go so far as to argue that the real New Yorkers are not those born and raised here, but rather the restless and ambitious provincials and foreigners attuned to the irresistable music of the metropolis – those excitable boys and girls who don't want to miss the ball. Here in America birth is not supposed to confer special priveleges and I see no reason to credit the taste or intelligence of those whose parents were wise enough to choose New York in which to spawn them.

Perhaps the greatest virtue of the city is that anyone can choose to call it home. I believe it takes approximately three months to become a New Yorker, although for some reason – a sort of special dispensation – it requires only three days or four days after debarking from either Haiti or the Soviet Union to become a New York cab driver. America proper may be a melting pot, but in New York there's little pressure to blend; nothing, and no one, is heterogeneous on the streets of Manhattan. You don't need to speak the language so long as you can count in dollars and cents. You won't be judged by your accent, but you will be judged by your shoes. Appearances count here. So look sharp.

Quintessentially American in its porousness, its broad democratic mien, its belief in the new and the fast and the dollar – New York is also a place which all other Americans regard with fear and loathing born out of combined envy and good common sense. Most red-blooded Americans consider New York a foreign capital – a combination of Babel, Sodom and Gommorah – and there is much to be said for this view. New York doesn't quite belong on such a young and psychologically rural continent. If there were truth in geography the island of Manhattan would be located out in the Gulf Stream about a thousand miles to the east. Not a European city, but not quite American either.

The product of a peripatetic childhood – bounced around Europe, Canada, and various corners of the United States – I considered myself stateless until I moved to Manhattan as a young adult. From the Williamsburg bridge, coming in by taxi from Kennedy airport, I thought the needle-nosed Chrysler and Empire State buildings looked like rocketships to glory. Like Dick Whttington, I would not have been entirely surprised to find the streets of my dream metropolis lined with gold and in fact, the first day I prowled the sidewalks of New York the concrete under my feet flashed and sparkled in the sunlight as if embedded with millions of tiny diamonds – a phenomenon I have observed many times since and which I call St Arno's fire, in honor of the *bon vivant*, New Yorker cartoonist and patron saint of the high life Peter Arno. I'm sure it happens elsewhere, and has to do with no doubt with quartz in the concrete or something, but I don't want to know about it. That day the streets were lined with diamonds and beautiful women moving rapidly toward glamorous engagements and I knew that I had come home for the first time in my life.

Ten years later, it is harder to ignore the beggars and bag ladies, the penniless, the limbless, the homeless and the hopeless here in the city of gross expectations. The fact is there are more of them. And the brash yellow sunlight indigenous to the canyons of Manhattan is being choked out by increasingly tall, dense thickets of concrete and glass shafts as the Mammon worship to which this city is a monument reaches a new pitch of fanaticism. But a perusal of this anthology cofirms that New York has always been too rich, too poor, too tall, too fast, too big, too loud, too dangerous. It is a city of excesses. And I can't seem to live anywhere else. Even at this late date, as the American Empire slouches into decline, New York seems to me to be the exact center of the world.

FIRST IMPRESSIONS

In 1827, FRANCES TROLLOPE, *mother of the novelist Anthony Trollope, left Britain with her husband for a new life on an Ohio farm. Their farming venture was a fiasco, but Mrs Trollope's vivid account of the New World,* Domestic Manners of the Americans, *published in 1832, was an international success.*

I have never seen the bay of Naples, I can therefore make no comparison, but my imagination is incapable of conceiving any thing of the kind more beautiful than the harbour of New York. Various and lovely are the objects which meet the eye on every side, but the naming them would only be to give a list of words, without conveying the faintest idea of the scene. I doubt if ever the pencil of Turner could do it justice, bright and glorious as it rose upon us. We seemed to enter the harbour of New York upon waves of liquid gold, and as we darted past the green isles which rise from its bosom, like guardian sentinels of the fair city, the setting sun stretched his horizontal beams farther and farther at each moment, as if to point out to us some new glory in the landscape.

. . . I think New York one of the finest cities I ever saw, and as much superior to every other in the Union (Philadelphia not excepted), as London to Liverpool, or Paris to Rouen. Its advantages of position are, perhaps, unequalled anywhere. Situated on an island, which I think it will one day cover, it rises like Venice, from the sea, and like that fairest of cities in the days of her glory, receives into its lap tribute of all the riches of the earth.

RICHARD COBDEN, *British politician and reformer, visited New York in 1835, at the age of thirty-one, and noted his immediate impressions in his diary.*

. . . beauty of the bay of New York as it opens out – *Never-Sink* the small hilly spot opposite highest land on the sea-board of the States – the bay would be more interesting if the shores were loftier like Naples or the Bosphorus – pass the narrows & enter the inner bay – beauty of this surpasses the other – number of small pleasure boats with young men taking excusions – Steam boats full of passengers – Staten Island on left with quarantine station a large building (in the distance reminding one of Somerset House or Greenwhich) close to the shore – Hoboken to the right on the East river – to the left the Hudson with the heights of the Hudson in the distance – the scene all round animated by the appearance of the small white houses erected on the shores – What beauty will this inner bay of New York present centuries hence when wealth & commerce shall have done their utmost to embellish this scene!

CHARLES DICKENS *toured America in 1842. He recounted his arrival in New York in* American Notes, *published later the same year.*

Then there lay stretched out before us, to the right, confused heaps of buildings, with here and there a spire or steeple, looking down upon the herd below; and here and there, again, a cloud of lazy smoke; and in the foreground a forest of ships' masts, cheery with flapping sails and waving flags. Crossing from among them to the opposite shore, were steam ferry-boats laden with people, coaches, horses, waggons, baskets, boxes: crossed and recrossed by other ferry-boats: all travelling to and fro: and never idle. Stately among these restless Insects, were two or three large ships, moving with slow majestic pace, as creatures of a prouder kind, disdainful of their puny journeys, and making for the broad sea. Beyond, were shining heights, and islands in the glancing river, and a distance scarcely less blue and bright than

'Breezy Day, New York Harbor' – painting by William Glackens, c. 1910.

the sky it seemed to meet. The city's hum and buzz, the clinking of capstans, the ringing of bells, the barking of dogs, the clattering of wheels, tingled in the listening ear. All of which life and stir, coming across the stirring water, caught new life and animation from its free companionship; and, sympathising with its buoyant spirits, glistened as it seemed in sport upon its surface, and hemmed the vessel round, and plashed the water high about her sides, and, floating her gallantly into the dock, flew off again to welcome other comers, and speed before them to the busy port.

I t was silent, the city of my dreams, marble and serene, due perhaps to the fact that in reality I knew nothing of crowds, poverty, the winds and storms of the inadequate that blow like dust along the paths of life. It was an amazing city, so far-flung, so beautiful, so dead. There were tracks of iron stalking through the air, and streets that were as canyons, and stairways that mounted in vast flights to noble plazas, and steps that led down into deep places where

In 1894, future novelist THEODORE DREISER *arrived penniless in New York. He recalled the city's impact in his essay 'The Color of a Great City' (1923).*

were, strangely enough, underworld silences. And there were parks and flowers and rivers. And then, after twenty years, here it stood, as amazing almost as my dream, save that in the waking the flush of life was over it. It possessed the tang of contests and dreams and enthusiasms and delights and terrors and despairs. Through its ways and canyons and open spaces and underground passages were running, seething, sparkling, darkling, a mass of beings such as my dream-city never knew.

The Russian social critic, novelist and playwright MAXIM GORKI arrived in New York after he was exiled from Czarist Russia for his participation in the failed Revolution of 1905. Socialists in New York prepared a gala reception but the newspapers lambasted him, dwelling particularly on the fact that he was not then married to the woman he was living with. He was evicted from his hotel, spurned by the literary notables of the day, and subsequently wrote a damning account of New York in The City of the Yellow Devil *(1906).*

Over earth and ocean hangs a fog well mixed with smoke, and a fine slow rain is falling over the dark buildings of the city and the muddy waters of the roadstead.

The immigrants gather at the ship's side and gaze silently about them with the curious eyes of hope and apprehension, fear and joy.

'Who's that?' a Polish girl asks softly, staring in wonder at the Statue of Liberty.

'The American god,' someone replies.

The massive figure of the bronze woman is covered from head to foot with verdigris. The cold face stares blindly through the fog, out to the wastes of ocean, as though the bronze is waiting for the sun to bring sight to its sightless eyes. There is very little ground under Liberty's feet, she appears to rise from the ocean on a pedestal of petrified waves. Her arm, raised aloft over the ocean and the masts of the ships, gives a proud majesty and beauty to her pose. The torch so tightly gripped in her hand seems about to burst into a bright flame, driving away the grey smoke and bathing all around in fierce and joyous light.

And around that insignificant strip of land on which she stands, huge iron vessels glide over the waters like prehistoric monsters, and tiny launches dart about like hungry beasts of prey. Sirens wail, angry whistles shrill, anchor chains clang, and the ocean waves grimly slap against the shore.

Everything is running, hurrying, vibrating tensely. The screws and paddles of the steamers rapidly thresh the water which is covered with a yellow foam and seamed with wrinkles.

Slowly the steamer makes her way through the throng of vessels. The faces of the immigrants look strangely grey and dull, with something of a sheeplike sameness about the eyes. Gathered at the ship's side, they stare in silence at the fog.

In this fog something incomprehensibly vast, emitting a hollow murmur, is born; it grows, its heavy odorous breath is carried to the people and its voice has a threatening and avid note.

This is a city. This is New York. Twenty-storeyed houses, dark soundless skyscrapers, stand on the shore. Square, lacking in any desire to be beautiful, the bulky, ponderous buildings tower gloomily and drearily. A haughty pride in its height, and its ugliness is felt in each house. There are no flowers at the windows and no children to be seen . . .

From this distance the city seems like a vast jaw, with uneven black teeth. It breathes clouds of black smoke into the sky and puffs like a glutton suffering from his obesity.

Entering the city is like getting into a stomach of stone and iron, a stomach that has swallowed several million people and is grinding and digesting them.

Design for Statue of Liberty by Auguste Bartholdi.

The small white steamer, *Peter Stuyvesant*, that delivered the immigrants from the stench and throb of the steerage to the stench and the throb of New York tenements, rolled slightly on the water beside the stone quay in the lee of the weathered barracks and new brick buildings of Ellis Island...

It was May of the year 1907, the year that was destined to bring the greatest number of immigrants to the shores of the United States. All that day, as on all the days since spring began, her decks had been thronged by hundreds upon hundreds of foreigners, natives from almost evey land in the world, the jowled

HENRY ROTH *'s novel* Call It Sleep *(1934) tells the story of a Jewish immigrant family in New York in the early twentieth century.*

11

'Steerage' – by Alfred Stieglitz, 1907.

close-cropped Teuton, the full-bearded Russian, the scraggly-whiskered Jew, and among them Slovak peasants with docile faces, smooth-cheeked and swarthy Armenians, pimply Greeks, Danes with wrinkled eyelids. All day her decks had been colourful, a matrix of the vivid costumes of other lands, the speckled green-and-yellow aprons, the flowered kerchief, embroidered homespun, the silver-braided sheepskin vest, the gaudy scarfs, yellow boots, fur caps, caftans, dull gabardines. All day the guttural, the high-pitched voices, the astonished cries, the gasps of wonder, reiterations of gladness had risen from her decks in a motley billow of sound. But now her decks were empty, quiet, spreading out under the sunlight almost as if the warm boards were relaxing from the strain and the pressure of the myriads of feet. All those steerage passengers of the ships that had docked that day who were permitted to enter had already entered – except two, a woman and a young child she carried in her arms. They had just come aboard escorted by a man.

About the appearance of these late comers there was very little that was unusual. The man had evidently spent some time in America and was now bringing his wife and child over from the other side. It might have been thought that he had spent most of his time in lower New York, for he paid only the scantest attention to the Statue of Liberty or to the city rising from the water or to the bridges spanning the East River – or perhaps he was merely too agitated to waste time on these wonders. . .

The truth was there was something quite untypical about their behaviour. The old peddler woman on the bench and the overalled men in the stern had seen enough husbands meeting their wives and children after a long absence to know how such people ought to behave. The most volatile races, such as the Italians, often danced for joy, whirled each other around, pirouetted in an ecstasy; Swedes sometimes just looked at each other, breathing through open mouths like a panting dog; Jews wept, jabbered, almost put each other's eyes out with the recklessness of their darting gestures; Poles roared and gripped each other at arm's length as though they meant to tear a handful of flesh; and after one pecking kiss, the English might be seen gravitating towards, but never achieving an embrace. But these two stood silent, apart; the man staring with aloof, offended eyes grimly down at the water – or if he turned his face towards his wife at all, it was only to glare in harsh contempt at the blue straw hat worn by the child in her arms, and then his hostile eyes would sweep about the deck to see if anyone else were observing them. And his wife beside him regarding him uneasily, appealingly. And the child against her breast looking from one to the other with watchful, frightened eyes. Altogether it was a very curious meeting.

They had been standing in this strange and silent manner for several minutes, when the woman, as if driven by the strain into action, tried to smile, and touching her husband's arm said timidly, 'And this is the Golden Land.' She spoke in Yiddish.

When the fourth day dawned even those who had spent the whole trip cooped up in their cabins showed up on deck. We saw the lights of New York even before the morning mist rose. As the boat entered the harbor the sky was clear and clean. The excitement grew the closer we got to the docks. We recognized the Statue of Liberty in the distance. Countless smaller

On the eve of the First World War, BERNARDO VEGA sailed into New York harbour, an impoverished but hopeful immigrant from

rural Puerto Rico. He was later to become a leading political and cultural figure in New York's Puerto Rican community, and recalled his odyssey in his Memoirs, *(1984).*

boats were sailing about in the harbor. In front of us rose the imposing sight of skyscrapers – the same skyline we had admired so often on postcards. Many of the passengers had only heard talk of New York, and stood with their mouths open, spellbound . . . Finally the *Coamo* docked at Hamilton Pier on Staten Island.

First to disembark were the passengers traveling first class – businessmen, well-to-do families, students. In second class, where I was, there were the emigrants, most of us *tabaqueros*, or cigar workers. We all boarded the ferry that crossed from Staten Island to lower Manhattan. We sighed as we set foot on solid ground. There, gaping before us, were the jaws of the iron dragon: the immense New York metropolis.

All of us new arrivals were well dressed. I mean, we had on our Sunday best. I myself was wearing a navy blue woolen suit (or *flus*, as they would say back home), a borsalino hat made of Italian straw, black shoes with pointy toes, a white vest, and a red tie. I would have been sporting a shiny wristwatch too, if

'Times Square Sector' – etching by Howard Cook, 1931.

a traveling companion hadn't warned me that in New York it was considered effeminate to wear things like that. So as soon as the city was in sight, and the boat was entering the harbor, I tossed my watch into the sea . . . And to think that it wasn't long before those wristwatches came into fashion and ended up being the rage!

And so I arrived in New York, without a watch.

The Battery, which as I found out later is what they call the tip of lower Manhattan where our ferry from Staten Island docked, was also a port of call for all the elevated trains. The Second, Third, Sixth, and Ninth Avenue lines all met there. I entered the huge station with Ambrosio Fernández, who had come down to meet me at the dock. The noise of the trains was deafening, and I felt as if I was drowning in the crowd. Funny, but now that I was on land I started to feel seasick. People were rushing about every which way, not seeming to know exactly where they were headed. Now and then one of them would cast a mocking glance at the funny-looking travelers with their suitcases and other baggage. Finally there I was in a subway car, crushed by the mobs of passengers, kept afloat only by the confidence I felt in the presence of my friend.

The train snaked along at breakneck speed. I pretended to take note of everything, my eyes like the golden deuce in a deck of Spanish cards. The further along we moved, and as the dingy buildings filed past my view, all the visions I had of the gorgeous splendor of New York vanished. The skyscrapers seemed like tall gravestones. I wondered why, if the United States was so rich, as surely it was, did its biggest city look so grotesque? At that moment I sensed for the first time that people in New York could not possibly be as happy as we used to think they were back home in Cayey.

FRIEND AL: I opened the serious here and beat them easy but I know you must of saw about it in the Chi papers. At that they don't give me no fair show in the Chi papers. One of the boys bought one here and I seen in it where I was lucky to win that game in Cleveland. If I knowed which one of them reporters wrote that I would punch his jaw.

Al I told you Boston was some town but this is the real one. I never seen nothing like it and I been going some since we got here. I walked down Broadway the Main Street last night and I run into a couple of the ball players and they took me to what they call the Garden but it ain't like the gardens at home because this one is indoors. We sat down to a table and had several drinks. Pretty soon one of the boys asked me if I was broke and I says No, why? He says You better get some lubricating oil and loosen up. I don't know what he meant but pretty soon when we had had a lot of drinks the waiter brings a check and hands it to me. It was for one dollar. I says Oh I ain't paying for all of them. The waiter says This is just for that last drink.

I thought the other boys would make a holler but they didn't say nothing. So I give him a dollar bill and even then he didn't act satisfied so I asked him what he was waiting for and he said Oh nothing, kind of sassy. I was going to bust him but the boys give me the sign to shut up and not to say nothing. I excused myself pretty soon because I wanted to get some air. I give my check for my hat to a boy and he brought my hat and I started going and he says Haven't you forgot something? I guess he must of thought I was wearing a overcoat.

In RING LARDNER *'s comic novel,* You Know Me Al, *(1916), the hero, a baseball pitcher from the sticks named Jack Keefe, narrates what he obstinately believes to be his triumphs in the Big Leagues in letters to his old hometown friend Al.*

15

Then I went down the Main Street again and some man stopped me and asked me did I want to go to the show. He said he had a ticket. I asked him what show and he said the Follies. I never heard of it but I told him I would go if he had a ticket to spare. He says I will spare you this one for three dollars. I says You must take me for some boob. He says No I wouldn't insult no boob. So I walks on but if he had of insulted me I would of busted him.

I went back to the hotel then and run into Kid Gleason. He asked me to take a walk with him so out I go again. We went to the corner and he bought me a beer. He don't drink nothing but pop himself. The two drinks was only ten cents so I says This is the place for me. He says Where have you been? and I told him about paying one dollar for three drinks. He says I see I will have to take charge of you. Don't go round with them ball players no more. When you want to go out and see the sights come to me and I will stear you. So to-night he is going to stear me. I will write to you from Philadelphia. *Your pal, Jack.*

Born in Missouri, the poet LANGSTON HUGHES emigrated to New York (by ship from the Gulf of Mexico) in the early twenties. He recalled the moment in his autobiography, The Big Sea *(1940).*

At last! New York was pretty, rising out of the bay in the sunset – the thrill of those towers of Manhattan with their million golden eyes, growing slowly taller and taller above the green water, until they looked as if they could almost touch the sky! Then Brooklyn Bridge, gigantic in the dusk! Then the necklaces of lights, glowing everywhere around us, as we docked on the Brooklyn side. All this made me feel it was better to come to New York than to any other city in the world.

I didn't know how to get to Harlem or where to stay after I got there, so I went that night with two Mexican friends I'd met on the boat, to a hotel off Times Square. One was a young mechanic, coming to take a course at an automobile school in Detroit and he kept saying, as the taxi carried us up town: 'But where are all the poor people? *Caramba!* Every one is dressed up here! Everybody wears shoes!' The other friend was an old man, coming to live with his son's family in Jersey. He kept saying: 'Where is the grass? Where will I keep my chickens? *Puta madre!* Is there no grass?' He had brought along a crate of game cocks, which he refused to surrender even to the bell boy in the crowded lobby of the hotel.

It was a gyp-joint hotel, between Broadway and Sixth. The clerk declared all their rooms came in suites, and he rented us a suite at nine dollars a day, each. We didn't want a suite. And we didn't want to pay nine dollars, but we didn't know where else to go that night, so we paid it, and each of us slept in an enormous bed, in an apartment that looked out onto a noisy street off the Great White Way.

Toward morning, the old man's chickens began to crow and woke me up, so we had breakfast early, shook hands, promised to write each other, and went our separate ways. I took the subway to Harlem and never saw either of them again.

Swiss architect LE CORBUSIER visited New York in 1936 and recorded his first impressions in When the Cathedrals Were White *(1944).*

Monday morning, when my ship stopped at Quarantine, I saw a fantastic, almost mystic city rising up in the mist. But the ship moves forward and the apparition is transformed into an image of incredible brutality and savagery. Here is certainly the most prominent manifestation of the power of modern times. This brutality and this savagery do not displease me. It is thus that great enterprises begin: by strength.

Not until we were sailing through the Jersey countryside did my spirits begin to rise. Then my old confidence and optimism revived, and I tried to plan my time in the North. I would work hard . . .

I dreamed with my eyes gazing blankly upon the landscape until I looked up to see a Red Cap frowning down. 'Buddy, are you getting off?' he said. 'If so, you better get started.'

'Oh, sure,' I said, beginning to move. 'Sure, but how do you get to Harlem?'

'That's easy,' he said. 'You just keep heading north.'

And while I got down my bags and my prize brief case, still as shiny as the night of the battle royal, he instructed me how to take the subway, then I struggled through the crowd.

Moving into the subway I was pushed along by the milling salt-and-pepper mob, seized in the back by a burly, blue-uniformed attendant about the size of Supercargo, and crammed, bags and all, into a train that was so crowded that everyone seemed to stand with his head back and his eyes bulging, like chickens frozen at the sound of danger. Then the door banged behind me and I was crushed against a huge woman in black who shook her head and smiled while I stared with horror at a large mole that arose out of the oily whiteness of her skin like a black mountain sweeping out of a rainwet plain. And all the while I could feel the rubbery softness of her flesh against the length of my body. I could neither turn sideways nor back away, nor set down my bags. I was trapped, so close that simply by nodding my head, I might have brushed her lips with mine. I wanted desperately to raise my hands to show her that it was against my will. I kept expecting her to scream, until finally the car lurched and I was able to free my left arm. I closed my eyes, holding desperately to my lapel. The car roared and swayed, pressing me hard against her, but when I took a furtive glance around no one was paying me the slightest attention. And even she seemed lost in her thoughts. The train seemed to plunge downhill now, only to lunge to a stop that shot me out upon a platform feeling like something regurgitated from the belly of a frantic whale. Wrestling with my bags, I swept along with the crowd, up the stairs into the hot street. I didn't care where I was, I would walk the rest of the way.

For a moment I stood before a shop window staring at my own reflection in the glass, trying to recover from the ride against the woman. I was limp, my clothing wet. 'But you're up North now,' I told myself, 'up North.' Yes, but suppose she had screamed . . . The next time I used the subway I'd always be sure to enter with my hands grasping my lapels and I'd keep them there until I left the train. Why, my God, they must have riots on those things all the time. Why hadn't I read about them?

I had never seen so many black people against a background of brick buildings, neon signs, plate glass and roaring traffic – not even on trips I had made with the debating team to New Orleans, Dallas or Birmingham. They were everywhere. So many, and moving along with so much tension and noise that I wasn't sure whether they were about to celebrate a holiday or join in a street fight. There were even black girls behind the counters of the Five and Ten as I passed. Then at the street intersection I had the shock of seeing a black policeman directing traffic – and there were white drivers in the traffic who obeyed his signals as though it was the most natural thing in the world. Sure I had heard of it, but this was *real*. My courage returned. This really was

The anonymous black hero of RALPH ELLISON*'s novel* Invisible Man *(1952) arrives in New York by train, fresh from a life spent in the segregated South.*

'New York, 1959' – photograph by Henri Cartier-Bresson.

17

Harlem, and now all the stories which I had heard of the city-within-a-city leaped alive in my mind ... For me this was not a city of realities, but of dreams; perhaps because I had always thought of my life as being confined to the South. And now as I struggled through the lines of people a new world of possibility suggested itself to me faintly, like a small voice that was barely audible in the roar of city sounds. I moved wide-eyed, trying to take the bombardment of impressions.

The English critic
CYRIL CONNOLLY *visited his expatriate friend W. H. Auden ('Wystan') in New York shortly after the Second World War. His first impressions are preserved in his book* Ideas and Places *(1953).*

Up at six to see New York in the darkness – sunrise, the Narrows, the first houses, the ferries, *l'aurore rose et verte*, the Statue of Liberty, skyscrapers in fog, general impression much more European than I had expected ... Tony and Wystan are there and we go off to lunch. Auden warns us of the perils of the big city, he seems obsessed with hold-ups, the proper use of the subway system, and with jumping to it at the traffic lights; his welcome is like that of the town mouse to the country mouse in the Disney film. I discover only later that his battle with the traffic lights is a kind of personal obsession with the machine age, a challenge to his desire to pass efficiently in the crowd. Hugging our wallets tightly and plunging over the crossings we proceed in short rushes to the Holliday bookshop, an oasis where carefully chosen books are sold like handmade cushions; here Wystan introduces the two new mice and leaves us, with instructions on how to take the subway back...

The new mice compare notes. Peter says the U.S.A. is a place where only the very rich can be the least different from anyone else, but where the poor are not crushed and stunted (as in England, where the upper class is twice as tall as the lower). Here, he said, the poor are picturesque and often beautiful – the true creators of the American dream – and that there was also a great poetry about the country where one travelled over it. On the other hand it was awful seeing nothing but copies – of buildings, houses, furniture, pictures, and where the originals were in private hands they gave no intimacy. I found the skyscrapers depressing, a huge black ferro-concrete architecture of necessity shutting out the light from the treeless streets.

TOM WOLFE, *born in Virginia in 1931, is the author of* The Electric Kool-Acid Test, The Kandy Kolored Tangerine Flake Streamline Baby, The Bonfire of the Vanities *and* In Our Time *(1980) in which this newcomer's vision of the city appears.*

Oh, to be young and come to New York and move into your first loft and look at the world with eyes that light up even the rotting fire-escape railings, even the buckling pressed-tin squares on the ceiling, even the sheet-metal shower stall with its belly dents and rusting seams, the soot granules embedded like blackheads in the dry rot of the window frames, the basin with the copper-green dripping-spigot stains in the cracks at the bottom, the door with its crowbar-notch history of twenty-five years of break-ins, the canvas-bottom chairs that cut off the circulation in the sural arteries of the leg, the indomitable roach that appears every morning in silhouette on the cord of the hot plate, the doomed yucca straining for light on the windowsill, the two cats nobody ever housebroke, the garbage trucks with the grinder whine, the leather freaks and health-shoe geeks, the punkers with chopped hair and Korean warm-up jackets, the herds of Uptown Boutique bohemians who arrive every weekend by radio-call cab, the bag ladies who sit on the standpipes swabbing the lesions on their ankles – oh, to be young and in New York and to have eyes that light up all things with the sweetest and most golden glow!

If we couldn't drink at Fitchton Academy, we could at least plan how and when we would drink away from school. Felix and I planned two big luncheons, which were becoming more like lost weekends. The first was to take place over Christmas vacation at Felix's place in New York City. I was excited. I had never been to New York City before, and Felix had told me it was easy to get served there. They often didn't ask for ID. Besides, his father would take us out to all the clubs.

What I wasn't prepared for were his parents and the way they lived. I'd never seen anything like it before. They lived in a hotel and drank an awful lot. They claimed to be looking for an apartment but never got around to finding one, so they were paying some huge daily fee to live in the Henry Hudson Hotel. I mean, it wasn't even a residential hotel. They'd stay in their rooms, watch TV, and order from room service. Felix's father was on some crazy diet where he'd order steak from room service, chew it 40 times till he got all the flavor out of it, then throw the pulp out the twenty-second-storey window. Felix's mother was a beer alcoholic, and it didn't take much to get her off. She'd hide bottles of Miller High Life all over the three-room suite.

The place was a nuthouse. When I arrived his father was standing in a scattered pile of sheet music, dressed only in his boxer shorts. He had run out of inspiration and was just standing there waiting to be inspired. He acted like W. C. Fields and kept muttering little phrases like, 'My wife, poor wretch' and 'Sucking mule!'

Felix's parents had both grown up in Iowa, where his father had studied music. He won a thousand-dollar prize for an original composition for bassoon and with that money he and his wife moved to New York City. It looked to me like New York had been their undoing. They both hated cities and didn't like to go out of the hotel. They seemed liked each other's albatross. There were no clocks in their hotel rooms, but Felix's mother said she could tell time by the flow of traffic on Eighth Avenue.

Because there wasn't room at the Henry Hudson, Felix's father put us in our own room at the Hotel Chelsea on 23rd Street. From there we were able to rendezvous to go drinking with him. We'd start drinking in our room around noon and were pretty ripped by the time the traditional cocktail hour came around. By dinner time we'd end up at one of the restaurants with his father. We tried them all. Keene's Chophouse, The Round Table, and Eddie Condon's, which Felix said was the most important spot, because Eddie drank so much. The Top of the Sixes wouldn't let us in because we didn't have ties and jackets, and not even Felix's father's reputation helped. We even ended up at the White Horse Tavern on New Year's Eve. I remember that well because it was 1960 and a big fat man raised his glass and said, 'Here's to the sexy sixties.'

Actor and monologist SPALDING GRAY recalled his first trip to New York as a fresh-faced New England prep school boy in his 'Booze, Cars, and College Girls' (1986).

KNICKERBOCKER TALES

*The Florentine explorer
GIOVANNI DA VERAZZANO
became the first European to
land in the bay in April 1524.
Verazzano reported his
discoveries to his employer,
the French King François I.*

While at anchor on this coast, there being no harbour to enter, we sent the boat on shore with twenty-five men to obtain water, but it was not possible to land without endangering the boat, on account of the immense high surf thrown up by the sea, as it was an open roadstead. Many of the natives came to the beach, indicating by various friendly signs that we might trust ourselves on shore. One of their noble deeds of friendship deserves to be made known to your Majesty. A young sailor was attempting to swim ashore through the surf to carry them some knick-knacks, as little bells, looking glasses, and other like trifles; when he came near three yards of them he tossed the things to them, and turned about to get back to the boat, but he was thrown over by the waves, and so dashed by them that he lay as it were dead upon the beach. When these people saw him in his situation, they ran and took him up by the head, legs and arms, and carried him to a distance from the surf; the young man, finding himself borne off in this way, uttered very loud shrieks in fear and dismay, which they answered as they could in their language, showing him that he had no cause for fear. Afterwards they laid him down at the foot of a little hill, when they took off his shirt and trowsers, and examined him, expressing the greatest astonishment at the whiteness of his skin. Our sailors in the boat seeing a great fire made up, and their companion placed very near it, full of fear, as is usual in all cases of novelty, imagined that the natives were about to roast him for food. But as soon as he had recovered his strength after a short stay with them, showing by signs that he wished to return aboard, they hugged him with great affection, and accompanied him to the shore, then leaving him, that he might feel more secure, they withdrew to a little hill, from which they watched him until he was safe in the boat.

*The Dutch established a
colony on Manhattan Island
in the early seventeenth
century. JASPER DANCKAERTS,
a member of a Dutch
Protestant sect, visited
New Amsterdam in October
1679, and recorded his
impressions in his diary.*

We remained in the house during the forenoon, but after having dined we went out about two o'clock to explore the island of *Manathans*. . .

We went from the city, following the Broadway, over the valley, or the fresh water. Upon both sides of this way were many habitations of negroes, mulattoes and whites. These negroes were formerly the proper slaves of the [West India] company, but, in consequence of the frequent changes and conquests of the country, they have obtained their freedom and settled themselves down where they have thought proper, and thus on this road, where they have ground enough to live on with their families. We left the village, called the Bouwerij, lying on the right hand, and went through the woods to New Harlem, a tolerably large village situated on the south side of the island, directly opposite the place where the northeast creek and the East river come together, situated about three hours journey from New Amsterdam, like as Old Harlem, in Europe, is situated about three hours distance from old Amsterdam.

'Winter Scene in Brooklyn' – painting by Francis Guy, resident in Brooklyn, 1817-20.

The number of Inhabitants in this Province are about 3000 families whereof almost one halfe are naturally Dutch a great part English and the rest French . . . As to their Religion they are very much divided. few of them intelligent & sincere but the most part ignorant & conceited, fickle & regardless. As to their wealth & disposition thereto yᵉ Dutch are rich & sparing, the English neither very rich nor too great husbands, the French are poor and therefore forced to be penurious: As to their way of trade & dealing they are all generally cunning and crafty but many of them not so just to their words as they should be.

. . . [such is] the wickedness & irreligion of the inhabitants which abounds in all parts of the Province & appear in so many shapes constituting so many sorts of sin that I can scarce tell which to begin withall.

. . . [there are] many in the City of New York whose daily practice is to frequent the taverns & to Carouse & game their night imployment. This course is the ruine & destruction of many merchants especially those of the Younger sort who carrying over with them a stock whether as Factor's or on their own

JOHN MILLER *served as chaplain to the English garrison in New York, recently seized from the Dutch, from 1692 to 1695. On the return voyage to England in 1695 his ship was captured by French privateers and Miller was imprisoned at St Malo, France, where he wrote his account of the people and the province of New York.*

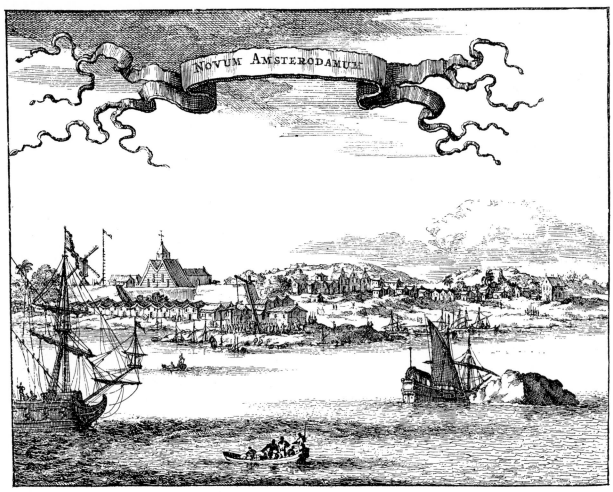

'The Dutch are rich and sparing' – New Amsterdam, 1671.

Account Spend even to prodigality till they find themselves bankrupt e'er they are aware.

In a town where this course of life is led by many tis no wonder if there be other vices in vogue because they are the naturall product of it such are cursing & Swearing to both of which People are here much accustomed some doing it in that frequent horrible & dreadfull manner as if they prided themselves both as to the number and invention of them this joyned with their profane Atheisticall & scoffing method of discourse makes their Company extreamly uneasy to sober & religious men who sometimes by reason of their affairs cannot help being of their society & becoming ear-witnesses of their blasphemy & folly. 'tis strange that men should ingage themselves so foolishly & run into ye Commission of so great a sin unto which they have no sufficient, often not a p^{r}tended, provocation & from which they reap no advantage nor any reall pleasure: & yet we see them even delight in it & no discourse is thought witty or eloquent except larded with oaths & execrations. . .

And the sage Oloffe dreamed a dream, – and lo, the good St Nicholas came riding over the tops of the trees, in that self-same wagon wherein he brings his yearly presents to children, and he descended hard by where the heroes of Communipaw had made their late repast. And he lit his pipe by the fire, and sat himself down and smoked; and as he smoked, the smoke from his pipe ascended into the air and spread like a cloud overhead. And Oloffe bethought him, and he hastened and climbed up to the top of one of the tallest trees, and saw that the smoke spread over a great extent of country; and as he considered it more attentively, he fancied that the great volume of smoke assumed a variety of marvellous forms, where in dim obscurity he saw shadowed out palaces and domes and lofty spires, all of which lasted but a moment, and then faded away, until the whole rolled off, and nothing but the green woods were left. And when St Nicholas had smoked his pipe, he twisted it in his hatband, and laying his finger beside his nose, gave the astonished Van Kortlandt a very significant look; then mounting his wagon, he returned over the treetops and disappeared.

And Van Kortlandt awoke from his sleep greatly instructed; and he aroused his companions and related his dream, and interpeted it, that it was the will of St Nicholas that they should settle down and build the city here; and that the smoke of the pipe was a type how vast would be the extent of the city, inasmuch as the volumes of its smoke would spread over a wide extent of country.

WASHINGTON IRVING *was the first internationally famous New York writer. A world traveller, the author of such tales as* Rip Van Winkle *and* The Legend of Sleepy Hollow, *Irving's first major work was an historical burlesque aimed at his fellow New Yorkers and published in 1809 under the pseudonym Diedrich Knickerbocker. In this excerpt from* A History of New York, *Knickerbocker recounts the dream of Oloffe Van Kortlandt, 'one of the first property speculators in these parts'.*

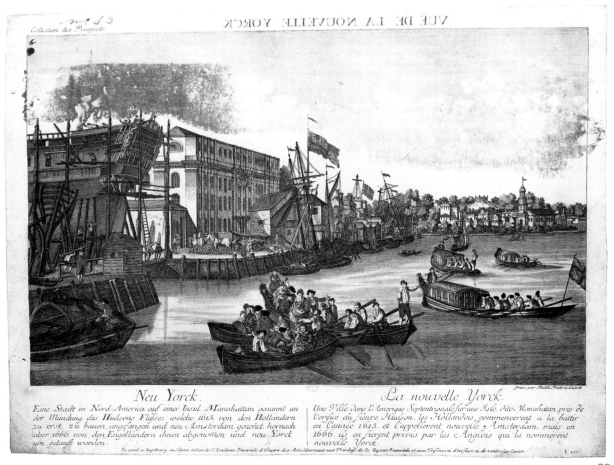

The English in New York, 1776.

And they all with one voice assented to this interpretation, excepting Mynheer Ten Broeck, who declared the meaning to be that it would be a city wherein a little fire would occasion a great smoke, or, in other words, a very vaporing little city; – both which interpretations have strangely come to pass!

The great object of their perilous expedition, therefore, being thus happily accomplished, the voyagers returned merrily to Communipaw – where they were received with great rejoicings. And here, calling a general meeting of all the wise men and the dignitaries of Pavonia, they related the whole history of their voyage, and of the dream of Oloffe Van Kortlandt. And the people lifted up their voices and blessed the good St Nicholas: and from that time forth the sage Van Kortlandt was held in more honor than ever, for his great talent at dreaming, and was pronounced a most useful citizen and a right good man – when he was asleep.

Poet and newspaper editor WILLIAM CULLEN BRYANT *re-created what was already thought of as 'old New York' in his 'Commemorative Address on Washington Irving' (1859).*

At the time that Washington Irving was born, the city of New York contained scarcely more than twenty thousand inhabitants. During the war its population had probably diminished. The town was scarcely built up to Warren Street; Broadway, a little beyond, was lost among grassy pastures and tilled fields; the Park, in which now stands our City Hall, was an open common; and beyond it gleamed, in a hollow among the meadows, a little sheet of fresh water, the Kolch, from which a sluggish rivulet stole through the low

Broadway and City Hall, 1819 – watercolour by Baron Axel Klinckowstrom.

grounds called Lispenard's Meadows, and, following the course of what is now Canal Street, entered the Hudson. With the exception of the little corner of the island below the present City Hall, the rural character of the whole region was unchanged, and the fresh air of the country entered New York at every street. The town at that time contained a mingled population, drawn from different countries; but the descendants of the old Dutch settlers formed a large proportion of the inhabitants, and these preserved many of their peculiar customs, and had not ceased to use the speech of their ancestors at their fireside. Many of them lived in the quaint old houses, built of small yellow bricks from Holland, with their notched gable-ends on the street, which have since been swept away with the language of those who built them . . .

. . . Those who know the island of New York as it now is, only see few traces of the beauty it wore before it was levelled and smoothed from side to side for the builder. Immediately without the little town it was charmingly diversified with heights and hollows, groves alternating with sunny openings, shining tracks of rivulets, quiet country-seats with trim gardens, broad avenues of trees, and lines of pleached hawthorn hedges. I came to New York in 1825, and I well recollect how much I admired the shores of the Hudson above Canal Street, where the dark rocks jutted far out into the water, with little bays between, above which drooped forest-trees overrun with wild vines. No less beautiful were the shores of the East River, where the orchards of the Stuyvesant estate reached to cliffs beetling over the water, and still farther on were inlets between rocky banks bristling with red cedars. Some idea of this beauty may be formed from looking at what remains of the natural shore of New York island, where the tides of the East River rush to and fro by the rocky verge of Jones's Wood.

Here wandered Irving in his youth, and allowed the aspect of that nature which he afterward portrayed so well to engrave itself on his heart; but his excursions were not confined to this island. He became familiar with the banks of the Hudson, the extraordinary beauty of which he was the first to describe. He made acquaintance with the Dutch neighborhoods sheltered by its hills — Nyack, Haverstraw, Sing Sing, and Sleepy Hollow, and with the majestic Highlands beyond. His rambles in another direction led him to ancient Communipaw, lying in its quiet recess by New York Bay; to the then peaceful Gowanus, now noisy with the passage of visitors to Greenwood and thronged with funerals; to Hoboken, Horsimus, and Paulus Hook, which has since become a city. A ferry-boat dancing on the rapid tides took him over to Brooklyn, now our flourishing and beautiful neighbor city; then a cluster of Dutch farms, whose possessors lived in broad, low houses, with stoops in front, overshadowed by trees.

Y ou will find that New York possesses the advantages of a capacious and excellent roadstead, a vast harbour, an unusually extensive natural basin, with two outlets to the sea, and a river that, in itself, might contain all the shipping of the earth. By means of the Sound, and its tributary waters, it has the closest connexion with the adjoining State of Connecticut; and, through the adjacent bays, small vessels penetrate in almost every direction into that of New Jersey. These are the channels by which the town receives its ordinary daily supplies . . .

American novelist JAMES FENIMORE COOPER *adopted the pseudonymous persona of a European aristocrat recounting his visit to the new American democracy in his* Notions of the Americans *(1828).*

New York stands central between the commerce of the north and that of the south. It is the first practicable port, at all seasons of the year, after you quit the mouth of the Chesapeake, going northward. It lies in the angle formed by the coast, and where the courses of Europe, to the West Indies, or to the Southern Atlantic, can be made direct. The ship from Virginia, or Louisiana, commonly passes within a day's sail of New York, on its way to Europe, and the coaster from Boston frequently stops at the wharfs of this city to deposit part of its freight before proceeding further south.

... in every great commercial community there is a tendency to create a common mart, where exchanges can be regulated, loans effected, cargoes vended in gross, and all other things connected with trade, transacted on a scale commensurate to the magnitude of the interests involved in its pursuits. The natural advantages of New York had indicated this port to the Americans for that spot, immediately after the restoration of the peace in 1783. Previously to that period, the whole proceedings of the colonies were more or less influenced by the policy of the mother country. But for a long time after the independence of the States was acknowledged, the possessors of the island of Manhattan had to contend for supremacy against a powerful rivalry. Philadelphia, distant less than a hundred miles, was not only more wealthy and more populous, but for many years it enjoyed the *éclat* and advantage of being the capital of the Union. Boston and Baltimore are both seaports of extensive connexions, and of great and enlightened enterprise. Against this serious competition, however, New York struggled with success; gradually obtaining the superiority in tonnage and inhabitants, until within a few years, when opposition silently yielded to the force of circumstances, and those towns which had so long been rivals became auxiliaries to her aggrandizement.

In the preface to his book Meyer Berger's New York *(1956), the veteran New York journalist reminded visitors that New York is a city with a long history, traces of which can still be found.*

Before you walk about New York you should know that a good bit of the city's history is written right into street signs. Visitors are seldom aware of that. The street called Wall, for example, actually had a wall. The Dutch ran it across the narrow part of Manhattan as protection against Indians. Broadway was, literally, The Broad Way. First it was an Indian path. The pioneers widened it for the carts they sent north, through the wall toward the upper island. In Maiden Lane almost 300 years ago, Dutch girls did the family wash in a stream that ran across the island there. At night they walked the lane with the village beaux who knew it as The Maiden's Path. A mill actually stood in Mill Street.

Up Marketfield Street (old Petticoat Lane) the Dutch women trudged to buy their cloth, meats, fish and vegetables from peddlers' carts. A canal once ran across Canal Street. Minetta Street follows the line of Minetta Brook. In Colonial times Cherry Street was a cherry orchard. Stone Street was New York's first paved street. The names of original farm owners on Manhattan Island crop up everywhere – Rutgers, Duane, Stuyvesant, Warren, Lispenard, Doyers, Pell. When you trace those names, you begin to get some hint of the early city and of the pioneers who built it. Your imagination can help you, then, to picture New York when it was pasture, orchard, meadow and dusty highway. The place wasn't always concrete and it wasn't always crowded. It just grew faster than any city in history.

One of the 'America Today' murals painted for the New School for Social Research in 1930/31 by Thomas Hart Benton.

THE CROWD

What hurrying human tides, or day or night!
What passions, winnings, losses, ardors, swim thy waters!
What whirls of evil, bliss and sorrow, stem thee!
What curious questioning glances – glints of love!
Leer, envy, scorn, contempt, hope, aspiration!
Thou portal – thou arena – thou of the myriad long-drawn lines and groups!
(Could but thy flagstones, curbs, façades, tell their inimitable tales;
Thy windows rich, and huge hotels – thy side-walks wide;)
Thou of the endless sliding, mincing, shuffling feet!
Thou, like the parti-colored world itself – like infinite, teeming, mocking life!
Thou visor'd, vast, unspeakable show and lesson!

Brooklyn-born poet
WALT WHITMAN *celebrated
the hordes of New York
in his poem 'Broadway'
(1880).*

27

'The crowd is something new . . .' – Times Square, 1937.

In 1843, at the age of twenty-five, poet and essayist HENRY THOREAU *visited New York, staying for several weeks with friends on Staten Island, then occupied by small, isolated rural and fishing villages. In this letter to his friend Ralph Waldo Emerson, Thoreau announced his discovery of 'something new' – the New York crowd.*

You must not count much upon what I can do or learn in New York. I feel a good way off here; and it is not to be visited, but seen and dwelt in. I have been there but once, and have been confined to the house since. Everything there disappoints me but the crowd; rather, I was disappointed with the rest before I came. I have no eyes for their churches, and what else they find to brag of. Though I know but little about Boston, yet what attracts me, in a quiet way, seems much meaner and more pretending than there, – libraries, pictures, and faces in the street. You don't know where any respectability inhabits. It is in the crowd in Chatham Street. The crowd is something new, and to be attended to. It is worth a thousand Trinity Churches and Exchanges . . . and will run over them and trample them under foot one day. There are two things I hear and am aware I live in the neighborhood of, – the roar of the sea and the hum of the city. I have just come from the beach (to find your letter), and I like it much. Everything there is on a grand and generous scale, – seaweed, water, and sand; and even the dead fishes, horses, and hogs have a rank, luxuriant odor; great shad-nets spread to dry; crabs and horseshoes crawling over the sand; clumsy boats, only for service, dancing like sea-fowl over the surf, and ships afar off going about their business.

Not in the solitude
Alone may man commune with heaven, or see
   Only in savage wood
And sunny vale, the present Deity;
   Or only hear his voice
Where the winds whisper and the waves rejoice.

   Even here do I behold
Thy steps, Almighty! – here, amidst the crowd,
   Through the great city rolled,
With everlasting murmur deep and loud –
   Choking the ways that wind
'Mongst the proud piles, the work of human kind.

   Thy golden sunshine comes
From the round heaven, and on their dwellings lies,
   And lights their inner homes;
For them thou fill'st with air the unbounded skies,
   And givest them the stores
Of ocean, and the harvests of its shores.

   Thy spirit is around,
Quickening the restless mass that sweeps along;
   And this eternal sound –
Voices and footfalls of the numberless throng –
   Like the resounding sea,
Or like the rainy tempest, speaks of thee.

   And when the hours of rest
Come, like a calm upon the mid-sea brine,
   Hushing its billowy breast –
The quiet of that moment too is thine;
   It breathes of Him who keeps
The vast and helpless city while it sleeps.

Poet and newspaper editor WILLIAM CULLEN BRYANT *lived and worked in New York for over fifty years. His 'Hymn to the City' was published in 1869.*

There now is your insular city of the Manhattoes, belted round by wharves as Indian isles by coral reefs – commerce surrounds it with her surf. Right and left, the streets take you waterward. Its extreme down-town is the Battery, where that noble mole is washed by waves, and cooled by breezes, which a few hours previous were out of sight of land. Look at the crowds of water-gazers there.

Circumambulate the city on a dreamy Sabbath afternoon. Go from Corlears Hook to Coenties Slip, and from thence, by Whitehall, northward. What do you see? – Posted like silent sentinels all around the town, stand thousands upon thousands of mortal men fixed in ocean reveries. Some leaning against the spiles; some seated upon the pier-heads; some looking over the bulwarks of ships from China; some high aloft in the rigging, as if striving to get a still better seaward peep. But these are all landsmen; of week days pent up in lath and plaster – tied to counters, nailed to benches, clinched to desks. How then is this? Are the green fields gone? What do they here?

But look! here come more crowds, pacing straight for the water, and seem-

In Moby Dick *(1851),* HERMAN MELVILLE, *a native New Yorker, described the Manhattan crowd's seemingly instinctive attraction to the surrounding waters.*

ingly bound for a dive. Strange! Nothing will content them but the extremest limit of the land; loitering under the shady lee of yonder warehouses will not suffice. No. They must get just as nigh the water as they possibly can without falling in. And there they stand – miles of them – leagues. Inlanders all, they come from lanes and alleys, streets and avenues – north, east, south, and west. Yet here they all unite. Tell me, does the magnetic virtue of the needles of the compasses of all those ships attract them thither?

THEODORE DREISER *described the ebb and flow of New York's working masses in 'The Color of a Great City' (1923).*

'the restless mass'

Have you ever arisen at dawn or earlier in New York and watched the outpouring in the meaner side-streets or avenues? It is a wondrous thing. It seems to have so little to do with the later, showier, brisker life of the day, and yet it has so very much. It is in the main so drab or shabby-smart at best, poor copies of what you see done more efficiently later in the day. Typewriter girls in almost stage or society costumes entering shabby offices; boys and men made up to look like actors and millionaires turning into the humblest institutions, where they are clerks or managers. These might be called the machinery of the city, after the elevators and street cars and wagons are excluded, the implements by which things are made to go.

Take your place on Williamsburg Bridge some morning, for instance, at say three or four o'clock, and watch the long, the quite unbroken line of Jews trundling pushcarts eastward to the great Wallabout Market over the bridge. A procession out of Assyria or Egypt or Chaldea, you might suppose, Biblical in quality; or, better yet, a huge chorus in some operatic dawn scene laid in Paris or Petrograd or here. A vast, silent mass it is, marching to the music of necessity. They are so grimy, so mechanistic, so elemental in their movements and needs. And later on you will find them seated or standing, with their little charcoal buckets or braziers to warm their hands and feet, in those gusty, icy streets of the East Side in winter, or coatless and almost shirtless in hot weather, open-mouthed for want of air. And they are New York, too – Bucharest and Lemberg and Odessa come to the Bowery, and adding rich, dark, colorful threads to the rug or tapestry which is New York.

Since these are but a portion, think of those other masses that come from the surrounding territory, north, south, east and west. The ferries – have you ever observed them in the morning? Or the bridges, railway terminals, and every elevated and subway exit?

Already at six and six-thirty in the morning they have begun to trickle small streams of human beings Manhattan or cityward, and by seven and seven-fifteen these streams have become sizable affairs. By seven-thirty and eight they have changed into heavy, turbulent rivers, and by eight-fifteen and eight-thirty and nine they are raging torrents, no less. They overflow all the streets and avenues and every available means of conveyance. They are pouring into all available doorways, shops, factories, office-buildings – those huge affairs towering so significantly above them. Here they stay all day long, causing those great hives and their adjacent streets to flush with a softness of color not indigenous to them, and then at night, between five and six, they are going again, pouring forth over the bridges and through the subways and across the ferries and out on the trains, until the last drop of them appears to have been exuded, and they are pocketed in some outlying side-street or village or metropolitan hall-room – and the great, turbulent night of the city is on once more.

I can never forget the East Side street where I lived as a boy.

It was a block from the notorious Bowery, a tenement canyon hung with fire-escapes, bed-clothing, and faces.

Always these faces at the tenement windows. The street never failed them. It was an immense excitement. It never slept. It roared like a sea. It exploded like fireworks.

People pushed and wrangled in the street. There were armies of howling pushcart peddlers. Women screamed, dogs barked and copulated. Babies cried.

A parrot cursed. Ragged kids played under truck-horses. Fat housewives fought from stoop to stoop. A beggar sang.

At the livery stable coach drivers lounged on a bench. They hee-hawed with laughter, they guzzled cans of beer.

Pimps, gamblers and red-nosed bums; peanut politicians, pugilists in sweaters; tinhorn sports and tall longshoremen in overalls. An endless pageant of East Side life passed through the wicker doors of Jake Wolf's saloon.

The saloon goat lay on the sidewalk, and dreamily consumed a *Police Gazette.*

East Side mothers with heroic bosoms pushed their baby carriages, gossiping. Horse cars jingled by. A tinker hammered at brass. Junkbells clanged.

Whirlwinds of dust and newspaper. The prostitutes laughed shrilly. A prophet passed, an old-clothes Jew with a white beard. Kids were dancing around the hurdy-gurdy. Two bums slugged each other.

Excitement, dirt, fighting, chaos! The sound of my street lifted like the blast of a great carnival or catastrophe. The noise was always in my ears. Even in sleep I could hear it; I can hear it now.

MICHAEL GOLD'S classic memoir, Jews Without Money *(1930), is filled with the pressing sights and sounds of the ghetto multitudes.*

Hardly a day goes by, you know, that some innocent bystander ain't shot in New York City. All you got to do is be innocent and stand by and they're gonna shoot you. The other day, there was four innocent people shot in one day – four innocent people – in New York City. Amazing. It's kind of hard to *find* four innocent people in New York.

In his popular thirties radio broadcasts, western humorist WILL ROGERS *often cast a jaundiced eye on big city life.*

'the cure of souls' Henry James

In DELMORE SCHWARTZ's *'Far Rockaway' (1939) the New York poet meditates on the great multitudes at play on one of the city's crowded beaches.*

The radiant soda of the seashore fashions
Fun, foam, and freedom. The sea laves
The shaven sand. And the light sways forward
On the self-destroying waves.

The rigor of the weekday is cast aside with shoes,
With business suits and the traffic's motion;
The lolling man lies with the passionate sun,
Or is drunken in the ocean.

A socialist health takes hold of the adult,
He is stripped of his class in the bathing-suit,
He returns to the children digging at summer,
A melon-like fruit.

O glittering and rocking and bursting and blue
– Eternities of sea and sky shadow no pleasure:
Time unheard moves and the heart of man is eaten
Consummately at leisure.

The novelist tangential on the boardwalk overhead
Seeks his cure of souls in his own anxious gaze.
'Here,' he says, 'With whom?' he asks, 'This?' he questions,
'What tedium, what blaze?'

'What satisfaction, fruit? What transit, heaven?
Criminal? justified? arrived at what June?'
That nervous conscience amid the concessions
Is a haunting, haunted moon.

'On the Street' – etching by Isabel Bishop, 1934.

Writer TRUMAN CAPOTE *defended the honour of a derided borough in his 'Brooklyn' (1946).*

As a group, Brooklynites form a persecuted minority; the uninventive persistence of not very urbane clowns has made any mention of their homeland a signal for compulsory guffaws; their dialect, appearance and manners have become, by way of such side-splitting propaganda, synonymous with the crudest, most vulgar aspects of contemporary life. All this, which perhaps began good-naturedly enough, has turned the razory road toward malice: an address in Brooklyn is now not altogether respectable. A peculiar irony, to be sure, for in this unfortunate region the average man, being on the edge of an outcast order, guards averageness with morbid intensity; he does, in fact, make of respectability a religion; still, insecurity makes for hypocrisy, and so he greets The Big Joke with the loudest hee-haw of all: 'Yaaah, ain't Brooklyn a kick – talk about funny!' Terribly funny, yes, but Brooklyn is also sad brutal provincial lonesome human silent sprawling raucous lost passionate subtle bitter immature innocent perverse tender mysterious, a place where Crane and Whitman found poems, a mythical dominion against whose shores the Coney Island sea laps a wintry lament. Here, scarcely anyone can give directions; nobody knows where anything is, even the oldest taxi driver seems uncertain; luckily, I've earned my degree in subway travel, though learning to ride these rails, which, buried in the stone, are like the veins found on fossilized fern, requires fiercer application, I'm sure, than working toward a master's. Rocking through the sunless, starless tunnels is an outward-bound feeling: the train, hurtling below unlikely land, seems destined for fog and mist, only the flash-by of familiar stations revealing our identities. Once, thundering under the river, I saw a girl, she was sixteen or so and being initiated into some sorority, I suspect, who carried a basket filled with little hearts cut from scarlet paper. 'Buy a lonely heart,' she wailed, passing through the car. 'Buy a lonely heart.' But the pale, expressionless passengers, none of whom needed one, merely flipped the pages of their *Daily News*.

Remember, when you're writing about New York,
Faces are as important as buildings.

Dive deep into the subway, that gallery of portraiture;
Bathe your eyes in that flood of bitter truth.
It is not lovely, it proves no theorems,
But there is no weariness it cannot heal.

Generalizers on human trouble,
Have you courage to face those faces?
You, and you, and you, seen only once,
Good-bye forever, and good luck.

The columnist and poet CHRISTOPHER MORLEY gives good advice for all students of the city in his poem 'When You're Writing'.

You ought to know a little about New York's millions that somehow doesn't reach the visitor through guide books and guided tours. They're not a special species. Around 98 per cent of them are simple folk living in curious provincialism in quiet flats and little houses 'way out beyond the glare and harshness of Times Square and the night-club belt. They pour into Manhattan Island from around 6 o'clock in the morning to around 9.30, to fill the skyscrapers, the factories, the department stores, and work at appointed tasks for eight hours, or more. At twilight the tide reverses and the subways, buses and ferries hurry them out again to Queens, to the Bronx, to Brooklyn, Staten Island.

They're not at their best in the morning and evening rush hours and you're not to judge them by their worried and harried look in those periods. If they push and crowd into the subways, it's because their jobs depend on their getting to them on time. If they huddle and jostle on the way out again, it's partly because suppers and families are waiting, or because there won't be too much time after shop or office closing to get home to change, eat, and keep a romantic date. Even courtship in a city of more than eight million often is hurried, except on week-ends.

You'll find, if you're in New York for more than a few days, that the mill-race way of living gets to be habit. You're a human chip in a fast-moving tide and by and by, without meaning to, you find you're accommodating your pace to the tempo.

Journalist MEYER BERGER was a familiar figure to millions of newspaper-addicted New Yorkers for over a generation. In Meyer Berger's New York *(1956) he urged visitors to take note of the ordinary people who make up this extraordinary community.*

'The glare and harshness of Times Square' – photograph by Louis Faurer.

People who come from less crowded cities are shocked when they first find themselves in the race. Those who can, flee from it. Men and women have written bitterly about it; have applied the literary quirt to New York and to its people. Some of this is justified, but mainly it comes from hasty judgment. Back in their own homes city dwellers are normal folk, content with normal living. They follow humble, normal family routines. On the Sabbath, when the work-a-day pace lets up, they put on their Sunday best as people in small towns do, to wend their way to quiet devotions in over 3,000 city churches. If you go to a neighborhood church in one of the outlying districts, you'll get the peaceful feel of it.

If you wander into Greenwich Village and come across men and women who affect Bohemian dress and the Bohemian manner, don't go away with the impression that they alone represent New York. The visitor from Flatbush and from Hunt's Point in the Bronx find them as strange as you do. If you stroll on the East Side of town and marvel at the splendor of specialty shops and at penthouses, be-furred matrons, pampered dogs, chauffeur-driven limousines and expensive restaurants, you ought to know that the stenographer from Brooklyn's Bushwick district and the clerk from Staten Island's Tottenville find them as extraordinary as you do. If you enter higher-priced night clubs and recoil from menu prices you can safely figure that 99 per cent of the city's eight million would react the same way.

There are roughly three New Yorks. There is, first, the New York of the man or woman who was born here, who takes the city for granted and accepts its size and its turbulence as natural and inevitable. Second, there is the New York of the commuter – the city that is devoured by locusts each day and spat out each night. Third, there is the New York of the person who was born somewhere else and came to New York in quest of something. Of these three trembling cities the greatest is the last – *the city of final destination, the city that is a goal*. It is this third city that accounts for New York's high-strung disposition, its poetical deportment, its dedication to the arts, and its incomparable achievements. Commuters give the city its tidal restlessness; natives give it solidity and continuity; but the settlers give it passion. And whether it is a farmer arriving from Italy to set up a small grocery store in a slum, or a young girl arriving from a small town in Mississippi to escape the indignity of being observed by her neighbors, or a boy arriving from the Corn Belt with a manuscript in his suitcase and a pain in his heart, it makes no difference: each embraces New York with the intense excitement of first love, each absorbs New York with the fresh eyes of an adventurer, each generates heat and light to dwarf the Consolidated Edison Company.

Essayist, critic, and long-time contributor to The New Yorker, *E. B. WHITE published his elegant paean to the metropolis, 'Here Is New York', in 1949.*

> As the stores close, a winter light
> opens air to iris blue,
> glint of frost through the smoke,
> grains of mica, salt of the sidewalk.
> As the buildings close, released autonomous
> feet patter the streets
> in hurry and stroll; balloon heads
> drift and dive above them; the bodies
> aren't really there.
> As the lights brighten, as the sky darkens,
> a woman with crooked heels says to another woman
> while they step along at a fair pace,
> *'You know, I'm telling you, what I love best
> is life. I love life! Even if I ever get
> to be old and wheezy – or limp! You know?
> Limping along? – I'd still . . .'* Out of hearing.
> To the multiple disordered tones
> of gears changing, a dance
> to the compass points, out, four-way river.
> Prospect of sky
> wedged into avenues, left at the ends of streets,
> west sky, east sky: more life tonight! A range
> of open time at winter's outskirts.

DENISE LEVERTOV, *born in England but an adoptive New Yorker since 1948, published her poem 'February Evening in New York' in 1960.*

THE MELTING POT

New York City isn't a melting pot,
it's a boiling pot.

– THOMAS E. DEWEY,
one-time Governor of New York State

*The Irish were the first
immigrant group to make
their mark in New York.
Often employed as casual
labourers, exploited by
employers, landlords, and
politicians, their lives in the
mid-nineteenth century were
difficult by any standards.*
JOHN MAGUIRE*, an Irish
journalist and politician,
visited America in 1866 to
survey the conditions of his
fellow countrymen and on his
return published his
observations in* The Irish in
America.

My informant was a great, broad-shouldered, red-haired Irishman, over six feet 'in his stocking vamps', and who, I may add, on the best authority, bore himself gallantly in the late war, under the banner of the Union. He was but a very young lad when, in 1848, he came to New York, with a companion of his own age, 'to better his fortune', as many a good Irishman had endeavoured to do before him. He possessed, besides splendid health and a capacity for hard work, a box of tools, a bundle of clothes, and a few pounds in gold – not a bad outfit for a good-tempered young Irishman, with a red head, broad shoulders, grand appetite, and fast rising to the six feet. The moment he landed his luggage was pounced upon by two runners, one seizing the box of tools, the other confiscating the clothes. The future American citizen assured his obliging friends that he was quite capable of carrying his own luggage; but no, they should relieve him – the stranger, and guest of the Republic – of that trouble. Each was in the interest of a different boarding-house, and each insisted that the young Irishman with the red head should go with him – a proposition that, to any but a New York runner, would seem, if not altogether impossible, at least most difficult of accomplishment. Not being able to oblige both the gentlemen, he could only oblige one; and as the tools were more valuable than the clothes, he followed in the path of the gentleman who had secured that portion of the 'plunder'. He remembers that the two gentlemen wore very pronounced green neckties, and spoke with a richness of accent that denoted special if not conscientious cultivation; and on his arrival at the boarding-house, he was cheered with the announcement that its proprietor was from 'the ould counthry, and loved every sod of it, God bless it!' In a manner truly paternal the host warned the two lads against the danger of the streets; and so darkly did he paint the horrors, and villanies, and murders of all kinds, that were sure to rain down upon their innocent heads, that the poor boys were frightened into a rigid seclusion from the world outside, and occupied their time as best they could, not forgetting 'the eating and the drinking' which the house afforded. The young Irishman with the red head imparted to the host the fact of his having a friend in Canal Street – 'wherever Canal Street was'; and that the friend had been some six years in New York,

'Hester Street' – painting by George Benjamin Luks (1867-1933)

and knew the place well, and was to procure employment for him as soon as they met; and he concluded by asking how he could get to Canal Street. 'Canal Street! – is it Canal Street? – why then what a mortal pity, and the stage to go just an hour before you entered this very door! My, my! that's unfortunate; isn't it? Well, no matter, there'll be another in two days' time, or three at farthest, and I'll be sure to see you sent there all right – depend your life on me when I say it,' said the jovial kindly host. For full forty-eight hours the two lads, who were as innocent as a brace of young goslings, endured the irksome monotony of the boarding-house, even though that abode of hospitality was cheered by the presence of its jovial host, who loved every sod of the 'ould counthry'; but human nature cannot endure beyond a certain limit – and the two lads resolved, in sheer desperation, to break bounds at any hazard. They roamed through the streets for some time, without any special ill befalling them. Meeting a policeman, the young fellow with the red head suggested to his companion the possibility of the official knowing something about Canal Street; and as his companion had nothing to urge against it, they approached that functionary, and boldly propounded the question to him – where Canal Street was, and how it could be reached? 'Why, then, my man,' replied the policeman, who also happened to be a compatriot, 'if you only follow your nose for the space of twenty minutes in that direction, you'll come to Canal Street, and no mistake about it; you'll see the name on the corner, in big letters, if you can read – as I suppose you can, for you look to be two decent boys.' Canal Street in twenty minutes! Here indeed was a pleasant surprise for the young fellows, who had been told to wait for the stage, which, according to the veracious host, 'was due in about another day'. Of course they did follow their respective noses until they actually reached Canal Street, found the number of the house in which their friend resided, and discovered the friend himself, to whom they recounted their brief adventures in New York. Thanks to the smartness of their acclimated friend, they recovered their effects, but not before they disbursed to the jovial host, who 'loved every sod of the ould counthry, God bless it!' more than would have enabled them to fare sumptuously at the Astor. And as the great strapping fellow – who had since seen many a brave man die with his face to the foe – told the tale of his first introduction to the Empire City, he actually looked sheepish at its recollection, and then laughed heartily at a simplicity which had long since become, with him, a weakness of the past.

'Italian Immigrant, East Side' – photograph by Lewis Hine, 1910.

The traveller who passes up Broadway, through Chatham Street, into the Bowery, up Houston Street, and then right to First Avenue will find himself in a section which has very little in common with the other parts of New York. The arrangement of the streets and the monotony of the brownstone dwellings are similar, but the height and detail of the houses, the inhabitants, and their language and customs differ greatly from those of the rest of New York. This is 'Kleindeutschland', or 'Deutschlandle', as the Germans call this part of the city...

Life in Kleindeutschland is almost the same as in the Old Country. Bakers, butchers, druggists – all are Germans. There is not a single business which is not run by Germans. Not only the shoemakers, tailors, barbers, physicians, grocers, and innkeepers are German, but the pastors and priests as well. There is even a German lending library where one can get all kinds of German books. The resident of Kleindeutschland need not even know English in order to make a living, which is a considerable attraction to the immigrant.

The shabby apartments are the only reminder that one is in America. Tailors or shoemakers use their living rooms as workshops, and there is scarcely space to move about. The smell in the house is not too pleasant, either, because the bedrooms have no windows, and there is a penetrating odor of sauerkraut. But the Germans do not care. They look forward to the time when they can afford a three-room apartment; and they would never willingly leave their beloved Kleindeutschland. The Americans who own all these buildings know this. That's why they do not consider improving the housing conditions. They like the Germans as tenants because they pay their rent, punctually, in advance, and keep the buildings neat and clean. The landlords are interested in keeping the German tenants crowded together because such buildings bring more profit than one-story houses...

In the decades after the failed revolutions of 1848, German immigrants arrived in New York in large numbers. This account of 'Kleindeutschland' – Little Germany – by KARL THEODOR GRIESINGER appeared in a German publication in 1863.

As I went walking up and down to take the evening air,
  (Sweet to meet upon the street, why must I be so shy?)
I saw him lay his hand upon her torn black hair;
  ('Little dirty Latin child, let the lady by!')

The women squatting on the stoops were slovenly and fat,
  (Lay me out in organdie, lay me out in lawn!)
And everywhere I stepped there was a baby or a cat;
  (Lord God in Heaven, will it never be dawn?)

The fruit-carts and clam-carts were ribald as a fair,
  (Pink nets and wet shells trodden under heel)
She had haggled from the fruit-man of his rotting ware;
  (I shall never get to sleep, the way I feel!)

He walked like a king through the filth and the clutter,
  (Sweet to meet upon the street, why did you glance me by?)
But he caught the quaint Italian quip she flung him from the gutter;
  (What can there be to cry about that I should lie and cry?)

He laid his darling hand upon her little black head,
  (I wish I were a ragged child with ear-rings in my ears!)
And he said she was a baggage to have said what she had said;
  (Truly I shall be ill unless I stop these tears!)

Italian migration to New York swelled in the last decades of the nineteenth century and the beginning of the twentieth. Many Italians settled in and around Greenwich Village. EDNA ST VINCENT MILLAY hints at the hostility between Italian and old New Yorkers in her poem 'Macdougal Street' (1920).

MICHAEL GOLD *'s memoir of his childhood in the Jewish ghetto on the Lower East Side,* Jews Without Money, *first appeared in 1930.*

At first my mother had feared going out to work in a cafeteria among Christians. But after a few days she settled easily into the life of the poly-glot kitchen, and learned to fight, scold, and mother the Poles, Germans, Italians, Irish and Negroes who worked there. They liked her, and soon called her 'Momma', which made her vain.

'You should hear how a big black dishwasher named Joe, how he comes to me today and says, "Momma, I'm going to quit. Every one is against me here because I am black," he says. "The whole world is against us black people."'

'So I said to him, "Joe, I am not against you. Don't be foolish, don't go out to be a bum again. The trouble with you here is you are lazy. If you would work harder the others would like you, too." So he said, "Momma, all right I'll stay." So that's how it is in the restaurant. They call me Momma, even the black ones.'

It was a large, high-priced cafeteria for business-men on lower Broadway. My mother was a chef's helper, and peeled and scoured tons of vegetables for cooking. Her wages were seven dollars a week.

She woke at five, cooked our breakfast at home, then had to walk a mile to her job. She came home at five-thirty, and made supper, cleaned the house, was busy on her feet until bedtime. It hurt my father's masculine pride to see his wife working for wages. But my mother liked it all; she was proud of earning money, and she liked her fights in the restaurant.

My dear, tireless, little dark-faced mother! Why did she always have to fight? Why did she have to give my father a new variety of headache with accounts of her battles for 'justice' in the cafeteria? The manager there was a fat blond Swede with a *Kaiserliche* mustache, and the manners of a Mussolini. All the workers feared this bull-necked tyrant, except my mother. She told him 'what was what'. When the meat was rotten, when the drains were clogged and smelly, or the dishwashers overworked, she told him so. She scolded him as if he were her child, and he listened meekly. The other workers fell into the habit of telling their complaints to my mother, and she would relay them to the Swedish manager.

'It's because he needs me,' said my mother proudly. 'That's why he lets me scold him. I am one of his best workers; he can depend on me in the rush. And he knows I am not like the other kitchen help; they work a day or two; then quit, but I stay on. So he's afraid to fire me, and I tell him what is what.'

It was one of those super-cafeterias, with flowers on the tables, a string orchestra during the lunch hour, and other trimmings. But my mother had no respect for it. She would never eat the lunch served there to the employees, but took along two cheese sandwiches from home.

'Your food is *Dreck*, it is fit only for pigs,' she told the manager bluntly. And once she begged me to promise never to eat hamburger steak in a restaurant when I grew up.

'Swear it to me, Mikey!' she said. 'Never, never eat hamburger!'

'I swear it, momma.'

'Poison!' she went on passionately. 'They don't care if they poison the people, so long as there's money in it. I've seen with my own eyes. If I could write English, I'd write a letter to all the newspapers.'

'Mind your own business!' my father growled. 'Such things are for Americans. It is their country and their hamburger steak.'

'Hurdy-Gurdy Ballet' – lithograph by Glenn O. Coleman, 1928.

The imprisoned life of the prison city
burns with a white blaze.
In the streets of the Jewish East Side
white fires burn still whiter.

I love to wander in the fieriness of the Jewish East Side,
to shove in and out of the cramped stalls and pushcarts,
breathing the smell and saltiness
of a feverish stripped life.
And always when, gazing, I see creep up through the whiteness
Jews bearded and from head to toe hung with
Ladies' and girls' dresses dragging them down,
and Jewish men, or women, with sick little birds
that for a penny pick out a fortune card and turn yearning and pleading eyes
    on the buyer,
and Jews pushing themselves along on two-wheeled platforms,
    blind cripples, who sit sunk down deep
in their shoulders and can see with their shoulders

H. LEIVICK was born in Russia and served imprisonment and Siberian exile for his socialist activities before coming to the United States in 1913, where he lived on the Lower East Side, whose life he celebrated years later in his poem 'Here Lives the Jewish People', translated by Cynthia Ozick.

41

the color and size of every thrown coin —
then I am roused by a buried longing, a boyhood longing
to be transformed into the lame beggar
who used to hop from street to street of our town
(Luria was his name)
and clatter with his crutch over sidewalks and thresholds.

Who knows, if sometimes I see the same beggar sitting on that barrow,
the beggar my boyhood craved? His blindness sees my staring.
Once the world was not imprisoned as now,
though white as now,
fiery and white.

Hour by hour I walk the streets of the Jewish East Side,
and in the fiery whiteness my eyes paint fantastic turrets,
elongated columns soaring up over the ruined stalls,
up to the emptied sky of New York.
Turrets hung all over their parapets with signs flashing and glowing:
Here Lives the Jewish People.

The imprisoned life of the prison city
slips into yellow-gray shadows
and in the streets of the Jewish East Side
the yellow-gray deepens.
Step by step the Jews dragging dresses for sale,
for ladies, for girls — they vanish around some corner;
the woman is carrying the cage with its sick little bird,
and the box still full of fortunes.
The blind cripple is trundling home
through streets cleared of pushcarts and stalls.
My longing grows. I let myself follow
the hard jutting shoulders of the cripple.
(Luria was his name.)
I am enticed by his progress, his nest-seeking.
Until suddenly I am knifed by a look,
the look of an eye sprung open in the middle of his back.

Stillness. Midnight.
Once the world was not as now,
dark and shadowed.

And in the darkness the turrets loom in earnest,
they that in the white flame of day were a dream;
they reveal themselves in all their vastness and roundness,
like the thick towers of fortresses.
Turrets hung all over their parapets with red warning signs:
Here Sleeps the Jewish People.

Stillness. Midnight.
The years of my childhood cry in me, the longing.

'Immigration' – painting by Ben Shahn.

I will not toy with it nor bend an inch.
Deep in the secret chambers of my heart
I muse my life-long hate, and without flinch
I bear it nobly as I live my part.
My being would be a skeleton, a shell,
If this dark Passion that fills my every mood,
And makes my heaven in the white world's hell,
Did not forever feed me vital blood.
I see the mighty city through a mist –
The strident trains that speed the goaded mass,
The poles and spires and towers vapor-kissed,
The fortressed port through which the great ships pass,
The tides, the wharves, the dens I contemplate,
Are sweet like wanton loves because I hate.

When poet CLAUDE McKAY *arrived in New York from his native Jamaica he found a city poisoned by racism. His bitter sonnet 'The White City' was published in 1920.*

For a generation JAMES WELDON JOHNSON *was one of New York's leading black politicians and educators. His book* Black Manhattan *(1930) chronicles the struggles of black people in the city from slavery in the eighteenth century to Harlem's cultural explosion in the 1920s.*

The fact that within New York, the greatest city of the New World, there is found the greatest single community anywhere of people descended from age-old Africa appears at a thoughtless glance to be the climax of the incongruous. Harlem is today the Negro metropolis and as such is everywhere known. In the history of New York the name Harlem has changed from Dutch to Irish to Jewish to Negro; but it is through this last change that it has gained its most widespread fame. Throughout colored America Harlem is the recognized Negro capital. Indeed, it is Mecca for the sightseer, the pleasure-seeker, the curious, the adventurous, the enterprising, the ambitious, and the talented of the entire Negro world: for the lure of it has reached down to every island of the Carib Sea and penetrated even into Africa. It is almost as well known to the white world, for it has been much talked and written about.

So here we have Harlem – not merely a colony or a community or a settlement – not at all a 'quarter' or a slum or a fringe – but a black city, located in the heart of white Manhattan, and containing more Negroes to the square mile than any other spot on earth. It strikes the uninformed observer as a phenomenon, a miracle straight out of the skies. . .

'A black city located in the heart of white Manhattan . . .' – Harlem, 1948.

... A visit to Harlem at night – the principal streets never deserted, gay crowds skipping from one place of amusement to another, lines of taxicabs and limousines standing under the sparkling lights of the entrances to the famous night-clubs, the subway kiosks swallowing and disgorging crowds all night long – gives the impression that Harlem never sleeps and that the inhabitants thereof jazz through existence. But, of course, no one can seriously think that the two hundred thousand and more Negroes in Harlem spend their nights on any such pleasance. Of a necessity the vast majority of them are ordinary, hard-working people, who spend their time in just about the same way that other ordinary, hard-working people do. Most of them have never seen the inside of a night-club. The great bulk of them are confronted with the stern necessity of making a living, of making both ends meet, of finding money to pay the rent and keep the children fed and clothed neatly enough to attend school; their waking hours are almost entirely consumed in this unromantic task. And it is a task in which they cannot escape running up against a barrier erected especially for them, a barrier which pens them off on the morass – no, the quicksands – of economic insecurity. Fewer jobs are open to them than to any other group; and in such jobs as they get, they are subject to the old rule, which still obtains, 'the last to be hired and the first to be fired'.

The year 1922 was especially hard on Puerto Ricans in New York. There seemed to be more people crammed into apartments than ever. As I recall, there were at least a dozen people – men, women, and children – in every room. I even knew of cases where three couples had to live in the same place. I can also remember families that worked it out so that the men would sleep during the day and the women at night. And in spite of this, new emigrants kept arriving from Puerto Rico.

That year there was almost total unemployment among Puerto Ricans. I knew men – honest, law-abiding citizens – who had to resort to bootlegging. Many were the families who stayed alive by selling rum under the counter. The other recourse was the numbers. Yes, *la bolita* was a means of survival for quite a few 'bankers' and countless numbers of runners.

People went to bed hungry and dreamed of numbers and symbols. Books for interpreting dreams, or *la charada* as they were called, could be found in nearly every home. In the Puerto Rican neighborhoods it was not uncommon to hear people in the streets saying, 'Lend me your *charada*. I had this weird dream last night.' 'Well, try playing 033.'

Whenever a family had to move out of its apartment they would use a hand cart. Beds, couches, and cots were usually all the furniture they had. Sometimes there would also be a rickety old table and some chairs. And, of course, there were kitchen utensils.

The buildings where Puerto Ricans lived were never painted. Broken windows were never repaired either, so that they had to fill the holes with pieces of cardboard or old rags. The only time there was any heat or hot water was the night before the landlord came around to collect the rent. Garbage collection in those neighborhoods was irregular at best. In fact, it's amazing that tuberculosis, prostitution, and delinquency were not more widespread than they were, and that, in spite of everything, Puerto Ricans did manage to survive under such unfavorable conditions.

The Puerto Rican community in New York began to grow – and to face increased prejudice and privation – in the years following the First World War, as BERNARDO VEGA *recalled in his* Memoirs *(1984).*

The Jewish Lower East Side immortalized by Michael Gold and the Yiddish poets is no more. Today it is a largely Puerto Rican neighbourhood, which has produced its own poetic chroniclers, not least MIGUEL PIÑERO, whose 'A Lower East Side Poem' was published in the 1970s.

Just once before I die
I want to climb up on a
tenement sky
to dream my lungs out till
I cry
then scatter my ashes thru
the Lower East Side

So let me sing my song tonight
let me feel out of sight
and let all eyes be dry
when they scatter my ashes thru
the Lower East Side

From Houston to 14th Street
from Second Avenue to the mighty D
here the hustlers & suckers meet
the faggots & freaks will all get high
on the ashes that have been scattered
thru the Lower East Side

There's no other place for me to be
there's no other place that I can see
there's no other town around that
brings you up or keeps you down
no food little heat sweeps by
fancy cars & pimp bars & juke saloons
& greasy spoons make my spirits fly
with my ashes scattered thru the
Lower East Side. . .

Police work in New York – photograph by Leonard Freed.

A thief a junkie I've been
committed every known sin
Jews & Gentiles. . . Bums and Men
of style. . . run away child
police shooting wild. . .
mother's futile wails. . . pushers
making sales. . . dope wheelers
& cocaine dealers. . . smoking pot
streets are hot & feed off those who
bleed to death. . .

So here I am look at me
I stand proud as you can see
pleased to be from the Lower East
a street fighting man
a problem of this land
I am the Philosopher of the Criminal Mind
a dweller of prison time
a cancer of rockerfeller's ghettocide
this concrete tomb is my home
to belong to survive you gotta be strong
you can't be shy less without request
someone will scatter your ashes thru
the Lower East Side

I don't wanna be buried in Puerto Rico
I don't wanna rest in long island cemetery
I wanna be near the stabbing shooting
gambling fighting & unnatural dying
& new birth crying
so please when I die. . .
don't take me far away
keep me near by
take my ashes and scatter them thru out
the Lower East Side. . .

Photograph by Leonard Freed.

A newly arrived Jewish immigrant entered a kosher restaurant on Delan-cey Street. The waiter who poured his water was – *Gottenyu!* – Chinese! And the Chinese servitor proceeded to rattle off the menu in fluent Yiddish, even unto the idiomatic grunts and sighs.

When the Jew was paying his bill, he asked the cashier, 'Are you the *bale-boss* [owner]?'

'Who else?'

'Well, I certainly enjoyed my dinner – and even more, the fact that your waiter speaks such excellent Yiddish!'

'Sha!' hissed the proprietor. 'He thinks we're teaching him English!'

This Jewish joke appeared in LEO ROSTEN's The Joys of Yiddish, *(1970).*

'The Building of Manhattan Bridge' – painting by Gerrit Albertus Beneker, 1908.

DEMOCRATIC ISLAND CITY

More and more, too, the *old name* absorbs into me – Manahatta,
'the place encircled by many swift tides and sparkling waters'.
How fit a name for America's great democratic island city!
The word itself, how beautiful! how aboriginal! how it seems
to rise with tall spires, glistening in sunshine, with such
New World atmosphere, vista and action.

WALT WHITMAN

With eager step and wrinkled brow,
    The busy sons of care
Disgusted with less splendid scenes
    To Federal Hall repair.

In order plac'd, they patient wait
    To seize each word that flies,
From what they hear they sigh or smile,
    Look cheerful, grave, or wise.

Within these walls the doctrines taught
    Are of such vast concern,
That all the world with one consent
    Here strives to live – and learn.

The timorous heart that cautious shuns
    All churches, but its own,
No more observes its wonted rules,
    But ventures here alone.

Four hours a day each rank alike.
    (They that can walk or crawl)
Leave children, business, shop and wife,
    And steer for Federal Hall.

From morning tasks of mending soals
    The cobbler hastes away;
At *three* returns and tells to Kate
    The business of the day.

The debtor, vext with early duns,
    Avoids his hated home
And here and there at random roves
    Till hours of Congress come.

New York City was the nation's first capital with headquarters in Federal Hall in lower Manhattan. The infant democracy was affectionately satirized by the New York poet and passionate American nationalist PHILIP FRENEAU, *who published 'Federal Hall' in the New York* Daily Advertiser *in 1790.*

The barber at the well-known time
        Forgets his lather'd man,
And leaves him, grac'd with half a beard,
        To shave it – as he can.

The taylor, plagu'd with *suits* on *suits*
        Neglects Sir Fopling's call,
Forsakes his goose, disdains his board,
        And flies to Federal Hall.

In his diary, PHILIP HONE, *businessman, one-time Whig Mayor, and fierce opponent of President Andrew Jackson's new popular democracy, recorded events in the city elections of 1834, contested by the rival Whig and Democratic organizations. The latter had its headquarters in Tammany Hall, which was to become a byword for municipal corruption. It drew its support (at this time and for generations after) from the immigrant and ethnic groups excluded by the old New York élite.*

Tuesday, April 8   The election for mayor and charter officers commenced this day with a degree of spirit and zeal in both parties never before witnessed. This is the first election for mayor by the people since the new law [abolishing property qualifications], and has acquired immense importance . . . The number of votes will be very great (probably thirty-five thousand); the Whig party, whose candidate for mayor is Mr Verplanck, are active, zealous, and confident of success. A great meeting was held yesterday at four o'clock, at the Exchange . . . and several resolutions were passed, one of which recommends to the merchants and traders to omit their usual attendance at the Exchange, and to close their stores and places of business at noon on each of the three days of the election, in order to devote their undivided attention to the great business of reform at the polls. This last suggestion has been in part observed; many stores are closed today, and several have notices on the doors that the inmates are gone to the polls to vote for Verplanck.

Thursday, April 10   Last day of the election; dreadful riots between the Irish and the Americans have again disturbed the public peace. The Mayor arrived with a strong body of watchmen, but they were attacked and overcome, and many of the watchmen are severely wounded. Eight of them were carried to the hospital where I went to visit them. The Mayor has ordered out Colonel Sanford's regiment and a troop of horse, and proper measures have been taken to preserve order, but we apprehend a dreadful night . . .

Friday, April 11   Such an excitement! So wonderful is the result of this election that all New York has been kept in a state of alarm; immense crowds have been collected at Masonic and Tammany Halls, but the greatest concourse was in front of the Exchange. The street was a dense mass of people. Partial returns were coming in every few minutes, and so close has been the vote that the Whigs at the Exchange and the small party for Jackson in front of the office of the 'Standard' opposite shouted alternately as the news was favourable to one or the other; and up to the last moment the result was doubtful, when, at the close of the canvass, the majority for Mr Lawrence, the Jackson candidate, out of the immense number of votes – thirty-five thousand one hundred and forty-one – was found to be one hundred and seventy-nine. There is no doubt, however, that we have elected a majority of aldermen and assistants. The Common Council is reformed, and we shall succeed in the great fall election. It is a signal triumph of good principles over violence, illegal voting, party discipline, and the influence of office-holders. . .

THE VOTING-PLACE, NO. 488 PEARL STREET, IN THE SIXTH WARD, NEW YORK CITY.

Elections of 1858, a Tammany strong-hold.

July, 1863 – The Draft Riots
No sleep. The sultriness pervades the air
And binds the brain – a dense oppression, such
As tawny tigers feel in matted shades,
Vexing their blood and making apt for ravage.
Beneath the stars the roofy desert spreads
Vacant as Libya. All is hushed near by.
Yet fitfully from far breaks a mixed surf
Off muffled sound, the Atheist roar of riot.
Yonder, where parching Sirius set in drought,
Balefully glares red Arson – there – and there.
The Town is taken by its rats – ship-rats
And rats of the wharves. All civil charms
And priestly spells which late held hearts in awe –
Fear-bound, subjected to a better sway
Than sway of self; these like a dream dissolve,
And man rebounds whole aeons back in nature.
Hail to the low dull rumble, dull and dead,
And ponderous drag that shakes the wall.
Wise Draco comes, deep in the midnight roll
Of black artillery; he comes, though late;
In code corroborating Calvin's creed
And cynic tyrannies of honest kings;
He comes, nor parleys; and the Town, redeemed,
Gives thanks devout; nor, being thankful, heeds
The grimy slur on the Republic's faith implied,
Which holds that Man is naturally good,
And – more – is Nature's Roman, never to be scourged.

Sympathy for the Southern Confederacy was widespread in New York during the Civil War. In 1863, Lincoln's decision to introduce conscription touched off days of rioting and murderous attacks on New York's small black community. The violence only came to an end when federal troops entered and subdued the city. HERMAN MELVILLE, a passionate opponent of slavery and supporter of the Union cause, published his poem 'The House-Top: A Night Piece' in 1866.

GEORGE TEMPLETON STRONG, *businessman, lawyer, and philanthropist, recorded his disgust with New York's corrupt political administration – under the rule of 'Boss' Tweed – in his diary in 1868.*

The state and city elections of 1894 produced a number of upsets. The former governor of New York State, David Bennett Hill, was defeated in his attempt to recapture the State House by Republican Levi Morton. The Republican ticket of William Strong, for Mayor, and John Goff, for city recorder, defeated the Tammany Hall ticket lead by 'Hughie' Grant and backed by 'Boss' Richard Croker. In this collection of remarks overheard in the street, novelist, poet and journalist STEPHEN CRANE offers a snapshot of New York democracy in action.

December 19 . . . The body politic of this city and country, judges, aldermen, councilmen, supervisors, and so on, our whole local government, is so diseased and so corrupt and so far gone that we can no longer count on any recuperative, restorative action of its vital forces. People talk of the pride a New Yorker must feel in his great city! To be a citizen of New York is a disgrace. A domicile on Manhattan Island is a thing to be confessed with apologies and humiliation. The New Yorker belongs to a community worse governed by lower and baser blackguard scum than any city in Western Christendom, or in the world, so far as I know . . .

'Hully chee! Everything's dumped!'

'S'cuse me, g'l'men, fer bein' s'noisy, but, fact is, I'm Repu'lican! What? Yessir! Morton by seventy-fi' thousan'. Yessir! I'm goin' holler thish time 'til I bust m' throat – tha's what I am.'

'Can you tell me, please, if the returns indicate that Goff has a chance?' 'Who? Goff? Well, I guess! He's running like a race-horse. He's dead in it.'

'That's all right. Wait 'til later. Then, you'll see. Morton never had a show. Hill will swamp him.'
'Oh, hurry up with your old slide. Put on another. Good thing – push it along. Ah, there we are. 'Morton's – plurality – over – Hill – is – estimated – at – 10,135.' Say, look at that, would you? Don't talk to me about the unterrified Democracy. The unterrified Democracy can be dog goned. There's more run than fight in them this trip. Hey, hurry up, Willie, give us another one. It's a good thing, but push it along.'

'Say, that magic lantern man is a big fakir. Lookatim pushin' ads in on us. Hey, take that out, will yeh? You ain't no bill-poster are yeh?'

'Strong has got a cinch. He wins in a walk. Ah there, Hughie, ah there.'

'Well, I guess not. If Hill wins this time, he's got to have iceboats on his feet. He ain't got a little chance.' . . .

'If Tammany wins this time, we might as well all quit the town and go to Camden. If we don't beat 'em now, we're a lot of duffers and we're only fit to stuff mattresses with.'

'Say, hear 'em yell ''Goff''. Popular? I guess yes.'
'He won't, hey? You just wait, me boy. If Hill can't carry this State at any time in any year, I'll make you a present of the Brooklyn bridge, and paint it a deep purple with gold stripes, all by myself.'

'Goff! Goff! John – W – Goff!'
'Goff! Goff! John – W – Goff!

'Voorhis and Taintor! They're the only two. The rest – '
'Well, this is what comes from monkeyin' with the people. You think you've got 'em all under a board when, first thing you know, they come out and belt you in the neck.'

Ever since the days of Tweed, Tammany Hall has, with the exception of a few brief periods, been the controlling force in the New York City Democracy, and has generally held the reins of government in the city itself. There have been honourable men in Tammany, and there have been occasions on which Tammany has acted well and has deserved well of the country; nevertheless, speaking broadly, it may be said that Tammany has always stood for what was worst in our political life, and especially in our municipal politics. The Tammany Hall organization is a machine of ideal perfection for its own purposes. It has as leaders a number of men of great ability in certain special directions. The rank and file of its members are recruited from the most ignorant portion of the city's population, coming from among the voters who can usually be voted in a mass by those who have influence over them. This influence is sometimes obtained by appeals to their prejudices and by the lowest art of the demagogue; sometimes it is obtained by downright corruption; sometimes it is obtained through the influence the local Tammany organizations exert on the social life of their neighborhoods. The District leaders are able in a hundred ways to benefit their followers. They try to get them work when they are idle; they provide amusement for them in the shape of picnics and steamboat excursions; and, in exceptional cases, they care for them when suffering from want or sickness; and they are always ready to help them when they have fallen into trouble with the representatives of the law. They thus get a very strong influence over a large class, the members of which are ordinarily fairly decent men, who work with reasonable industry at their trades, but who never get far ahead, who at times fall into want, and who sometimes have kinsfolk of semi-criminal type. These men are apt to regard the saloon as their clubhouse; often, indeed, the saloons are the headquarters of the District political organizations, and become in a double sense the true social centres of neighborhood life.

THEODORE ROOSEVELT, soldier, historian, politician, and ultimately twenty-sixth President of the United States, was deeply involved in New York City politics for many years, and even served as Commissioner of Police in the 1890s. In his book New York *(1903) he explained the origin and power of the local Democratic clubhouse bosses whom he had fought for so many years.*

A man is shouting from a soapbox at Second Avenue and Houston in front of the Cosmopolitan Café: '. . . these fellers, men . . . wageslaves like I was . . . are sittin on your chest . . . they're takin the food outer your mouths. Where's all the pretty girls I used to see walkin up and down the bullevard? Look for em in the uptown cabarets. . . They squeeze us dry friends . . . feller workers, slaves I'd oughter say . . . they take our work and our ideers and our women . . . They build their Plaza Hotels and their millionaire's clubs and their million dollar theayters and their battleships and what do they leave us? . . . They leave us shopsickness an the rickets and a lot of dirty streets full of garbage cans . . . You look pale you fellers . . . You need blood . . . Why dont you get some blood in your veins? . . . Back in Russia the poor people. . . not so much poorer'n we are . . . believe in wampires, things come suck your blood at night . . . That's what Capitalism is, a wampire that suck your blood . . . day . . . and . . . night.'

It is beginning to snow. The flakes are giltedged where they pass the streetlamp. Through the plate glass the Cosmopolitan Café full of blue and green opal rifts of smoke looks like a muddy aquarium; faces blob whitely round the tables like ill-assorted fishes. Umbrellas begin to bob in clusters up the snow-mottled street. The orator turns up his collar and walks briskly east along Houston, holding the muddy soapbox away from his trousers.

Soapbox orators were a common sight in the city for generations, as novelist JOHN DOS PASSOS *observed in* Manhattan Transfer *(1925).*

Radical journalist JOSEPH NORTH *published this account of New York City's biggest taxi strike in the periodical* New Masses *in 1934.*

Tammany Boss, William Tweed, and friends depicted as 'A Group of Vultures Waiting for the Storm to Blow Over' by cartoonist Thomas Nast, 1871.

Men who ply the streets for their livelihood develop a characteristic attitude: the highways belong to them. When they go on strike, be they taxicab drivers, or traction employees, the authorities may well expect the major pyrotechnics of revolt. The police nightstick can flail from day to night, it cannot dislodge the idea. The Mayor may cajole and storm in turn from dawn to dusk but the men of the streets stay on the streets. The streets are theirs – not only the gutters. As the New York cabbies say in their juicy lingo that springs partly from their slum derivations, partly from their enforced association with the night-life characters of a big city, and partly from the peculiar conditions of their trade: 'What? Them weasels tell us to get off the streets? Spit on them! Push me off, rat!'

The strike of the New York cabmen stands unique in American labor history: it is, to date, the biggest in the industry and possesses connotations of great importance to all American workingmen. Forty thousand cabmen abandoned their wheels for the sake of an independent union, and against the strait jacket of a company union . . .

The trio of policemen bivouacked across the street and dawn found them cracking slats to heap on the fire. Three ruddy faced cops – 'mugs' – pretended to ignore the hackies picketing the Parmelee garage at 23rd Street and Eleventh Avenue. One patrolman picked a carrot from the gutter and fed a blanketed horse, deliberately turning his massive blue-coated back on the strikers. Acoss the street this hackie, Leo Chazner, strike placards flapping aganst his chest and back, eyed him obliquely. 'I been in the racket seventeen years,' he told me. 'I never seen a strike like this one. The beauty part of it is, kid, we're making history for the whole woild. The eyes of the woild is on us – the New York hackies.'

He marched up and back, hackman's cap and worn overcoat. Every time he passed the garage entry he peeped inside. 'What a sight! Look at them, kid, look at them! Two hundred and fifty of 'em crowding the walls.' Within, shiny cabs, row on row, stretched a full block to the next wall – phalanxes of beautiful cars – eerily silent, something uncanny about them like all machines when the human factor is extracted. . .

. . .The previous night the strikers had swirled across Broadway, leaving a wake of wreckage which plunged the iron deep in the Parmelee, Radio, and Terminal fleet operators. Cabs lay on their sides, the wheels grotesquely whirling; here and there they burst into flames, scabs fled down the street pursued by strikers, while mounted police picked their way through the streets at the fore and rear of the demonstrations. The cabbies' 'Educational Committee' was on the job. Parmelee, Radio, and Terminal fleet owners spent thousands of dollars for full-page advertisemets in the commercial press moaning 'Vandals!' and calling for the military. 'Take the scabs off the street and there won't be no violence,' the hackies responded. 'Who's driving them cabs? Chicago gunmen wit' soft hats: say, did you ever see a hackie on duty wit' a soft hat? That's the Parmelee Chicago gunmen'. . .

A massive youth, pug-nosed and Irish, they called him Pondsie, was recounting the demonstration the delegation of cabbies received at the Communist district convention in the Coliseum the other night. 'We walks in and the Communists go crazy. They stand up, about a million of 'em, and start singing. We go up on the platform and they give us the spotlight.' The crowd about him listened intently. 'Then when they come to the chorus of the song they're sing-ing they give us the Communist salute.' His left fist – a huge affair – goes up in a sort of short uppercut. 'Know what their salute is?' he asks, looking around the room. 'The left hook.' And he demonstrates it again and again. The others in the room watching him, try the salute, too. I notice a youth with a palm cross on his lapel, giving the left hook. (It was Palm Sunday.) 'And then,' Pondsie finishes his story, 'they have a collection. Man, they raked the coin in wit' dishes on broomsticks. 'Bout three hundred bucks them Communists give us.'

The lad with the palm cross on his lapel raises his eyebrows. 'Three hundred bucks!' He shoots a few left hooks in the air. 'If them Communists are wit' us, I'm wit' them. Left hook!' he shouts. The others chorus, 'Left hook . . . left hook . . .'

'Election Night Bonfire' – lithograph by Glenn O. Coleman, 1928.

That long and lonely fight in the Bronx is ended. We have lost a great New Yorker and a great American. It is sad that the passing of Fiorello LaGuar-dia should have been pitiful. He was a man to provoke violent reactions – anger, hatred, enthusiasm, love, exasperation, devotion, anything but pity. He who loved combat, crowds, five-alarm fires, rough-and-tumble debate on street corners and on the floor of Congress, tumult and crisis, with all the ardor of a mischievous and exhibitionistic small boy, should not have had to wrestle unseen with a stealthy death. He should have died splendidly in battle, not slowly shrinking into skin and bone on a sickbed, restless, impatient, and frus-trated, a giant spirit in a shrunken child's body, watching with dismay as the world moved through misery he had tried to alleviate toward a new tragedy his unheeded warnings foresaw. This, for the Little Flower, the Mayor, Butch, the Hat, was a cruel end.

Fiorello LaGuardia was Mayor of New York City for twelve years, perhaps the most popular and respected figure ever to hold that testing office. Independent journalist I. F. STONE *published his tribute to the 'Little Flower' on his death in 1947.*

'Mayor LaGuardia, 1934' – by Peggy Bacon.

LaGuardia's background was of that richly composite and polyglot kind that is America's glory, however much it may depress the anemic D.A.R. [Daughters of the American Revolution]. He was half Italian, half Jewish, and wholly American. He was born in New York but spent his childhood and youth in Arizona. From the Southwest he brought more than a fondness for sombrero-brimmed hats so broad they made the stout little fellow look like a perambulating mushroom; he brought something of the breezy independence of the frontier. No figure in American politics ever thumbed his nose so brashly at party regularity and got away with it. In the midst of the smug Coolidge era, when the party bosses tried to get rid of this maverick Republican, he defied them and was re-elected to Congress as a Socialist. He was a New Dealer before the New Deal; the leader of a rebel Republican faction which rode herd on the Hooverites in the early '30s, fought hard for relief, blocked the sales tax, and in 1932 triumphantly put through Congress the Norris-LaGuardia anti-injunction act, forerunner of the Wagner Act and LaGuardia's greatest legislative achievement.

What were the qualities and circumstances which enabled LaGuardia to serve fourteen years in Congress, to be elected Mayor of New York for three consecutive terms, to become a national and international figure, without that loyalty to party machine which is ordinarily an essential to success in American politics? He survived in Congress because his base was on the East Side, among the poor and the politically advanced. He succeeded without a machine in New York because Tammany mismanagement, a leftward tide, and a sense of civic responsibility made it possible for LaGuardia to muster a coalition which ranged from Wall Street bankers to Union Square labor leaders. He gave the city competent, honest, and reasonably progressive government for twelve years – the best mayor New York ever had. Though he was as temperamental as an operatic tenor, and as flamboyant as a prima donna, LaGuardia was a tireless and capable administrator. He was a natural-born popular leader for a democratic people: straightforward in speech, free from cant and hypocrisy, shrewdly and disarmingly candid in tight spots, with a flair for the direct and the dramatic.

To protest against Prohibition, LaGuardia brewed beer in his own office in Washington. To illustrate a speech on the high cost of living after World War I, he waved a lamb chop before a startled House of Representatives. To show his contempt for Hoover during the '30s, he gave his own White House invitations to street urchins. To make Midwestern farmers realize the need abroad, LaGuardia went on a personal tour as head of UNRRA [a relief agency]; at one rally, in Minnesota, he mounted a farm wagon, held aloft a loaf of bread, and ripped off six slices to show assembled farmers an entire day's food allowance in some European countries – 'And mark you, there's no gravy goes with it.' This was not demagogy. LaGuardia was not a demagogue; he was not one to mouth irresponsible nonsense to inflame a crowd. But he knew how to capture popular imagination. He knew how to translate abstractions into concrete and vivid realities. He could talk the ordinary man's language as no ordinary man could talk it – he had the gift of plain, direct, and salty speech. Fiorello was no ivory-tower intellectual.

Ultimate power over public policy in New York is invisible and unelected. It is exercised by a loose confederation of bankers, bond underwriters, members of public authorities, the big insurance companies, political fundraisers, publishers, law firms, builders, judges, backroom politicians, and some union leaders.

The power of this interlocking network of elites is based on the control of institutions, money, property, and the law-making process. It endures no matter who the voters elect as mayor, governor, or president. Its collective power, when organized, is greater than the elected, representative government.

This permanent government is not an invincible conspiracy. It is only the creative self-interest of the rich. It sometimes can be beaten, as when 50,000 residents of Co-op City waged a thirteen-month rent strike in 1975-76 that successfully conquered a rent increase. Or when neighborhood activists stopped the Lower Manhattan Expressway in 1967.

The permanent government is not as monolithic now as it was a decade ago, when Nelson Rockefeller and the men around him controlled public and private power to a terrifying extent.

The balance of power within this elite group shifts. A few years ago the real-estate developers and construction unions had more influence than they do now. But with the onset of the recession, foreclosures, and the fiscal crisis, the banks and financial institutions that control lines of credit, bonds, venture capital, and mortgages became much more important. But our point is this: Whenever an assemblyman casts a vote, or when a public-works project is begun, or when a developer gets a zoning variance to build a highrise, or when federal funds come into a district, or when a decision is made to raise the interest rates that the banks charge the city – in all these situations, the real decision-makers are usually off stage, and unknown to the public. This means the average citizen does not know who is controlling his or her life.

In The Abuse of Power *(1977), journalists* JACK NEWFIELD *and* PAUL OBRUL *described what they called the city's 'permanent government'.*

STREETLIFE

HELEN KELLER, *blind and deaf from infancy, vividly imagined the sensations of New York City streetlife in her book* Midstream *(1929).*

Cut off as I am, it is inevitable that I should sometimes feel like a shadow walking in a shadowy world. When this happens I ask to be taken to New York City. Always I return home weary but I have the comforting certainty that mankind is real flesh and I myself am not a dream . . .

New York has a special interest for me when it is wrapped in fog. Then it behaves very much like a blind person. I once crossed from Jersey City to Manhattan in dense fog. The ferry-boat felt its way cautiously through the river traffic. More timid than a blind man, its horn brayed incessantly. Fog-bound, surrounded by menacing, unseen craft and dangers, it halted every now and then as a blind man halts at a crowded thoroughfare crossing, tapping his cane, tense and anxious . . .

I usually know what part of the city I am in by the odors. There are as many smells as there are philosophies. I have never had time to gather and classify my olfactory impressions of different cities, but it would be an interesting subject. I find it quite natural to think of places by their characteristic smells.

Fifth Avenue, for example, has a different odor from any other part of New York or elsewhere. Indeed, it is a very odorous street. It may sound like a joke to say that it has an aristocratic smell; but it has, nevertheless. As I walk along its even pavements, I recognize expensive perfumes, powders, creams, choice flowers, and pleasant exhalations from the houses. In the residential section I smell delicate food, silken draperies, and rich tapestries. Sometimes, when a door opens as I pass, I know what kind of cosmetics the occupants of the house use. I know if there is an open fire, if they burn wood or soft coal, if they roast their coffee, if they use candles, if the house has been shut up for a long time, if it has been painted or newly decorated, and if the cleaners are at work in it . . .

Eugene Gant, the hero of THOMAS WOLFE*'s autobiographical novel* Of Time and the River *(1935), is wont to spend his solitary nights prowling the streets of the city, a habit he finds difficulty in explaining to his upper crust hostess, Mrs Pierce.*

Mrs Pierce stood at the foot of the stairs surveying this young stranger from the outside world with a tolerant but glacially detached smile of impersonal curiosity:

'. . . Joel tells me that you like to stay up all night and prowl around. What do you do on these prowling expeditions?'

He wanted to answer her with simple eloquence and grace and warmth, he wanted to paint a picture of his midnight wanderings that would hold her there in fascinated interest, but the glacial impersonality of the woman's smile, the proud and haughty magnificence of her person, froze all the ardors of enthusiasm and conviction with which, he felt, he might have spoken, it even seemed to numb and thicken the muscles of his tongue, and he stood there gaping at her awkwardly, cutting a sorry figure, and flushing crimson with anger and vexation at his lame, stupid, halting tongue, and stammered out, replying:

'Harlem' – painting by Edward Burra, 1939.

'I – I walk,' he mumbled. 'I – I take walks.'

'You – *what*?' she said kindly enough, but sharply, with a kind of peremptory authority that told him that she must already be growing weary and impatient of his stammering, incoherent speech, his mumbling awkwardness:

'Oh – *walk*!' she cried, with an air of swift enlightenment, as if her puzzled mind had just succeeded in translating his jargon. 'Oh,' she said quietly, and looked at him for a moment steadily with her fixed and glacial smile, 'you do.'

. . .after a moment, as she continued to look at him with her brilliant, glacial, detached, yet not unkindly smile, she continued:

'And what do you do on these walks? Where do you go?'

– Where? Where? Where indeed? His mind groped desperately over the whole nocturnal pattern of the city – over the lean, gaunt webbing of Manhattan with the barren angularity of its streets, the splintered, glacial soar of its terrific buildings, and the silent, frozen harshness of its streets of old brown houses, grimy brick and rusty, age-encrusted stone.

Oh, he thought that he could tell her all that could be told, that youth could know, that any man had ever known about night and time and darkness, and about the city's dark and secret heart, and what lay buried in the dark and secret heart of all America. . .

Yes, he thought that he could tell her all this, but when he spoke, with thickened tongue, a numb and desperate constraint, all that he could mutter thickly was: 'I – I walk.'

'But *where*?' she said, a trifle more sharply, still looking at him with her glacial, curious smile. 'That's what I'd like to know. Where do you go? What do you see that's so interesting? What do you find that's worth staying up all night for? Where do you go when you make these expeditions?' she again demanded. 'Up to Broadway?'

'Yes,' he mumbled thickly, '– sometimes – and sometimes – I go down town.'

'Down town?' the cool incisive inflection of the voice, the glacial gray-green of the eye bored through him like a steel-blue drill. 'Down town *where*? To the Battery?'

'Y-y-yes – sometimes. . . And – and along the East Side too,' he mumbled. '*Where*?' she cried sharply, smiling, but manifestly impatient with his mumbled, tongue-tied answers. '*Oh* – the East Side!' she cried again, with the air of glacial enlightenment. '– In the tenement section!'

'Yes – yes,' he stumbled on desperately, '– and along Fourteenth Street and Second Avenue – and Grand Street – and – and Delancey – and – and the Bowery – and all the docks and piers and all,' he blurted out, conscious of Joel's eager, radiant smile of hopeful kindness, and the miserable clown he was making of himself.

'But I should think you would find all that dreadfully boring.' Mrs Pierce's voice was now tinged with cool and mild surprise. 'And awfuly ugly, isn't it? . . . I mean, if you've got to prowl around at night, you might hunt for something a little more attractive than the East Side, couldn't you? . . . After all, we still have Riverside Drive – I suppose even that has changed a great deal, but in my childhood it was quite a lovely place. Or the Park?' she said, a little more kindly and persuasively. 'If you want to take a walk before going to bed, why wouldn't it be better to take it in the Park – where you could see an occasional tree or a little grass . . . Or even Fifth Avenue and around Washington Square

– that used to be quite pleasant! But the East *Side*! Heavens! My dear boy, what on earth do you ever find in a place like that to interest you?'

He was absolutely speechless, congealed, actually terrified by the haughty magnificence, the glacial and almost inhuman detachment, of her person. His mouth gaped, he gulped, his lips quivered and made soundless efforts for a moment, and then he stammered:

'You – you find – you find – p-p-p-people there,' he said.

'*People?*' Again, her thin eyebrows arched in fine surprise. 'But of course you find people there! You find people everywhere you go.'

Walk down any street in the soft violet light. Make the mind blank. A thousand sensations assault you at once from every direction. Here man is still furred and feathered; here cyst and quartz still speak. There are audible, voluble buildings with sheet-metal visors and windows that sweat; places of worship too, where the children drape themselves about the porticos like

Brooklynite HENRY MILLER *evoked the complex sensual and sentimental experience of New York's streets in his novel* Sexus *(1946).*

'The lean, giant webbing of Manhattan' – photograph by Berenice Abbott, 1932.

contortionists; rolling, ambulant streets where nothing stands still, nothing is fixed, nothing is comprehensible except through the eyes and mind of a dreamer. Hallucinating streets too, where suddenly all is silence, all is barren, as if after the passing of a plague. Streets that cough, streets that throb like a fevered temple, streets to die on and not a soul take notice. Strange, frangipanic streets, in which attar of roses mingles with the acrid bite of leek and scallion. Slippered streets, which echo with the pat and slap of lazy feet. Streets out of Euclid, which can be explained only by logic and theorem...

Pervading all, suspended between the layers of the skin like a distillate of ruddy smoke, is the secondary sexual sweat – public, Orphic, mammalian – a heavy incense smuggled in by night on velvet pads of musk. No one is immune, not even the Mongoloid idiot. It washes over you like the brush and passage of camisoled breasts. In a light rain it makes an invisible etherial mud. It is of every hour, even when rabbits are boiled to a stew. It glistens in the tubes, the follicles, the papillaries. As the earth slowly wheels, the stoops and banisters turn and the children with them; in the murky haze of sultry nights all that is terrene, volupt and fatidical hums like a zither. A heavy wheel plated

'Third Avenue, 1928' – lithograph by Glenn O. Coleman.

with fodder and feather-beds, with little sweet-oil lamps and drops of pure animal sweat. All goes round and round, creaking, wobbling, lumbering, whimpering sometimes, but round and round and round. Then, if you become very still, standing on a stoop, for instance, and carefully think no thoughts, a myopic, bestial clarity besets your vision. There is a wheel, there are spokes, and there is a hub. And in the center of the hub there is – exactly nothing. It is where the grease goes, and the axle. And you are there, in the center of nothingness, sentient, fully expanded, whirring with the whir of planetary wheels. Everything becomes alive and meaningful, even yesterday's snot which clings to the door knob. Everything sags and droops, is mossed with wear and care; everything has been looked at thousands of times, rubbed and caressed by the occipital eye...

An abandoned church, a For Rent sign defacing its baroque façade, towers black and broken at the corner of this lost square; sparrows nest among the stone flowers carved above its chalked-up door (Kilroy Was Here, Seymour Loves Betty, You Stink!); inside, where sunlight falls on shattered pews, all manner of stray beasts have found a home: one sees misty cats watching from its windows, hears queer animal cries, and neighborhood children, who dare each other to enter there, come forth toting bones they claim as human (yeah, they is so! I'm tellin' yuh; the guy was kilt). Definitive in its ugliness, the church for me symbolizes some elements of Brooklyn: if a similar structure were destroyed, I have the uneasy premonition that another, equally old and monstrous, would swiftly be erected, for Brooklyn, or the chain of cities so-called, has, unlike Manhattan, no interest in architectural change. Nor is it lenient toward the individual: in despair one views the quite endless stretches of look-alike bungalows, gingerbread and brownstones, the inevitable empty, ashy lot where the sad, sweet, violent children, gathering leaves and tenement-wood, make October bonfires, the sad, sweet children chasing down these glassy August streets to Kill the Kike! Kill the Wop! Kill the Dinge! – a custom of this country where the mental architecture, like the houses, is changeless.

The Southern writer TRUMAN CAPOTE lived in Brooklyn when he first came to the city after the Second World War. In his essay 'Brooklyn' (1946), he carefully observed his new environment.

Every now and then, seeking to rid my mind of thoughts of death and doom, I get up early and go down to Fulton Fish Market. I usually arrive around five-thirty, and take a walk through the two huge open-fronted market sheds, the Old Market and the New Market, whose fronts rest on South Street and whose backs rest on piles in the East River. At that time, a little while before the trading begins, the stands in the sheds are heaped high and spilling over with forty to sixty kinds of finfish and shellfish from the East Coast, the West Coast, the Gulf Coast, and half a dozen foreign countries. The smoky riverbank dawn, the racket the fishmongers make, the seaweedy smell, and the sight of this plentifulness always give me a feeling of well-being, and sometimes they elate me. I wander among the stands for an hour or so. Then I go into a cheerful market restaurant named Sloppy Louie's and eat a big, inexpensive, invigorating breakfast – a kippered herring and scrambled eggs, or a shad-roe omelet, or split sea scallops and bacon, or some other breakfast specialty of the place.

'Up in the Old Hotel', like many of journalist JOSEPH MITCHELL's chronicles of out-of-the-way New York, first appeared in the New Yorker and was published later in The Bottom of the Harbor (1959).

'Sidewalk Fisherman' is a
sketch by newspaperman
MEYER BERGER *from his
book* The Eight Million
(1942).

Sam Schultz has always been hydrophobic. Even as a kid, in a Central Park rowboat he would go white with fear of the water. When he grew up and friends invited him on fishing parties he'd always refuse, saying he had a tendency to seasickness. It took a vast economic disturbance, the depression, to throw him into grate fishing when all his natural instincts were against it, but today he is probably the world's champion grate fisherman, the man who can haul up coins from subway gratings with more efficiency than anybody else in the business. Grate fishing was a primitive art when Sam became identified with it after losing his job as a truckman's helper seven years ago. It was just something that bums worked at for beer money. Sam has made it an exact science, and he earns a living by it.

Sam works with a few feet of light twine and a plummet of his own design – a piece of steel five inches long, an eighth of an inch thick, and about an inch and three quarters wide, just right to lower through the grate slot. He lets it down endways until it gets to the bottom, and then lets it fall broadside on the coin. Sam will point out that his five-inch plummet thus covers a potential working area of almost ten inches. The flat side of the plummet is greased so that the coin sticks to it; all Sam has to do then is to haul away and he's got the money. The bums of the grate-fishing industry use tiny weights for plummets and have to maneuver their lines a long time before they hit. 'My way,' Sam

Etching by Isabel Bishop, 1953.

will tell you, 'is pure headwoik.'

Sam's second and equally important contribution toward uplift of the industry was an all-weather stickum to take the place of the chewing gum or taxicab-wheel grease which the bums use on their casting plummets. Chewing gum was all right in summer but it hardened at the first frost. Taxi grease worked into your pores, got under your fingernails, and made your hands untidy. It took months of experiment before Sam found the right thing – white petroleum jelly, or vaseline. A thin coat of this on the plummet will pull pennies, dimes, nickels, and even big money out of any subway grate, come frost or heat wave.

Sam buys the vaseline in the Liggett's drugstore on Times Square. The clerks there know him now and they plop the jar on the counter the minute he walks in. A single jar will last a month in winter and about three weeks in summer, if you husband it and don't oversmear, which is the general fault of amateurs. Runoff, because of heat, accounts for the extra summer waste, and so far Sam hasn't found a way around that. When you're after big money (quarters and halves), it is better to thicken the vaseline coating on your plummet, but not too much. Sam figures, for example, that proper bait for a silver dollar would be around a sixteenth of an inch. That's pure theory, because cartwheels are practically extinct in New York and he has never had a chance to work on one.

Under the seeming disorder of the old city, wherever the old city is working successfully, is a marvelous order for maintaining the safety of the streets and the freedom of the city. It is a complex order. Its essence is intricacy of sidewalk use, bringing with it a constant succession of eyes. This order is all composed of movement and change, and although it is life, not art, we may fancifully call it the art form of the city and liken it to the dance – not to a simple-minded precision dance with everyone kicking up at the same time, twirling in unison and bowing off en masse, but to an intricate ballet in which the individual dancers and ensembles all have distinctive parts which miraculously reinforce each other and compose an orderly whole. The ballet of the good city sidewalk never repeats itself from place to place, and in any one place is always replete with new improvisations.

The stretch of Hudson Street where I live is each day the scene of an intricate sidewalk ballet. I make my own first entrance into it a little after eight when I put out the garbage can, surely a prosaic occupation, but I enjoy my part, my little clang, as the droves of junior high school students walk by the center of the stage dropping candy wrappers. (How do they eat so much candy so early in the morning?)

While I sweep up the wrappers I watch the other rituals of morning: Mr Halpert unlocking the laundry's handcart from its mooring to a cellar door, Joe Cornacchia's son-in-law stacking out the empty crates from the delicatessen, the barber bringing out his sidewalk folding chair, Mr Goldstein arranging the coils of wire which proclaim the hardware store is open, the wife of the tenement's superintendent depositing her chunky three-year-old with a toy mandolin on the stoop, the vantage point from which he is learning the English his mother cannot speak. Now the primary children, heading for St Luke's, dribble through to the south; the children for St Veronica's cross, heading to the west, and the children for P.S. 41, heading toward the east. Two new entrances are

JANE JACOBS' book, The Death and Life of Great American Cities, *caused a furore when it appeared in 1961. As one of the first investigations into the nature of inner-city decay it led many people to rethink old ideas about urban planning and what, exactly, we expect from life in a big city.*

'The world of the street belonged to the kid alone' – photograph by Leonard Freed.

being made from the wings: well-dressed and even elegant women and men with brief cases emerge from doorways and side streets. Most of these are heading for the bus and subways, but some hover on the curbs, stopping taxis which have miraculously appeared at the right moment, for the taxis are part of a wider morning ritual: having dropped passengers from midtown in the downtown financial district, they are now bringing downtowners up to midtown. Simultaneously, a number of women in housedresses have emerged and as they crisscross with one another they pause for quick conversations that sound with either laughter or joint indignation, never, it seems, anything between. It is time for me to hurry to work too, and I exchange my ritual farewell with Mr Lofaro, the short, thick-bodied, white-aproned fruit man who stands outside his doorway a little up the street, his arms folded, his feet planted, looking solid as earth itself. We nod; we each glance quickly up and down the street, then look back to each other and smile. We have done this many a morning for more than ten years, and we both know what it means: All is well.

In the daytime Harlem looks kinda dirty and the people a little drab and down. But at night, man, it's a swinging place, especially Spanish Harlem. The lights transform everything into life and movement and blend the different colors into a magic cover-all that makes the drabness and garbage, wailing kids and tired people invisible. Shoes and clothes that by day look beat and worn out, at night take on a reflected splendor that the blazing multi-colored lights burn on them. Everyone seems to develop a sense of urgent rhythm and you get the impression that you have to walk with a sense of timing.

The daytime pain fades alongside the feeling of belonging and just being in swing with all the humming kicks going on around you. I'd stand on a corner and close my eyes and look at everything through my nose. I'd sniff deep and see the *cuchifritos* and hot dogs, stale sweat and dried urine. I'd smell the worn-out mothers with six or seven kids, and the nonpatient fathers beating the hell out of them. My nose would get a high-pitch tingling from the gritty wailing and bouncing red light of a squad car passing the scene like a bat out of Harlem, going to cool some trouble, or maybe cause some.

I'd walk on Lexington Avenue, where a lot of things were going on, and hear the long, strung-out voice of a junkie, 'Hey, man, you got a couple of charlies you can lend me?'. . .

I'd meet my boys, and all the other hearing and seeing suddenly became unimportant. Only my boys were the important kick, and for good reasons – if I had boys, I had respect and no other clique would make me open game. Besides, they gave me a feeling of belonging, of prestige, of accomplishment; I felt *grande* and bad. Sometimes the thoughts would start flapping around inside me about the three worlds I lived in – the world of home, the world of school (no more of that, though), and the world of street. The street was the best damn one. It was like all the guys shouting out, 'Hey, man, this is our kick.'

The worlds of home and school were made up of rules laid down by adults who had forgotten the feeling of what it means to be a kid but expected a kid to remember to be an adult – something he hadn't gotten to yet. The world of street belonged to the kid alone. There he could earn his own rights, prestige, his good-o stick of living. It was like being a knight of old, like being ten feet tall.

PIRI THOMAS*'s novel of New York streetlife* Down These Mean Streets *appeared in 1967.*

NOEL RICO's poem
'The First Place' is set in the
tense Puerto Rican slums of
present-day New York.

Conga beats pouring out a window
makes the curtains tremble
A man is laughing
A woman leans out
a window her fingers running
through her hair over her blouse
down to her thighs
I hear Ismael Miranda
singing
A mulata with cheeks
red as two drops of blood
walks past me
pushing a baby carriage

A little girl is cutting open the face
of the sidewalk with a piece of red chalk. . .
The jewish store owner
turns keys in hundreds of locks,
he dreams that thieves
grow out of the sidewalk
like plants
when no one is around

on the corner by the police phone
two boys are stealing a drunk's money
as he sleeps
on an old piece of newspaper
garbage dancing
at his feet
to a rhythm
played by the cold

it is a mambo
lined with ice.

In SAUL BELLOW's novel
Mr Sammler's Planet (1969),
the protagonist, a survivor of
the Nazi concentration
camps, examines the city
with a jaundiced eye.

On Second Avenue the springtime scraping of roller skates was heard on hollow, brittle sidewalks, a soothing harshness. Turning from the new New York of massed apartments into the older New York of brownstone and wrought-iron, Sammler saw through large black circles in a fence daffodils and tulips, the mouths of these flowers open and glowing, but on the pure yellow the fallout of soot already was sprinkled. You might in this city become a flower-washer . . .

. . . Sammler had learned to be careful on public paths in New York, invariably dog-fouled. Within the iron-railed plots the green lights of the grass were all but put out, burned by animal excrements. The sycamores, blemished bark, but very nice, brown and white, getting ready to cough up leaves. Red brick, the Friends Seminary, and ruddy coarse warm stone, broad, clumsy, solid, the Episcopal church, St George's. Sammler had heard that the original J. Pierpont Morgan had been an usher there . . . At St George's, Sundays, the god of stockbrokers could breathe easy awhile in the riotous city. In thought, Mr

Street vendor, New York (1985).

Sammler was testy with White Protestant America for not keeping better order. Cowardly surrender. Not a strong ruling class. Eager in a secret humiliating way to come down and mingle with all the minority mobs, and scream against themselves. And the clergy? Beating swords into plowshares? No, rather converting dog collars into G strings. But this was neither here nor there.

. . . He noted a female bum drunkenly sleeping like a dugong, a sea cow's belly rising, legs swollen purple; a short dress, a mini-rag. At a corner of the fence, a wino was sullenly pissing on newspapers and old leaves. Cops seldom bothered about these old-fashioned derelicts. Younger people, autochthonous-looking, were also here. Bare feet, the boys like Bombay beggars, beards clotted, breathing rich hair from their nostrils, heads coming through woolen ponchos, somewhat Peruvian. Natives of somewhere. Innocent, devoid of aggression, opting out, much like Ferdinand the Bull. No *corrida* for them; only smelling flowers under the lovely cork tree. How similar also to the Eloi of H. G. Wells' fantasy *The Time Machine*. Lovely young human cattle herded by the cannibalistic Morlocks who lived a subterranean life and feared light and fire. Yes, that tough brave little old fellow Wells had had prophetic visions after all. . .

THE YELLOW DEVIL

In Boston they ask, How much does he know?
In New York, How much is he worth?
MARK TWAIN

Mammon, n. The god of the world's leading religion.
His chief temple is in the holy city of New York.

AMBROSE BIERCE, The Devil's Dictionary

For Russian social critic, novelist, and playwright MAXIM GORKI *New York was* The City of the Yellow Devil, *the title he gave to the little book he published in 1906, recounting his visit to the city in the previous year.*

People hurry to and fro on the pavements, in every direction the streets take. They are sucked up by the deep pores in the stone walls. The exultant rumble of iron, the loud piercing whine of electricity, the clatter of work on some new steel construction or on new walls of stone, drown out human voices as a storm at sea drowns the cries of the birds.

The people's faces wear an expression of immobile calm; not one of them, apparently, is aware of his misfortune in being the slave of life, nourishment for the city monster. In their pitiable arrogance they imagine themselves to be the masters of their fate; consciousness of their independence gleams occasionally in their eyes, but clearly they do not understand that this is only the independence of the axe in the carpenter's hand, the hammer in the smith's hand, the brick in the hand of that unseen bricklayer, who, with a sly chuckle, is building one vast but cramping prison for all. There are many virile faces among them, but in each face, one notices the teeth first of all. Inner freedom, the freedom of the spirit, does not shine in these people's eyes. And their freedomless energy reminds one of the cold gleam of a knife that has not yet been blunted. It is the freedom of blind tools in the hands of the Yellow Devil – Gold.

This is the first time I have seen so monstrous a city, and never before have people seemed to me so insignificant, so enslaved. At the same time nowhere have I met people so tragicomically satisfied with themselves as are these in this voracious and filthy stomach of the glutton, who has grown into an imbecile from greed and, with the wild bellowing of an animal, devours brains and nerves. . .

On 14 October 1835, PHILIP HONE, *prominent businessman and one-time mayor of New York, noted in his diary the frantic trade in company stocks which had already become a feature of Wall Street life.*

The gambling in stocks in Wall street has arrived at such a pitch, and the sudden reverses of fortune are so frequent, that it is a matter of every-day intelligence that some unlucky rascal has lost other people's money to a large amount, and run away, or been caught and consigned to the hands of justice. It is one taken from the mass; there is some swearing among the losers, some regret on the part of the immediate friends of the defaulter, but the chasm on the face of society which his detection and removal occasions is filled up in a day or two. They go to work again to cheat each other, and the catastrophe of Monday is forgotten by Saturday night.

'The Chrysler Building Under Construction' – painting by Earl Horter, 1931.

When FREDERICK MARRYAT, *English novelist and seaman, visited New York in 1837, the city was in the midst of one of its periodic business crashes, as he recorded in his* Diary in America *(1838).*

A visit, to make it agreeable to both parties, should be well timed. My appearance at New York was very much like bursting into a friend's house with a merry face when there is a death in it – with the sudden change from levity to condolence. 'Any other time most happy to see you. You find us in a very unfortunate situation.'

'Indeed I'm very – very sorry.'

Two hundred and sixty houses have already failed, and no one knows where it is to end. Suspicion, fear, and misfortune have taken possession of the city. Had I not been aware of the cause, I should have imagined that the plague was raging, and I had the description of Defoe before me.

Not a smile on one countenance among the crowd who pass and repass; hurried steps, careworn faces, rapid exchanges of salutation, or hasty communication of anticipated ruin before the sun goes down. Here two or three are gathered on one side, whispering and watching that they are not over-heard; there a solitary, with his arms folded and his hat slouched, brooding over departed affluence. Mechanics, thrown out of employment, are pacing up and down with the air of famished wolves. The violent shock has been communicated, like that of electricity, through the country to a distance of hundreds of miles. Canals, railroads, and all public works, have been discontinued, and the Irish emigrant leans against his shanty, with his spade idle in his hand, and starves, as his thoughts wander back to his own Emerald Isle.

The Americans delight in the hyperbole; in fact they hardly have a metaphor without it. During this crash, when every day fifteen or twenty merchants' names appeared in the newspapers as bankrupts, one party, not in a very good humour, was hastening down Broadway, when he was run against by another whose temper was equally unamiable. This collision aroused the choler of both.

'What the devil do you mean, sir?' cried one; 'I've a great mind to knock you into *the middle of next week.*'

This occurring on a Saturday, the wrath of the other was checked by the recollection of how very favourable such a blow would be to his present circumstances.

'Will you! by heavens, then pray do; it's just the thing I want, for how else I am to get over next Monday and the acceptances I must take up, is more than I can tell.'

All the banks have stopped payment in specie, and there is not a dollar to be had. I walked down Wall Street, and had a convincing proof of the great demand for money, for somebody picked my pocket.

The Depression of 1857 was one of the worst downturns seen in the American economy in the nineteenth century. Lawyer GEORGE TEMPLETON STRONG *recorded its devastation in his diary on 22 October, 1857.*

D epression continues. Though there may be little side-eddies that some people look at with joy, the tide is still running out and everything is drifting down with it, or else stuck fast already on the black mud flats of insolvency and destined to rot there and perish long before the tide comes back again. . .

We are a very sick people just now. The outward and visible signs of disease, the cutaneous symptoms, are many. Walking down Broadway you pass great $200,000 buildings begun last spring or summer that have gone up two stories, and stopped, and may stand unfinished and desolate for years, or on which six Celts are working instead of sixty. Almost every shop has its placards (*written* not *printed*) announcing a great sacrifice, vast reduction of prices, sales at less than cost ... In Wall Street every man carries Pressure, Anxiety, Loss, written on his forehead. This is far the worst period of public calamity and distress I've ever seen, and I fear it is but the beginning.

Few commercial capitals have ever grown with more marvellous rapidity than New York. The great merchants and men of affairs who have built up her material prosperity, have not merely enriched themselves and their city; they have also played no inconsiderable part in that rapid opening up of the American continent during the present century, which has been rendered possible by the eagerness and far-reaching business ambition of commercial adventurers, wielding the wonderful tools forged by the science of our day. The merchant, the 'railroad king', the capitalist who works or gambles for

John Jacob Astor and Cornelius Vanderbilt were two of New York's most legendary millionaires. THEODORE ROOSEVELT *described their careers in his book* New York *(1903).*

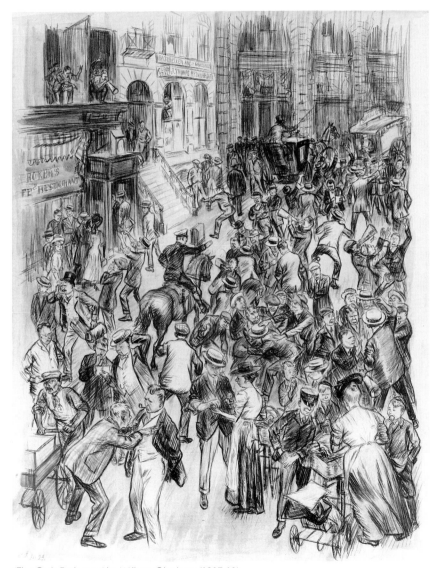

'The Curb Exchange' by William Glackens (1907-10).

colossal stakes, bending to his purpose an intellect in its way as shrewd and virile as that of any statesman or warrior, – all these, and their compeers, are and have been among the most striking and important, although far from the noblest, figures of nineteeth-century America.

Two New Yorkers of great note in this way may be instanced as representatives of their class, – John Jacob Astor and Cornelius Vanderbilt. Astor was originally a German pedler, who came to the city immediately after the close of the Revolution. He went into the retail fur-trade, and by energy, thrift, and far-sightedness, soon pushed his way up so as to be able to command a large amount of capital; and he forthwith embarked on ventures more extensive in scale. The fur-trade was then in the North almost what the trade in gold and silver had been in the South. Vast fortunes were made in it, and the career of the fur-trader was checkered by romantic successes and hazardous vicissitudes. Astor made money with great rapidity, and entered on a course of rivalry with the huge fur companies of Canada. Finally, in 1809, he organized the American Fur Company, under the auspices of the State of New York, with no less a purpose than the establishment of a settlement of trappers and fur-traders at the mouth of the Columbia. He sent his parties out both by sea and overland, established his posts, and drove a thriving trade; and doubtless he would have anticipated by a generation the permanent settlement of Oregon, if the war had not broken out, and his colony been destroyed by the British. The most substantial portion of his fortune was made out of successful ventures in New York City real estate; and at his death he was one of the five richest men in the world. His greatest service to the city was founding the Astor Library.

Vanderbilt was a Staten Island boy, whose parents were very poor, and who therefore had to work for his living at an early age. Before the War of 1812, when a lad in his teens, he had been himself sailing a sloop as a ferry-boat, between Staten Island and New York, and soon had saved enough money to start a small line of them. After the war he saw the possibilities of the steamboat, and began to run one as captain, owning a share in it as well. He shortly saved enough to become his own capitalist, and removed to New York in 1829. He organized steam lines on the Hudson and Sound, making money hand over hand; and in 1849 – the period of the California gold fever – he turned his attention to ocean steamships, and for several years carried on a famous contest with the Pacific Mail Steamship Company, for the traffic across the Isthmus to California. He was drawn into antagonism with the filibuster Walker, because of his connection with the Central American States, and became one of the forces which compassed that gray-eyed adventurer's downfall. Then he took to building and managing railways, and speculating in them, and by the end of his days had amassed a colossal fortune. The history of the Wall Street speculations in which he took part, forms much the least attractive portion of the record of his life.

'The Chrysler Building' by Howard Cook.

In the twenties, New York was a place to spend money. Any and everything could be bought, as the critic, journalist, and acerbic

It roars with life like the Bagdad of the Sassanians. These great capitals of antiquity, in fact, were squalid villages compared to it, as Rome was after their kind, and Paris, Berlin and London are to-day. There is little in New York that does not issue out of money. It is not a town of ideas; it is not even a town of causes. But what issues out of money is often extremely brilliant, and I believe that it is more brilliant in New York than it has ever been anywhere else. A truly overwhelming opulence envelops the whole place, even the slums. The slaves who keep it going may dwell in vile cubicles, but they are hauled to and from their work by machinery that costs hundreds of millions, and when they fare forth to recreate themselves for to-morrow's tasks they are felled and made dumb by a gaudiness that would have floored John Paleologus himself. Has any one ever figured out, in hard cash, the value of the objects of art stored upon Manhattan Island? I narrow it to paintings, and bar out all the good ones. What would it cost to replace even the bad ones? Or all the statuary, bronzes, hangings, pottery, and bogus antiques? Or the tons of bangles, chains of pearls, stomachers, necklaces, and other baubles? Assemble all the diamonds into one colossal stone, and you will have a weapon to slay Behemoth. The crowds pour in daily, bringing the gold wrung from iron and coal, hog and cow. It is invisible, for they carry it in checks, but it is real for all that. Every dollar earned in Kansas or Montana finds it way, soon or late, to New York, and if there is a part of it that goes back, there is also a part of it that sticks.

wit H. L. MENCKEN noted in one of the essays collected in his Prejudices, Sixth Series, *(1927).*

Noon on Union Square. Selling out. Must vacate. WE HAVE MADE A TERRIBLE MISTAKE. Kneeling on the dusty asphalt little boys shine shoes lowshoes tans buttonshoes oxfords. The sun shines like a dandelion on the toe of each new-shined shoe. Right this way buddy, mister miss maam at the back of the store our new line of fancy tweeds highest value lowest price . . . Gents, misses, ladies, cutrate . . . WE HAVE MADE A TERRIBLE MISTAKE. Must vacate.

Noon sunlight spirals dimly into the chopsuey joint. Muted music spirals Hindustan. He eats fooyong, she eats chowmein. They dance with their mouths full, slim blue jumper squeezed to black slick suit, peroxide curls against black slick hair.

Down Fourteenth Street, Glory Glory comes the Army, striding lasses, Glory Glory four abreast, the rotund shining, navy blue, Salvation Army band.

Highest value, lowest price. Must vacate. WE HAVE MADE A TERRIBLE MISTAKE. Must vacate.

Business life has always been hard in New York. JOHN DOS PASSOS *captured its poignancy in this passage from his novel* Manhattan Transfer *(1925).*

The terrible, cold, cruel part is Wall Street. Rivers of gold flow there from all over the earth, and death comes with it. There as nowhere else you feel a total absence of the spirit: herds of men who cannot count past three, herds more who cannot get past six, scorn for pure science, and demoniacal respect for the present. And the terrible thing is that the crowd who fills the street believes that the world will always be the same, and that it is their duty to move the huge machine day and night forever. The perfect result of a Protestant morality that I, as a (thank God) typical Spaniard, found unnerving. I was lucky enough to see with my own eyes the recent crash, where they lost various billions of dollars, a rabble of dead money that slid off into the sea, and never as then, amid suicides, hysteria, and groups of fainters, have I felt the sensation of real death, death without hope, death that is nothing but rottenness, for the spectacle was terrifying but devoid of greatness. And I, who come from a country where, as the great poet Unamuno said, 'at night the earth climbs to the sky', I felt something like a divine urge to bombard that whole shadowy defile where ambulances collected suicides whose hands were full of rings.

The Wall Street Crash of 1929 reverberated around the world, plunging one capitalist economy after another into crisis. FEDERICO GARCIA LORCA *was visiting New York at the time, composing the poems which would later be collected under the title* Poet in New York. *On his return to Spain, he described his impressions of the city in a series of lectures given to accompany readings of the poems.*

Wall Street, 1929.

Who is there still remembers
The fame of the giant city of New York
In the decade after the Great War?

What a melting pot was America in those days – celebrated by poets!
God's own country!
Invoked just by the initials of its names:
U.S.A.
Like an unmistakable childhood friend whom everyone knows.

What people they were! Their boxers the strongest!
Their inventors the most practical! Their trains the fastest!
And also the most crowded!
And it all looked like lasting a thousand years
For the people of the city of New York put it about themselves:
That their city was built on the rock and hence
Indestructible.

Truly their whole system of communal life was beyond compare.
What fame! What a century! ⋅

Admittedly that century lasted
A bare eight years.

For one day there ran through the world the rumour of strange collapses
On a famous continent, and its banknotes, hoarded only yesterday,
Were rejected in disgust like rotten stinking fish.

Today, when the word has gone round
That these people are bankrupt
We on the other continents (which are indeed bankrupt as well)
See many things differently and, so we think, more clearly.

What of the skyscrapers?
We observe them more coolly.
What contemptible hovels skyscrapers are when they no longer yield rents!
Rising so high, full of poverty? Touching the clouds, full of debt?
What of the railroad trains?
In the railroad trains, which resemble hotels on wheels, they say
Often nobody lives.
He travels nowhere
With incomparable rapidity.
What of the bridges? The longest in the world, they now link
Scrapheap with scrapheap.
And what of the people?

Here I was in New York, city of prose and fantasy, of capitalist automatism, its streets a triumph of cubism; its moral philosophy that of the dollar. New York impressed me tremendously because, more than any other city in the world, it is the fullest expression of our modern age.

In this extract from his poem 'Late Lamented Fame of the Giant City of New York' (1929), German poet and playwright BERTOLT BRECHT *comments ironically on success in the light of the Great Crash.*

Pan-Am building under construction.

The international revolutionary LEON TROTSKY *recalled his brief stay in New York in his* My Life *(1929).*

After the Second World War, New York was seized by successive waves of development and redevelopment. In 1956 LEWIS MUMFORD devoted one of his regular architectural columns in the New Yorker *magazine to an attack on the power of high finance.*

The frantic effort to crowd the central district of Manhattan with enough tall office buildings to make traffic a permanent tangle is rapidly approaching complete success. Already, after ten in the morning, a reasonably healthy pedestrian can get across town faster than the most skillful taxi-driver. All this may persuade someone in authority to suggest turning the midtown district into a vast pedestrian mall, closed to private vehicles during the day, as some of the narrow streets in the financial district are now. Unfortunately, the load of pedestrians has likewise become so heavy, not merely at the lunch hour or during Christmas shopping but during most of the day, that the walker is frequently slowed down to the exhausting creep of the car or the bus. One would think that this situation might cause some serious thought among the bankers and investors and business enterprisers who have been fostering this congestion, admittedly with the sanction of the municipality's zoning laws. Their lack of concern for the end product has been explained to me by one of the most successful of our urban space men. 'Money,' he said, giving the word the sort of halo a Roman might attach to his tutelary deity, 'is not interested in looking further ahead than the next five years.' If this truly represents the prevailing mood, the people who are so ebulliently strangling the economic life of New York and canceling out, one by one, every sound reason for living here must consider that New York is expendable.

Traders on the floor of the New York Stock Exchange try to cope with the Crash of October, 1987.

'May Day in the city' (1859) – the traditional day for moving house in old New York.

UPHEAVAL

How this city marches northward! The progress of 1835 and 1836 was nothing to the luxuriant, rank growth of this year. Streets are springing up, whole strata of sandstone have transferred themselves from their ancient resting-places to look down on bustling thoroughfares for long years to come. Wealth is rushing in upon us like a freshet.

Within the span of a generation, the open spaces and the natural vistas began to disappear. The older beer gardens, like Niblo's Garden, gardens that had frequently preserved the trees and open space of a whole block, were wiped out: only in the further reaches of the city did they remain, like Unter den Linden on upper Broadway, and like the roadhouses which dotted the more or less open country that remained on the West Side above 125th Street until the end of the century. The rocky base of Manhattan, always

Lawyer GEORGE TEMPLETON STRONG *noted the city's rapid growth in his diary on 27 October 1850.*

In his essay 'America and Alfred Stieglitz' (1934), social and architectural critic LEWIS MUMFORD *reflected on New York's rapid transformation in the decades following the Civil War.*

unkind to life, steadily lost its filament of soil. The trees in the streets became more infrequent as the city grew; and their leaves grew sear before autumn came. Even the great Boulevard above Sixty-fifth Street, which the ignoble Tweed had planted along Broadway for his own pecuniary benefit, sacrificed its magnificent trees to the first subway; while only the ailanthus tree, quick growing and lean living, kept the back yards occasionally green, to gladden the lonely young men and women from the country, who faced their first year in the city from hall bedrooms on the top-floor rear of unamiable boarding-houses. And as the city grew, it grew away from its old markets: one of the last of these, to prove more reminiscent of the old than anticipatory of the new, was the Jefferson Market, with its medieval German tower, at Eighth Street. Vanishing from the consciousness of most Manhattanites were the open markets that had once brought the touch of the sea and the country to its streets, connecting farmstead and city home by means of little boats that plied the Hudson and Long Island Sound.

The water and the soil, as the prime environment of life, were becoming 'immaterial', that is to say, they were of no use to the canny minds that were promoting the metropolis, unless they could be described in a legal document, appraised quantitatively, and converted ultimately into cash. A farm became for the speculator a place that might be converted into building lots: in that process, indeed, lay the meaning of this feverish growth, this anxious speculation, this reckless transformation of the quick into the dead. People staked out claims on the farther parts of the city in the way that prospectors stake out claims in a gold rush. There was always the chance that some negligible patch of earth might become, in the course of the city's growth, a gold mine. That was magic. In the atmosphere of magic, the desire to get something for nothing, a whole population hoped and breathed and lived. That in reality the environment was becoming unfit for human habitation in the process did not concern the midas-fingered gentlemen who ruled the city, nor did it affect the dull-fingered million who lacked that golden touch: their dreams were framed within the same heaven. Lacking the reality, they fed on the gilded lubricities of Mr Bennett's, Mr Pulitzer's, and Mr Hearst's newspapers.

In 1904 novelist HENRY JAMES *returned to his native New York after an absence of over twenty years. He found the city profoundly changed by the tremendous forces of high finance, as he reported in his* The American Scene *(1907).*

You see the pin-cushion in profile, so to speak, on passing between Jersey City and Twenty-third Street, but you get it broadside on, this loose nosegay of architectural flowers, if you skirt the Battery, well out, and embrace the whole plantation. Then the 'American beauty', the rose of interminable stem, becomes the token of the cluster at large . . . Such growths, you feel, have confessedly arisen but to be 'picked', in time, with a shears; nipped short off, by waiting fate, as soon as 'science', applied to gain, has put upon the table, from far up its sleeve, some more winning card. Crowned not only with no history, but with no credible possibility of time for history, and consecrated by no uses save the commercial at any cost, they are simply the most piercing notes in that concert of the expensively provisional into which your supreme sense of New York resolves itself. They never begin to speak to you, in the manner of the builded majesties of the world as we have heretofore known such – towers or temples or fortesses or palaces – with the authority of things of permanence or even of things of long duration. One story is good only till

'Pennsylvania Station Excavation' – painting by George Bellows.

another is told, and skyscrapers are the last word of economic ingenuity only till another word be written. This shall be possibly a word of still uglier meaning, but the vocabulary of thrift at any price shows boundless resources, and the consciousness of that truth, the consciousness of the finite, the menaced, the essentially *invented* state, twinkles ever, to my perception, in the thousand glassy eyes of these giants of the mere market.

In 1982 New York will likely have so expanded that, if the same ratio of growth in population continues for the coming fifty years as has held for the past fifty, its census will show a community of close to 50,000,000; and its boundary limits including a goodly share of Long Island, as well as absorbing White Plains, Yonkers, and other contiguous territory northward. East River will have been filled in, and hundreds of acres of the Hudson River bed reclaimed.

Buildings will possibly be from 200 to 250 stories in height. Triple-deck elevators, vacuum-tube escalators, and other vertical travel will be so improved

In his New York, the Wonder City *(1932) the pseudonymous author* W. PARKER CHASE *imagined the city of the future.*

81

as to whisk tenants upwards at a speed surpassing all imagination at this time.

Traffic arrangements will no doubt have provided for several tiers of elevated roadways and noiseless railways – built on extended balconies flanking the enormous skyscrapers, or passing directly through them . . . so as to keep the streets cleared for '*air-taxi*' ships.

It may be a simple matter for one to eat breakfast in New York and attend the Follies Bergere in Paris that evening. Those who for some reason still prefer to *sleep* in Chicago, may be included among New York commuters.

Versifier OGDEN NASH *eulogized the recently demolished Sixth Avenue El – an elevated railway line – in his poem* Good Intentions *(1942).*

Let this be my tardy farewell
To the erstwhile Sixth Avenue El.
Though no longer a native New Yorker
My aesthetic eye is a corker;
The El had a twelve-foot clearance
And I notice its disappearance.
New York was to many a kingdom
Where business or pleasure bringdom,
But I got there so seldom
To me 'twas Sixth Avenue Eldom.
It never got anyone downer
Than this timid out-of-towner;
It ran like an iron entrail
Midway 'twixt Penn and Grand Central;
It staggered column by column
From the Battery up to Harlem,
And no matter wherever went you
The Sixth Avenue El went too.
You'd be riding from Park to Madison
While leafing through Steele or Addison.
And fleeter than meter could tell
You'd be twisting under the El;
Be you headed south or north
On Lexington, Park or Fourth
Any whither you wished to flit,
Lay the El between you and it.
Farewell, O El, farewell;
I was once of your clientele.
Although I'm no longer Manhattanized
I'm glad that we met and fraternized.

Having created Jones and Orchard Beaches, the West Side Highway, the Belt Parkway, and the Triborough Bridge, Robert Moses turned his attention to the Bronx in the fifties. Cultural historian MARSHAL BERMAN *witnessed the upheaval*

But then, in the spring and fall of 1953, Moses began to loom over my life in a new way: he proclaimed that he was about to ram an immense expressway, unprecedented in scale, expense and difficulty of construction, through our neighborhood's heart. At first we couldn't believe it; it seemed to come from another world. First of all, hardly any of us owned cars: the neighborhood itself, and the subways leading downtown, defined the flow of our lives. Besides, even if the city needed the road – or was it the state that needed the road? (in Moses' operations, the location of power and authority was never clear, except for Moses himself) – they surely couldn't mean what the stories seemed to say: that the road would be blasted directly through a dozen solid, settled, densely populated neighborhoods like our own; that something like 60,000 working- and lower-middle-class people, mostly Jews, but with many Italians, Irish and Blacks thrown in, would be thrown out of their homes. The Jews of the Bronx were nonplussed: could a fellow-Jew really want to do this to us? (We had little idea of what kind of Jew he was, or of how much we were all an obstruction in his path.) And even if he did want to do it, we were sure it couldn't happen here, not in America. We were still basking in the afterglow of the New Deal: the government was *our* government, and it would come through to protect us in the end. And yet, before we knew it, steam shovels and bulldozers were there, and people were getting notice that they had better clear out fast. They looked numbly at the wreckers, at the disappearing streets, at each other, and they went. Moses was coming through, and no temporal or spiritual power could block his way.

For ten years, through the late 1950s and early 1960s, the center of the Bronx was pounded and blasted and smashed. My friends and I would stand on the parapet of the Grand Concourse, where 174th Street had been, and survey the work's progress — the immense steam shovels and bulldozers and timber and steel beams, the hundreds of workers in their variously colored hard hats, the giant cranes reaching far above the Bronx's tallest roofs, the dynamite blasts and tremors, the wild, jagged crags of rock newly torn, the vistas of devastation stretching for miles to the east and west as far as the eye could see — and marvel to see our ordinary nice neighborhood transformed into sublime, spectacular ruins.

In college, when I discovered Piranesi, I felt instantly at home. Or I would return from the Columbia library to the construction site and feel myself in the midst of the last act of Goethe's *Faust*. (You had to hand it to Moses: his works gave you ideas.) Only there was no humanistic triumph here to offset the destruction. Indeed, when construction was done, the real ruin of the Bronx had just begun. Miles of streets alongside the road were choked with dust and fumes and deafening noise — most strikingly, the roar of trucks of a size and power that the Bronx had never seen, hauling heavy cargoes through the city, bound for Long Island or New England, for New Jersey and all points south, all through the day and night. Apartment houses that had been settled and stable for twenty years emptied out, often virtually overnight; large and impoverished Black and Hispanic families, fleeing even worse slums, were moved in wholesale, often under the auspices of the Welfare Department, which even paid inflated rents, spreading panic and accelerating flight. At the same time, the construction had destroyed many commercial blocks, cut others off from most of their customers and left the storekeepers not only close to bankruptcy but, in their enforced isolation, increasingly vulnerable to crime. The borough's great open market, along Bathgate Avenue, still flourishing in the late 1950s, was decimated; a year after the road came through, what was left went up in smoke. Thus depopulated, economically depleted, emotionally shattered — as bad as the physical damage had been the inner wounds were worse — the Bronx was ripe for all the dreaded spirals of urban blight.

Moses seemed to glory in the devastation. When he was asked, shortly after the Cross-Bronx road's completion, if urban expressways like this didn't pose special human problems, he replied impatiently that 'there's very little hard-

caused by the building of Moses's Cross-Bronx Expressway and recalled it in his book All That Is Solid Melts in the Air *(1982).*

ship in the thing. There's a little discomfort and even that is exaggerated.' Compared with his earlier, rural and suburban highways, the only difference here was that 'There are more houses in the way . . . more people in the way – that's all.' He boasted that 'When you operate in an overbuilt metropolis, you have to hack your way with a meat axe.'

In this extract from his poem 'An Urban Convalescence' (1962) New York-born poet JAMES MERRILL *contemplates the city's ever-changing streets.*

Out for a walk, after a week in bed,
I find them tearing up part of my block
And, chilled through, dazed and lonely, join the dozen
In meek attitudes, watching a huge crane
Fumble luxuriously in the filth of years.
Her jaws dribble rubble. An old man
Laughs and curses in her brain,
Bringing to mind the close of *The White Goddess*.

As usual in New York, everything is torn down
Before you have had time to care for it.
Head bowed, at the shrine of noise, let me try to recall
What building stood here. Was there a building at all?
I have lived on this same street for a decade.

'Ripe for the dreaded spiral of urban blight' – St Ann's Avenue, South Bronx.

What makes New York so dreadful, I believe, is mainly the fact that the vast majority of its people have been forced to rid themselves of one of the oldest and most powerful of human instincts – the instinct to make a permanent home. Crowded, shoved about and exploited without mercy, they have lost the feeling that any part of the earth belongs to them, and so they simply camp out like tramps, waiting for the constables to rush in and chase them away. I am not speaking here of the poor (God knows how they exist in New York at all!); I am speaking of the well-to-do, even of the rich. The very richest man, in New York, is never quite sure that the house he lives in now will be his next year – that he will be able to resist the constant pressure of business expansion and rising land values. . .

His house gives way to a flat – one offering perhaps half the room for his goods and chattels that his house offered. Next year he is in a smaller flat, and three-fourths of his goods and chattels have vanished. A few years more, and his is in two or three rooms. Finally, he lands in an hotel. At this point he ceases to exist as the head of a house. His quarters are precisely like the quarters of 50,000 other men. The front he presents to the world is simply an anonymous door on a gloomy corridor. Inside, he lives like a sardine in a can. Such a habitation, it must be plain, cannot be called a home. A home is not a mere transient shelter: its essence lies in its permanence, in its capacity for accretion and solidification, in its quality of representing, in all its details, the personalities of the people who live in it . . .

This concept of the home cannot survive the mode of life that prevails in New York. I have seen it go to pieces under my eyes in the houses of my own friends. The intense crowding in the town, and the restlessness and unhappiness that go with it, make it almost impossible for anyone to accumulate the materials of a home – the trivial, fortuitous and often grotesque things that gather around a family, as glories and debts gather around a state. The New Yorker lacks the room to house them: he thus learns to live without them. In the end he is a stranger in the house he lives in.

New York is a vertical city, under the sign of the new times. It is a catastrophe with which a too hasty destiny has overwhelmed courageous and confident people, though a beautiful and worthy catastrophe. Nothing is lost. Faced with difficulties, New York falters. Still streaming with sweat from its exertions, wiping off its forehead, it sees what it has done and suddenly realizes: 'Well, we didn't get it done properly. Let's start over again!' New York has such courage and enthusiasm that everything can be begun again, sent back to the building yard and made into something still greater, something mastered! These people are not on the point of going to sleep. In reality, the city is hardly more than twenty years old, that is the city which I am talking about, the city which is vertical and on the scale of the new times. . .

Wasteful of the past, she [New York] gambles Futurity. Day, how can I hold you? Already last night's news has gone blaze up my chimney to light this morning's fire. Coming outdoors early I found a fallen dragonfly cold on a garden stone, numb with the first night's frost. I put him on the sun-dial to study those crystal wings, and hoped meridian would revive him. At lunch he was gone, like my eager morning light. So with New York. As we draw breath

Living conditions in New York have been notoriously cramped and often inhuman. Critic H. L. MENCKEN *wondered at the phenomenon in an essay in his* Prejudices, Fifth Series *(1926).*

Swiss architect LE CORBUSIER *observed New York's volatile profile on his visit in 1936, and celebrated it in his book* When the Cathedrals Were White.

In 'New York One Way', written in 1939, CHRISTOPHER MORLEY *contemplates the city from the vantage of a cottage in rural Long Island.*

she alters. By the hour these words are in print they seem elderly in sentiment. Even her daylight changes faster than elsewhere. It jets a thousand slopes and angles on every piebald street. Her sunset, prismed through such perpendiculars, has almost Andes tint. The crosstown byways, cut so deep, are shadowed soonest; we forget that her summits later than all others hold the slipping sun. Light is her monogram; she signs it again with brilliance all her own. 'How great a bonfire the savages of New York kindle for their evening meal!'

ADA LOUISE HUXTABLE,
long-time architecture critic
for the New York Times,
published her essay
'Death by Development' in
Will They Ever Finish
Bruckner Boulevard? *(1970).*

They are terse headline notices – 'Three Town Houses Bought by High-Rise Builder', 'Midtown Expansion Forcing Music Street to Sing Swan Song', 'Real Estate Deal in Village', On the surface, a factual, newsprint chronicle of urban change; underneath, the death of a city by 'development'. . .

In New York, neighborhoods fall like dominoes. Everyone knows about the small electrical supply stores uprooted by the World Trade Center; the thrift and antique shops chased by the apartment builders from Third Avenue: the small businesses, bars and coffee dealers displaced from the lower Manhattan waterfront by office construction; the artists' lofts eliminated in the Village for more luxury apartments.

What follows demolition is preordained by the divine right of development. There will be the same new buildings out of the same old mold, sleekly commercial or shoddily residential; and in the ground floor store space of all, as if by some holy decree, there will be banks.

Even an expanding Rockefeller Center has repudiated the superior planning principles of organized massing and multi-level circulation that added a superb urban heart to midtown. Its subsequent preoccupation has just been to make the façades blend. Somehow, it fell over Sixth Avenue on the way to 48th Street. New York, anyone? Come and get it before it is too late. This seems like a death-wish city.

Veteran New Yorker
KATE SIMON *meditated on*
the changing urban
landscape in the introduction
to her book New York,
Places and Pleasures *(1971).*

The writer on New York City writes on swiftly rushing waters or, to confuse a metaphor, rides an escalator with few still platforms, relentlessly propelled by an invention of Kafka. It is stimulating and discouraging: a report written two or three years ago may have the wistful charms of remembrances of things past, cherished and often unusable. Where is that wonderful Ukrainian restaurant like the kitchen of a generous peasant? Where is that Provençal restaurant full of sound and fury? What happened to the manners of that nice young Italian waiter? Who took the gargoyles off that silly, engaging old building? Evaporated into wisps of nostalgia. . .

Much of the city, particularly the East Side and the tip of the island, seems to have been the victim of a roaring, obsessed giantess of a housewife, maniacally energetic, who keeps screaming. 'Tear it up! Knock it down! Throw it away! Let's get it cleaned up! Let's make it neat!' We have, with the result that the endlessly fascinating contrasts of large, bold buildings and small, diffident houses have been drained and further flattened by a unanimity of design which gives buildings of different purpose the same face: a school looks like a supermarket which looks like a garage which looks like a shop which looks like a church. Third Avenue, which was a tour of many worlds, is becoming a blind, glossy stare of houses which, the more their glass reveals, the less humanity they give off. . .

'Construction' – lithograph by Thomas Hart Benton, 1929.

What's new? you ask. Almost everything. As always in New York, to wake up in the morning is to find a new city. The bewildered upper East Side is reluctantly yielding its remaining sausage and paprika locations to new shops — alien, repetitious chic, cloaked in the broad mantle of 'Interiors'. The Italian greengrocer who made a garden of the sidewalk at Second Avenue and 81st Street is gone. During the night gremlins in slim, exquisitely fitted trousers papered the walls in fruity Edwardian patterns, hung them with 'fun' sconces (screaming rococo), placed a bentwood rocker in the middle of the sloped wooden floor next to a *santo* with shattered fingers, in the window, an *art nouveau* brush and mirror set, swollen with lotus blossoms and rueful profiles. *Voilà*, an antique shop. These of course, as you remember, existed before, but not in such overwhelming numbers and in such strong color combinations, every kitchen its own Albers. Every storeroom and cellar has been ransacked for beaded bags, limp old clothing, cane and bentwood chairs and clothes racks; lumpy cut glass is treasure; the wild bright fungus of 'Tiffany' lamps plagues every ceiling. Along with Grand Rapids, ball-clawed monsters, and dead old iceboxes, these make up non-style style called 'Americana', the things your grandmother yearned to throw out but couldn't afford to.

In the nuclear age, New York looked less permanent than ever, as E. B. WHITE *observed in his essay, 'Here is New York' (1949).*

The subtlest change in New York is something people don't speak much about but that is in everyone's mind. The city, for the first time in its long history, is destructible. A single flight of planes no bigger than a wedge of geese can quickly end this island fantasy, burn the towers, crumble the bridges, turn the underground passages into lethal chambers, cremate the millions. The intimation of mortality is part of New York now: in the sound of jets overhead, in the black headlines of the latest edition.

All dwellers in cities must live with the stubborn fact of annihilation; in New York the fact is somewhat more concentrated because of the concentration of the city itself, and because, of all targets, New York has a certain clear priority. In the mind of whatever perverted dreamer might loose the lightning, New York must hold a steady irresistible charm.

REAL CHARACTERS

Gŏ'tham *n*. 1. town proverbial for folly. 2. (colloq.) New York City.

THE CONCISE OXFORD DICTIONARY

A man from Mars landed on Second Avenue and looked into a store window, fascinated. Finally, he entered the shop and asked the owner: 'What are those little wheels in the window?'

'Wheels? What wheels?'

The Martian pointed.

'Those aren't wheels,' smiled the *baleboss*, 'They're called *bagels*. We eat them . . . Here, try one.'

The Martian bit into a *bagel* and smacked his lips. 'Man! This would go great with cream cheese and lox.'

LEO ROSTEN *'s* The Joys of Yiddish *(1970) is, among other things, a treasury of New York Jewish humour.*

'Astor Place' – painting by Francis Criss, 1932.

As a southerner who made
his home in New York,
O. HENRY was acutely
aware that in the rest of the
country New Yorkers
enjoyed a reputation for
peculiar behaviour, as he
showed in his story 'New
York by Camp Fire Light'
(1907).

Away out in the Creek Nation we learned things about New York.
We were on a hunting trip, and were camped one night on the bank of a little stream. Bud Kingsbury was our skilled hunter and guide, and it was from his lips that we had explanations of Manhattan and the queer folks that inhabit it . . .

'The most visible and peculiar trait of New York folks,' answered Bud, 'is New York. Most of 'em has New York on the brain. They have heard of other places, such as Waco, and Paris, and Hot Springs, and London; but they don't believe in 'em. They think that town is all Merino. Now to show you how much they care for their village I'll tell you about one of 'em that strayed out as far as the Triangle B while I was working there.

'This New Yorker come out there looking for a job on the ranch. He said he was a good horseback rider, and there were pieces of tanbark hanging on his clothes yet from his riding school.

'Well, for a while they put him to keeping books in the ranch store, for he was a devil at figures. But he got tired of that, and asked for something more in the line of activity. The boys on the ranch like him all right, but he made us tired shouting New York all the time. Every night he'd tell us about East River and J. P. Morgan and the Eden Musee and Hetty Green and Central Park till we used to throw tin plates and branding irons at him.

'Tattoo – Shave – Haircut' – etching by Reginald Marsh, 1932.

'One day this chap gets on a pitching pony, and the pony kind of sidled up his back and went to eating grass while the New Yorker was coming down.

'He come down on his head on a chunk of mesquite wood, and he didn't show any designs toward getting up again. We laid him out in a tent, and he begun to look pretty dead. So Gideon Pease saddles up and burns the wind for old Doc Sleeper's residence in Dogtown, thirty miles away.

'The doctor comes over and he investigates the patient.

'"Boys," says he, "you might as well go to playing seven-up for his saddle and clothes, for his head's fractured and if he lives ten minutes it will be a re-markable case of longevity."

'Of course we didn't gamble for the poor rooster's saddle — that was one of Doc's jokes. But we stood around feeling solemn, and all of us forgive him for having talked us to death about New York.

'I never saw anybody about to hand in his checks act more peaceful than this fellow. His eyes were fixed 'way up in the air, and he was using rambling words to himself all about sweet music and beautiful streets and white-robed forms, and he was smiling like dying was a pleasure.

'"He's about gone now," said Doc "Whenever they begin to think they see heaven it's all off."

'Blamed if that New York man didn't sit right up when he heard the Doc say that.

'"Say," says he, kind of disappointed, "was that heaven? Confound it all, I thought it was Broadway. Some of you fellows get my clothes. I'm going to get up."

'And I'll be blamed,' concluded Bud, 'if he wasn't on the train with a ticket for New York in his pocket four days afterward!'

The Crossroads of the World were cold and windswept. The subway gratings breathed mustily and strongly when trains came by. Each sudden exhalation scattered cellophane wrappers, cigar bands, and grimy papers on the sidewalk in front of the United Cigar store. . .

Strange creatures came by: a man with a screwed-up face staring bleakly ahead in blind despair, his neck pulled down in a grimy tan raincoat; an old man with a matted beard. He stooped to pick up cigarette ends. These he thrust into a soiled shopping bag. His eyes never lifted. . .

A crowd of newspaper vendors had assembled on the corner. One was a tall, thin youth. His front teeth showed through a lip widely severed by an old surgical cut. Meech, the dark-eyed man at the corner stand, spoke up.

'Give him an interview,' he said. 'He's The Killer. Give the guy an interview, Killer.'

Killer stared at me out of hollow eyes. He sucked in his thin, unshaved cheeks.

'I don't want no notoriety,' he said. He muttered about the papers he was stuck with and moved off toward Eighth Avenue. Meech apologized for The Killer.

'He's a wack,' Meech said, 'You know. He's shell-shocked from eatin' pea-nuts. How we call him The Killer: he won a dance contest in Brooklyn and he knocked them dead, and that's how we give him the rib and call him The Killer.'

In his columns in the New York Times *and other papers, journalist* MEYER BERGER *covered every aspect of the city's life, including the strange individuals who only come out at night in* 'Broadway Blackout', *published in his book* The Eight Million *(1942).*

A bent old woman, tightly wrapped in a shapeless gray coat, with a kettle-shaped old black felt covering her neck and forehead, came slowly by. She held out a small box of chewing gum, an automatic gesture. The sidewalk was bare of pedestrians where she stood. She stopped at the haberdashery and you wondered what there was about overgay shirts and gaudy ties in the window that could so hold her attention. She stared at the display for five minutes before she resumed her southward trudge.

One of the men came out of the cigar store with a flashlight. He held it close to the grating. It threw a pale light on countless bits of paper and cellophane, but at the last north gate, in front of the Rialto, he saw something.

'There's a quarter down there,' he said, 'in the corner.'

Meech said the fishers would be along any minute. It was three o'clock. In the cigar shop a strange little woman leaned against the mirrored wall. She seemed out of a drawing, like a bad job in soft clay. Her imitation brown fur coat looked like something left in a wet corner. She was reading a playbill.

'That's Broadway Rose,' Meech said.

He said that Broadway Rose came to the store every morning around three o'clock. Every morning she leans on the mirrored wall and reads a playbill or a pamphlet, something picked out of the street.

'Three hundred sixty-five days she comes and does the same thing,' Meech

'I was happy, I was bubbly drunk' – photograph by Louis Faurer.

said. 'Around four o'clock she buys a pack of butts, always a different kind, and she goes out and takes the Eighth Avenue subway.'

The man with the light defended Broadway Rose.

'She's a religious woman,' he said, righteously. 'She's got education.'

A shabby man came out of the cigar store. He told Meech that a crippled man, 'a good-dressed fella,' had put a dime on Rose's arm because he thought she was penniless.

'So she shakes this dime off on the floor,' the shabby man related. 'She says it ain't her dime.'

'Broadway Rose has got plenty of jack,' the man with the light said. 'Plenty.'

Broadway Rose folded the playbill. She bought her cigarettes and put them in her lumpy, knitted bag. She made awkward feminine gestures at the fan of dead hair lumped under her shapeless velvet hat and headed upstreet, toward Eighth Avenue.

The Square, north of the Crossroads, was a black pit now. It was almost four o'clock. Only one or two neon signs glowed redly through the dark.

'The fishers won't come no more,' Meech said.

I looked around at the garbage trucks, loading at the restaurants. The Rialto lights were out. It was blowing colder.

I was happy I was bubbly drunk
The street was dark
I waved to a young policeman
He smiled
I went up to him and like a flood of gold
Told him all about my prison youth
About how noble and great the convicts were
And about how I just returned from Europe
Which wasn't half as enlightening as prison
And he listened attentively I told no lie
Everything was truth and humor
He laughed
He laughed
And it made me so happy I said:
'Absolve it all, kiss me!'
'No no no no!' he said
      and hurried away.

Poet GREGORY CORSO, *a native New Yorker, celebrated his own eccentric behaviour in his poem 'Second Night in N.Y.C. After 3 Years' (1962).*

In September we started going regularly to a two-story bar/restaurant on Park Avenue South off Union Square that Mickey Ruskin had opened in late '65. It was called Max's Kansas City and it became the ultimate hangout. Max's was the farthest uptown of any of the restaurants Mickey had ever operated. He'd had a place on East 7th Street called Deux Mégots that later became the Paradox, and then he'd had the Ninth Circle, a Village bar with a format similar to what Max's would have, and then an Avenue B bar called the Annex. Mickey had always been attracted to the downtown art atmosphere – at Deux Mégots, he'd held poetry readings – and now painters and poets were starting to drift into Max's. The art heavies would group around the bar and the kids would be in the back room, basically.

In the sixties, artist, film-maker and promoter ANDY WARHOL *frequented Max's Kansas City, restaurant, bar and second home to a mixed crowd of artists, trendies, and street urchins. He painted a vivid picture of the place in his book* Popism: Andy Warhol's History of the Sixties *(1980).*

Max's Kansas City was the exact place where Pop Art and pop life came together in New York in the sixties – teeny boppers and sculptors, rock stars and poets from St Mark's Place, Hollywood actors checking out what the underground actors were all about, boutique owners and models, modern dancers and go-go dancers – everybody went to Max's and everything got homogenized there. . .

I started going to Max's a lot. Mickey was an art fan, so I'd give him a painting and he'd give us credit, and everybody in our group could just sign for their dinners until the credit was used up. It was a really pleasant arrangement.

The back room at Max's, lit by Dan Flavin's red light piece, was where everybody wound up every night. After all the parties were over and all the bars and all the discotheques closed up, you'd go on to Max's and meet up with everybody – and it was like going home, only better.

Max's became the showcase for all the fashion changes that had been taking place at the art openings and shows: now people weren't going to the art openings to show off their new looks – they just skipped all the preliminaries and went straight to Max's. Fashion wasn't what you wore someplace anymore; it was the whole reason for going. The event itself was optional – the way Max's functioned as a fashion gallery proved that. Kids would crowd around the security mirror over the night deposit slot in the bank next door ('Last mirror before Max's') to check themselves out for the long walk from the front door, past the bar, past all the fringe tables in the middle, and finally into the club room in the back.

Max's is where I started meeting the really young kids who had dropped out of school and been running around the streets for a couple of years – hard-looking, beautiful little girls with perfect makeup and fabulous clothes, and you'd find out later they were fifteen and already had a baby. These kids really knew how to dress, they had just the right fashion instincts, somehow. They were a type of kid I hadn't been around much before. Although they weren't educated like the Boston crowd or the San Remo crowd, they were very sharp in a comical sort of way – I mean, they certainly knew how to put each other down, standing on chairs and screaming insults. Like, if Gerard walked in with his fashion look really together and had that very serious Roman god-like expression on his face that people get when they think they're looking good, one of the little girls at Max's (the Twin-Twats, they were called) would jump up on the stable and swoon. 'Oh my God, it's Apollo! Oh, Apollo, will you sit with us tonight?'

I couldn't decide if these kids were intelligent but crazy, or just plain pea-brained with a flair for comedy and clothes. It was impossible to tell whether their problem was lack of intelligence or lack of sanity.

Writer KATE SIMON *drew a thumbnail sketch of that legendary character, the New York waiter, in her book* New York, Places and Pleasures *(1971).*

The New Yorker waiter is also superior, but for different reasons. It is simply that he knows more than you do about everything. He disapproves of your taste in food and clothing, your gauche manners, your miserliness, and sometimes, it seems, your very existence, which he tries to ignore. After you've been seated and the great presence has slowly approached and let its luster shine on you, you ask. 'How is the duck?' The presence turns its long lids on you, lets a pitying gleam emerge from under them, and intones, 'Duck is an insi-i-i-pid animal,' erasing at one stroke all ducks and your weakened ego. This waiter is often French or Italian and, though his native tastes may run to *pasta* and scratchy wine, he considers himself the sacred vessel of the secrets of Escoffier and Brillat-Savarin; his carefully maintained accent, he hopes, will join him to the great kitchens of Paris and Rome, though he may have come directly from a grim village in the Auvergne or in Sicily. The Jewish waiter is The Father – the father as doctor, the father as disciplinarian, the father as critic and, of course, protector; leaping from role to role, he makes an erratic and fascinating composite. When he is the protector, he will advise you to fold your coat neatly and put it on the nice chair there and he will guard it and watch 'nobody should spill on it'. As the disciplinarian, he will respond to 'What kind of jam have you for the blintzes?' with 'Jam is jam!' in the tone of outraged patience used to stop a nagging child. Should you order eggs fried rather than scrambled, as he approves of them, he will whip out his order book, keep his pencil ostentatiously poised, scrutinize you with the look of 'You're going to be trouble but I'm ready for you' and mutter in a voice rich with sarcasm, 'Ah, ha. Fancy customers!' The critic in him swings the lash wide: busboys are ignorant and lazy, bosses are oafs who rise to prosperity by trampling on waiters, customers are knaves or maniacs; in short, life would not be worth living except for the enchantments of complaining.

The doctor-father is his most engaging and annoying role. As if you were describing symptoms, he listens solemnly to your order, and then silently evaluates it. After a weighty pause, he offers you his learned advice: 'If you're going to have the steak, you shouldn't eat soup with dumplings before, it'll lay heavy on your stomach. Have a little nice chicken liver first.' 'Maybe you shouldn't have fried chicken so late; boiled is better for you.' 'You want creamed spinach? Carrots is healthier.' 'No potatoes? Whatsamatter, you're not fat. It's not nice a woman should look like a stick.' You will escape his solicitude only by succumbing to his superior knowledge of digestive matters, whether it pleases you or not.

His female counterpart, the delicatessen waitress, is less diagnostic and even more affectionate. 'Why don't you finish? You don't like it, honey?' – when you've left a crust of a sandwich built like the Great Wall of China. She dashes around, as jealous and busy as the bride's mother: 'More pickles?'; 'More coleslaw?'; 'honey', 'dearie', 'sweetie', bestowing the quick awareness of true love.

'New York on the brain.'

In his book O America *(1977) Italian author* LUIGI BARZINI *recalls his encounter with one of New York's Mafia dons.*

Don Turi lived in a decayed section of Brooklyn in a house surrounded by an iron fence. The house was old, but the fence was new. Don Turi was a kindly old gentleman, fat but still fast on his feet like an old house cat. He had watchful and alert black eyes, younger than his face; wore a woollen peaked cap indoors and a travel rug over his shoulders to protect himself from colds. He received me in a room whose walls were practically papered with framed photographs from the old country. There were peasant brides and grooms galore, some of the girls in their ancient costumes; young men in the last war's military uniforms, and some in *carabinieri* dress uniform holding the regulation Napoleonic hat with plume . . . There were also many priests, nuns, monks, and one bishop smiling benignly at me.

Don Turi sat on an American straight-backed armchair, with a silent and attentive young man sitting behind him, his oldest son. Oldest sons are always present at their Sicilian fathers' more important interviews and never speak, because their job is more or less that of what is now known as a tape recorder. They must listen and remember, in case something happens to the old man, but they cannot be played back by third parties. Don Turi spoke his obscure dialect, slowly and with royal dignity. He seemed to use the *pluralis majestatis* like the Pope, but, in fact, when he said 'we', he literally meant many men, the *amici* and *gli amici degli amici*. This is, more or less, what I think he said:

'Mike told me what you have done for him. It shows you have generous sentiments and are a gallant young man one can rely on. This is very rare among North Italians, Americans, and other foreigners. We thank you. We're in your debt. We never forget our debts. You know that. We never forget wrongs done to us, either. Someday you may need our help, Don Luigi, even when I am no longer here.' (Mike and his son murmured, 'As late as possible, with the help of God,' as automatically as the faithful answered '. . . *qui tollit peccata mundi*' when the priest said '*Agnus Dei* . . .') 'That day,' Don Turi continued, 'you can count on us, provided, of course, your request agrees with the laws of honor. Not today, however, the way you suggest. Mike says you want to defend the Sicilians' name from defamation, explain to the American public what laws we obey, and how we help each other like brothers in this strange, difficult, and hostile country.' (That, of course, was the explanation I had given Mike.) 'It is a noble wish. We commend you. But I'm afraid the moment is not opportune. We're at war. We Sicilians in America must think of ourselves like the Jews in Egypt before the Exodus. Everybody around us is our enemy and our oppressor. We have to be very prudent. Prudence, the Church teaches us, is one of the cardinal virtues. We showed our trust in you when we agreed to receive you in our house. But we cannot go further. Whatever you might write will be either accurate or wrong. If accurate, you will not be able to produce proof when it is denied and you will be accused by some of betraying us. Something unpleasant might happen to you. If it was wrong or exaggerated, it certainly would not have been worth your while to come and see me. Whether accurate or inaccurate, what you might write will be misunderstood anyway. Nobody understands (or wants to understand) us. You'll be bothered by the police, who are dull, ignorant, corrupt, and brutal people, mostly Irish. They will never leave you alone in order to get my name and my address, which they already have anyway. Yours is a dangerous errand, believe me, you yourself do not realize how dangerous. For your own sake it is my duty to discourage you, as I would discourage a grandson of mine. Some other time, perhaps, but not now.' He gave me a glass of sweet wine with a biscuit, then shook my hand, and dismissed me, walking me ceremoniously to the iron garden gate. That was the end of that.

Actor SPALDING GRAY*'s monologue 'Nobody Wanted to Sit Behind a Desk' was published in his* Sex and Death to the Age 14 *in 1986.*

I took the Lexington Avenue subway, and walking across town on my way down to Renée's, I saw a guy I used to pass on my way to Unemployment. He used to write messages in chalk on the sidewalk below Canal Street, on the corner of Chambers and Broadway. Rather articulate Marxist messages. I'd always pictured him living in a lean-to in the Catskills, taking a Trailways down to New York City to do this. Now he'd moved uptown, he had a knapsack and a dog with him. And his message had evolved. This one read: 'The Devil's nun

Photograph by Leonard Freed.

is a topless waitress who works in the Devil's church. The top looks good but the bottom smells like the Devil.' This was written in chalk. I was trying to imagine what the devil smelled like, and the best I could come up with is the orangutan at the Central Park Zoo.

By now I needed a sanctuary. I was so happy to reach Renée's loft and be in her arms again. She said, 'Hi, hon! How you doin'?' And her whole body welcomed me like a big flesh couch, but the hallways were dirty and the loft was dark and her neighbors were playing 'We Are Family.' I wanted out. I had to get out and get some light. I told Renée, 'I gotta get out. I gotta get out and get some of that stuff they loosely call air!' No green trees in downtown New York, and she was living in the Cancer Belt.

So I walked up to Washington Square to sit on a park bench in the October sun. I was just sitting there trying to relax, and there was a guy next to me, a young man with a beard, dressed in a business suit. But as I sat there I began to notice out of the corner of my eye that he had no socks on and that the entire suit was coming apart at the seams. And he was deep into the process of delousing himself. In fact, when he lifted his arm I saw a whole nest of them seething there in his armpit. I was thinking: Why, why am I seeing all this madness? I turned to my right and a woman started in on me. She said, 'The safest place, the only place I can go to now – I can't go any further – is Washington Square, because I'm afraid they're gonna lock me up for being crazy. I had a friend who came up from Virginia and she disappeared into a mental institution. So Washington Square, that's about as far as I can walk.' She had wanted to become a good secretary. That had been her ambition. She'd been married twice – both of them had been one-night stands. The second time she was married, she had a real big wedding, and they got divorced the next day. She kept saying, 'And it was a big wedding. A big wedding.' Now she was married again. She said that she was crazy, and I asked her how she got that way, and she said a friend of hers talked too much. It drove her nuts.

Then I saw the flag man. He was wearing a construction helmet with American flag decals all over it and had a rolled-up flag between his thighs. He had no teeth, and every so often, he'd pull the flag out from his crotch, unfurl it, wrap himself in it and sing 'I Love America.' Beautiful. I went over to talk to him and he said that he had gone crazy when he smoked his first marijuana cigarette and realized that the system was corrupt. Now he was getting paid for being crazy. He was on welfare. He was a virgin, and he slept with the American flag. I said, 'Don't you realize the American flag is just a symbol?' He said, 'Not for me. I sleep with it. And one of these days I'm going to get such an erection here in this park, that I'm going to be able to hang the flag on it.' He also had love letters to President Carter stuffed in his crotch. Love letters proclaiming his love for America.

I walked over to the Dance Theatre Workshop on West 19th to look over the space. I talked to Bob Applegarth about my upcoming performances, and left. I started down the steps and saw a woman collapsed at the bottom of the stairs. It looked like she had fallen. She had one hand in her pocket and with her other hand she was twisting her hair. Her eyes were rolling, looking up at me. Totally mad. I could smell her two flights up. I stopped. I thought she had a gun in her pocket. Then I thought, no, no, no, it's too small. It's too small a pocket. But she had a kind of intensity, a silence. Her eyes were young, and they were still soft, and they were rolling like an animal's. I was scared. I thought she'd scream and leap on me. So I came down the stairs, and I knelt beside her, and just as I did she blurted out, 'Ya gotta cigarette? Ya got some reefer?' I said I didn't have either of those things. She said that she used to be a dancer in Florida and that she was 26 years old. I said, 'Do you realize that you're in the hallway of the Dance Theatre Workshop?' She said, 'No, no.' I thought she was an ex-DTW dancer. But she slept in different doorways. She said, 'Look, all I need is a million dollars. Then I can get an apartment. 'I thought: She's not crazy. I said, 'Where are you from?' She said, 'Las Vegas. I love it there. I've got to get back.' I said, 'Why do you like it in Las Vegas?' She said, 'Because there are no hoodlums.' I said 'Why not?' She said, 'They lock them up.' I said, 'I know, I've been locked up for six days there myself.'

I thought of taking her home, to wash her, to clean her up. And then I thought . . . No.

'City Interior' – by Charles Sheeler, 1936.

WHO'D WANT TO LIVE THERE?

on't go wandering about the streets or parks unnecessarily in the evening. The degrading confession and warning is necessary, that New York is one of the most crime-haunted and dangerous cities in Christendom. There are hundreds – thousands – of infernal rascals among our floating population; street boys, grown up into rowdies, and the brutal scum of vile city ignorance and filth; shoulder-hitters and thieves, expelled, some of them, from distant

Poet WALT WHITMAN, a great defender of New York, nonetheless felt obliged to offer this advice to tourists in Life Illustrated in 1856.

San Franciso, vomited back among us to practice their criminal occupations, who will sneak up behind you, or pretend drunkenness and run against you, or inquire the way, or the hour, and snatch your watch, or take you unawares, like Brooks, knock you on the head, and rob you before you can even cry out. If you have evening errands, go circumspectly through respectable streets. If you are lost, ask a direction at a respectable store, or from the blue-coated and starred policeman, whom you will probably discern every square or two.

The Triangle Shirt Waist Company fire of the early twentieth century took many lives and alerted New Yorkers to the appalling conditions endured by thousands of women workers in the garment industry. Yiddish novelist SHOLEM ASCH *recreated the episode in his novel* East River *(1946).*

The Triangle firm was housed in a modern building, practically a skyscraper, situated on the edge of the enormous open square in the heart of the city. The factory took up several floors of the building. The offices, showrooms, and cutting rooms were on the lower floors. On the ninth floor about two hundred and thirty girls and a few men worked at sewing machines. Other hands worked on the eighth floor. The tenth floor housed the finishers, cleaners, and examiners. Besides a large number of men, cutters and pressers, Triangle employed more than seven hundred girls.

Entrance and exit to the ninth floor were furnished by two doors, one opposite the other. One of them, the one giving on the stairway on the Washington Square side, was always kept locked. The other door opened on the corridor and elevator leading to Greene Street. This door was constantly guarded by a watchman who looked the girls over each time they left the shop. His beady eyes were like exploring, impudent fingers, making sure that a girl didn't have a blouse or a stray piece of material concealed under her dress or coat. Nor did he hesitate to paw them for a more thorough inspection. There was no other way for the girls to enter or leave the shop except through the door guarded by the watchman.

March twenty-fifth fell on a Saturday. Through the wide windows overlooking Washington Place the afternoon sky was snow-laden and gloomy. The ninth floor bustled with activity. Rows of girls sat at the sewing machines, the electric bulbs gleaming over their bowed heads. The work was going on at full speed; all the girls were hurrying to get through with the day's work so as to get home as early as possible. Although Saturday was a full working day, the girls were permitted to leave an hour earlier if the day's quota was disposed of. Saturday was payday, another inducement to hurry; everyone had plans for the evening, to go visiting, to go shopping, to go to the movies or to a dance.

Mary and Sarah sat at adjoining machines. As they worked they chatted of their evening plans. The electricity-driven leather belts of the machines clattered so noisily they were barely able to hear one another. . .

As they talked above the whirr of the machines a sudden quiet fell on the shop; even the machines sounded subdued. Something seemed to be happening at the far end of the room. Sarah stood up to see what was going on. Mary scrambled up beside her. They could see nothing.

'What is it?' Mary asked in sudden alarm.

'I don't know,' Sarah answered.

All at once they saw puffs of thick smoke coming up between the cracks of the floor boards near the door leading to the elevator. Forked flames of fire followed the smoke. All the fright in the world broke out in a chorus of hysterical screams.

'Fire! Fire! Fire!'

Panic swept through the room. There was the noise of running feet, the clatter of chairs and stools being thrown over. The two girls began to run with the rest.

The running mob pushed them toward the exit door on the Greene Street side. It was near the door leading to the elevator that the flames were licking through the planks of the floor. They remembered that no stairway descended from the corridor. The elevator was the only exit. They would be trapped in the corridor by the flames. The smoke and fire coming through the floor near the door terrified them. The crowd veered and dashed to the other side of the loft, where the door led to the stairway that went down to Washington Place. Mary and Sarah, holding each other by the hand, ran with the rest.

They stumbled over chairs and upended stools. They were blocked by hysterical girls who were too terrified to move. Sarah and Mary tried to drag some of them along with them. Here and there tongues of fire were coming up through the floor. Around the sewing machines the heaps of remnants of material and trimmings, silks, linings, padded cotton, the oil-soaked rags which the girls used to clean the machines after oiling them, blazed into flame. The oil-soaked rags were the first to catch fire, setting alight the piles of cuttings and feeding the flames from one machine to the next. The grease-covered machines themselves began to blaze together with piles of material on them. The fire grew in volume by the minute. It spread like a stream overflowing its banks. The waves of living flame licked at the skirts of the fleeing, screaming, trapped girls.

Women workers in a New York sweat-shop, 1888.

Italian mother and child, New York, 1890 – photograph by Jacob Riis.

Poet DELMORE SCHWARTZ *published 'Sonnet: O City, City' in his* In Dreams Begin Responsibilities *(1938).*

To live between terms, to live where death
    Has his loud picture in the subway tide,
Being amid six million souls, their breath
An empty song suppressed on every side,
Where the sliding auto's catastrophe
Is a gust past the curb, where numb and high
The office building rises to its tyranny,
Is our anguished diminution until we die.

Whence, if ever, shall come the actuality
Of a voice speaking the mind's knowing,
The sunlight bright on the green windowshade,
And the self articulate, affectionate, and flowing,
Ease, warmth, light, the utter showing,
When in the white bed all things are made.

Southern-born writer TRUMAN CAPOTE *evoked a sweltering city summer in his essay 'New York' (1946),*

August. Although the morning papers said simply fair and warm, it was apparent by noon that something exceptional was happening, and office workers, drifting back from lunch with the dazed, desperate expression of chilren being bullied, began to dial Weather. Toward midafternoon, as the heat losed in like a hand over a murder victim's mouth, the city thrashed and twisted, but with its outcry muffled, its hurry hampered, its ambitions hindered, it was like a dry fountain, some useless monument, and so sank into a coma. The steaming willow-limp stretches of Central Park were like a battlefield where many have fallen: rows of exhausted casualties lay crumpled in the dead-still shade, while newspaper photographers, documenting the disaster, moved sepulchrally among them. At night, hot weather opens the skull of a city, exposing its white brain and its central nerves, which sizzle like the inside of an electric-light bulb.

What happens to a dream deferred?

Does it dry up
like a raisin in the sun?
Or fester like a sore –
And then run?
Does it stink like rotten meat?
Or crust and sugar over –
like a syrupy sweet?

Maybe it just sags
like a heavy load.

Or does it explode?

LANGSTON HUGHES's
*poem 'Harlem' appeared in
his* Montage of a Dream
Deferred *(1951).*

On the Avenue, through air tinted crimson
By neon over the bars, the rain is falling.
You stood once on Houston, among panhandlers and winos
Who weave the eastern ranges, learning to be free,
To not care, to be knocked flat and to get up clear-headed
Spitting the curses out. 'Now be nice,'
The proprietor threatens: 'Be nice,' he cajoles.
'Fuck you,' the bum shouts as he is hoisted again,
'God fuck your mother.' (In the empty doorway,
Hunched on the empty crate, the crone gives no sign.)

That night a wildcat cab whined crosstown on 7th.
You knew even the traffic lights were made by God,
The red splashes growing dimmer the farther away
You looked, and away up at 14th, a few green stars;
And without sequence, and nearly all at once,
The red lights blinked into green,
And just before there was one complete Avenue of green,
The little green stars in the distance blinked.

It is night, and raining. You look down
Towards Houston in the rain, the living streets,
Where instants of transcendence
Drift in oceans of loathing and fear, like lanternfishes,
Or phosphorus flashing in the sea, or the feverish light
Skin is said to give off when the swimmer drowns at night.

From the blind gut Pitt to the East River of Fishes
The Avenue cobbles a swath through the discolored air,
A roadway of refuse from the teeming shores and ghettos
And the Caribbean Paradise, into the new ghetto and new paradise,
This God-forsaken Avenue bearing the initial of of Christ
Through the haste and carelessness of the ages,
The sea standing in heaps, which keeps on collapsing,
Where the drowned suffer a C-change,
And remain the common poor.

GALWAY KINNELL's *long
poem* The Avenue Bearing
the Initial of Christ into the
New World *(1960)
transforms the sights,
sounds, and smells of
Avenue C on the Lower East
Side into a drama of urban
horror.*

*Harlem-born novelist
JAMES BALDWIN spent
much of his life abroad.
In* Another Country *(1962)
he portrays New York
through the eyes of a black
New Yorker recently returned
to the city after an absence
of many years.*

New York seemed very strange indeed. It might, almost, for strange barbarity of manner and custom, for the sense of danger and horror barely sleeping beneath the rough, gregarious surface, have been some impenetrably exotic city of the East. So superbly was it in the present that it seemed to have nothing to do with the passage of time: time might have dismissed it as thoroughly as it had dismissed Carthage and Pompeii. It seemed to have no sense whatever of the exigencies of human life; it was so familiar and so public that it became, at last, the most despairingly private of cities. One was continually being jostled, yet longed, at the same time, for the sense of others, for a human touch; and if one was never – it was the general complaint – left alone in New York, one had, still, to fight very hard in order not to perish of loneliness. This fight, carried on in so many different ways, created the strange climate of the city. The girls along Fifth Avenue wore their bright clothes like semaphores, trying helplessly to bring to the male attention the news of their mysterious trouble. The men could not read this message. They strode purposefully along, wearing little anonymous hats, or bareheaded, with youthfully parted hair, or crew cuts, accoutred with attaché cases, rushing, on the evidence, to the smoking cars of trains. In this haven, they opened up their newspapers and caught up on the day's bad news. Or they were to be found, as five o'clock fell, in discreetly dim, anonymously appointed bars, uneasy, in brittle, uneasy, female company, pouring down joyless martinis.

This note of despair, of buried despair, was insistently, constantly struck. It stalked all the New York avenues, roamed all the New York streets; was as present in Sutton Place, where . . . the great often gathered, as it was in Greenwich Village, where he had rented an apartment and been appalled to see what time had done to people he had once known well. He could not escape the feeling that a kind of plague was raging, though it was officially and publicly and privately denied. Even the young seemed blighted – seemed most blighted of all. The boys in their blue jeans ran together, scarcely daring to trust one another, but united, like their elders, in a boyish distrust of the girls. Their very walk, a kind of anti-erotic, knee-action lope, was a parody of locomotion and of manhood. They seemed to be shrinking away from any contact with their flamboyantly and paradoxically outlined private parts. They seemed – but could it be true? and how had it happened? – to be at home with, accustomed to, brutality and indifference, and to be terrified of human affection. In some strange way they did not seem to feel that they were worthy of it.

Singer BOB DYLAN *turned
up in Greenwich Village fresh
from his native Midwest in
1960, and composed his
sarcastic tribute to the big
city, 'Hard Times in New
York Town', in 1962.*

Old New York City is a friendly old town,
From Washington Heights to Harlem on down.
There's a-mighty many people all millin' all around,
They'll kick you when you're up and knock you when you're down.
It's hard times in the city,
Livin' down in New York town.

Well, it's up in the mornin' tryin' to find a job of work.
Stand in one place till your feet begin to hurt.
If you got a lot o' money you can make yourself merry,
If you only got a nickel, it's the Staten Island Ferry.
And it's hard times in the city,
Livin' down in New York town.

They say the neon lights are bright
On Broadway
They say there's always a magic in the air
On Broadway
But when you're walking down the street
And you ain't got enough to eat
The glitter all rubs off
And you're nowhere
On Broadway

'On Broadway', a hit song
for the Drifters in 1963, was
written by BARRY MANN,
CYNTHIA WEILL, JERRY
LEIBER, and MIKE STOLLER.

the radio that was not on
was playing loud enough
to be heard from the 1st floor
to the 21st floor & the roof
but all the tenants had turned
on their television sets
and stereo record players
at full blast from the 1st day
they moved into the projects
making hearing impossible

in matter of seconds
our father which art in the backseat
of a lincoln continental limousine
known in some circles as Mister Clean
will give the housing authority
the middle finger sign
and all the tenants will find
themselves on the 21st floor
and the only way you will be able
to see the streets again
will be by jumping out the window

isolation is the name of the game
you do not know
your next door neighbors name
your next door neighbor
does not know your name
you have been living on
the same floor since this
so-called promisedland opened
the only way you get to know each other
is after one or the other dies

everybody has a headache
in these human file cabinets
known as the housing projects

Puerto Rican-born poet
PEDRO PIETRI published the
long poem '3170 Broadway'
in his book Puerto Rican
Obituary (1973).

'The glitter all rubs off.'

Poet ALLEN GINSBERG
*has made his home on New
York's Lower East Side for
many years. His poem
'Mugging' (of which this is
the first part) appeared in his
volume* Mind Breaths *in
1977.*

Tonite I walked out of my red apartment door on East tenth street's dusk –
Walked out my home ten years, walked out in my honking neighborhood
Tonite at seven walked out past garbage cans chained to concrete anchors
Walked under black painted fire escapes, giant castiron plate covering a hole
in ground
– Crossed the street, traffic lite red, thirteen bus roaring by liquor store,
past corner pharmacy iron grated, past Coca Cola & My-Lai poster fading
scraped on brick
Past Chinese Laundry wood door'd, & broken cement stoop steps For Rent
hall painted green & purple Puerto Rican style
Along E. 10th's glass splattered pavement, kid blacks & Spanish oiled hair
adolescents' crowded house fronts –
Ah, tonite I walked out on my block NY City under humid summer sky Hallow-
een,
thinking what happened Timothy Leary joining brain police for a season?
thinking what's all this Weathermen, secrecy & selfrighteousness beyond
reason – F.B.I. plots?
Walked past a taxicab controlling the bottle strewn curb –
past young fellows with their umbrella handles & canes leaning against rav-
aged Buick
– and as I looked at the crowd of kids on the stoop – a boy stepped up, put his
arm around my neck
tenderly I thought for a moment, squeezed harder, his umbrella handle
against my skull,
and his friends took my arm, a young brown companion tripped his foot
'gainst my ankle –
as I went down shouting Om Ah Hūṁ to gangs of lovers on the stoop watching
slowly appreciating, why this is a raid, these strangers mean strange business
with what – my pockets, bald head, broken-healed-bone leg, my softshoes,
my heart –
Have they knives? Om Ah Hūṁ – Have they sharp metal wood to shove in eye
ear ass? Om Ah Hūṁ
& slowly reclined on the pavement, struggling to keep my woolen bag of
poetry address calendar & Leary-lawyer notes hung from my shoulder
dragged in my neat orlon shirt over the crossbar of a broken metal door
dragged slowly onto the fire-soiled floor an abandoned store, laundry candy
counter 1929 –
now a mess of papers & pillows & plastic covers cracked cockroach-corpsed
ground –
my wallet back pocket passed over the iron foot step guard
and fell out, stole by God Muggers' lost fingers, Strange – my bank money for
a week
old broken wallet – and dreary plastic contents – Ammex card & Manf.
Hanover Trust Credit too – business card from Mr Spears British Home Mini-
ster Drug Squad – my draft card – membership ACLU & Naropa Institute
Instructor's identification
Om Ah Hūṁ I continued chanting Om Ah Hūṁ
Putting my palm on the neck of an 18 year old boy fingering my back pocket

'glass spattered pavement'

crying 'Where's the money'
'Oh Ah Hūṁ there isn't any'
My card Chief Boo-Hoo Neo American Church New Jersey & Lower East Side
Om Ah Hūṁ – what not forgotten crowded wallet – Mobil Credit, Shell? old
    lovers addresses on cardboard pieces, booksellers calling cards –
– 'Shut up or we'll murder you' – 'Om Ah Hūṁ take it easy'
Lying on the floor shall I shout more loud? – the metal door closed on black-
    ness
one boy felt my broken healed ankle, looking for hundred dollar bills behind
    my stocking weren't even there – a third boy untied my Seiko Hong Kong
    watch rough from right wrist leaving a clasp-prick skin tiny bruise
'Shut up and we'll get out of here' – and so they left,
as I rose from the cardboard mattress thinking Om Ah Hūṁ didn't stop em
    enough,
the tone of voice too loud – my shoulder bag with 10,000 dollars full of poetry
    left on the broken floor –

We have just moved to New York, and outside the window at this very moment a man is parking a twenty-foot car in a nineteen-foot space. He has been working at it for ten minutes. It is a classic illustration of the New York temperament. If this man were a San Franciscan, he would give up and go play tennis. If a Washingtonian, he would already have a reserved parking space. Getting a reserved parking space is what Washington is all about. When it comes to parking, the true Washingtonian makes Machiavelli look like Anne of Green Gables.

The New Yorker, however, has to fit life into spaces too small for it. What he calls home would look like a couple of closets to most Americans, yet the New Yorker manages not only to live there but also to grow trees and cockroaches right on the premises.

A window affording a view of the sky is something to boast about. Getting a seat on the subway is an exciting start to his day. On such a day, he suspects, the gods may even favor him with a lunch table expansive enough to contain not only his pastrami but also a dish of pickles and a glass for the cream soda.

The sight of a nineteen-foot parking space makes him giddy with delight. The average $250,000 town house is only seventeen feet wide. Is it a wonder that a nineteen-foot parking space looks to him like a berth fit for the QE2?. . .

Trying to fit life into spaces too small for it takes a toll on civilization. Blood pressure among New Yorkers is probably always high. One goes through life most days with temperature just one degree below the boiling point. It takes very little to push it into the danger zone.

New Yorkers instinctively realize this about each other, and, recognizing the danger, try to avoid encroaching on each other's limited life space.

This may be why New Yorkers instinctively avoid making eye contact with each other in crowded places, why they 'look right through you', as dismayed visitors often complain. They are not looking right through you at all; they are discreetly avoiding an intrusion into your space. They sense the danger in a place where a one-degree temperature rise can mean an explosion.

New York Times *columnist* RUSSELL BAKER *published his article 'Spaced In' in 1974.*

'The most wretched urban slum in America.'

In their book
The Abuse of Power *journalists*
JACK NEWFIELD *and*
PAUL OBRUL *portrayed the
state of the city in the wake
of the great financial crisis of
1977.*

A walker in New York today can see many symbols and omens of its doom. In a single police precinct in Brooklyn – the 77th – seven people are murdered during one hot summer weekend. At the South Bronx Neighborhood Youth Corps Center, a thousand teenagers line up by midnight for a chance at fifty summer jobs when the doors open the next morning at 7:30.

In East Harlem, a fourteen-year-old boy is dead of a heroin overdose. It doesn't even make the papers; in 1970, a twelve-year-old named Walter Vandermeer died of an OD, so it is not 'news' any more.

At 122nd Street in East Harlem, a $45-million apartment development called Taino Towers stands vacant and vandalized. There is no money to complete the thirty-five-story buildings, which were intended for poor and middle-income families. Most of the windows are broken, and even the large, outdoor lighting fixtures have been stolen. The city fathers say that the architecturally distinctive project is 90 per cent completed.

In the Bronx, 435 families, mostly working-class Italian, have been evicted to make way for a 'new Fordham Hospital'. The city has spent $6 million on site acquisition and relocation, and another $1.5 million for architectural design, but the money has run out. No new hospital has been built. The money has been wasted. The families have been evicted for nothing. Where their homes once stood, there are today three blocks of rubble, garbage, beer cans, broken bottles, and dead trees.

In Brooklyn, the Lindsay Park housing development is falling apart nine years after it was opened at a gala ceremony. It is a $47-million middle-income cooperative development. But large shards of plaster are falling down from the ceilings of 3000 apartments. The roofs of all seven of the project's high-rise buildings leak seriously.

In Times Square, a blind man is mugged and his seeing-eye dog stolen by junkies. On Fox Street, a nine-year-old girl is raped and thrown off a rooftop. On 111th Street, parents are begging money on the street to pay for the funeral of their baby, who fell out of a tenement window. In Harlem, two men freeze to death in a slum building owned by a landlord named Gold, who lives in Miami.

In the Bronx, Hans Kabel, seventy-eight years old, and his wife Emma, seventy-six, commit suicide together after being robbed and terrorized in their own small apartment. They leave a suicide note behind that says, 'We don't want to live in fear any more.'

The slums of the Mott Haven community in the Bronx have bred a new strain of 'super-rat' that is immune to poison. Super-rats eat warfarin and other 'anti-coagulants' with no ill effect. The new rat mutations, often sixteen or eighteen inches long, have survived the Bureau of Pest Control's costly extermination campaigns. When the city fired more and more sanitation workers, more and more garbage accumulated in the South Bronx, and more and more super-rats bred and passed immunity on to their offspring. By the summer of 1976 the Bureau of Pest Control had discovered that almost 15 per cent of the city's estimated 9 million rats could eat ten times the normally lethal dose of poison without dying. The Bureau of Pest Control has had to fire almost 500 employees during the last two years, as part of a budget cutback. But this will mean more children bitten by rats, and more disease spread by rats and rat droppings. . .

By the early 1970s, the South Bronx was perhaps the most wretched urban slum in America – its only rival Brooklyn's Brownsville. The infant mortality rate there was 29 per 1000 births. In 1970 the average median family income in the South Bronx was $5,200, compared to the city-wide average of $9,682. The South Bronx has a quarter of all New York's reported cases of malnutrition and 16 per cent of all its cases of venereal disease. In 1972 less than 6 per cent of the public-school pupils could read at grade level. Three out of every four housing units were below standard and in violation of housing and health codes. There were 6000 abandoned buildings. Residents ran wires from an abandoned building with electricity to an inhabited one with none. Street gangs were armed with automatic weapons, and packs of wild dogs lived in the abandoned buildings.

'The Subway' – painting by George Tooker, 1950.

BAGHDAD-ON-SUBWAY

The sheer pace of life in New York creates a certain kind of personality, as poet, novelist, and columnist CHRISTOPHER MORLEY *observed in 'Epitaph for Any New Yorker'.*

I, who all my life had hurried,
    Came to Peter's crowded gate;
And, as usual, was worried,
    Fearing that I might be late.
So, when I began to jostle
    (I forgot that I was dead)
Patient smiled the old Apostle:
    'Take your Eternity,' he said.

Satirist MARK TWAIN *frowned on the ill-manners displayed in the New York street cars in his 'The Sex in New York' (1867).*

They do not treat women with as much deference in New York as we of the provinces think they ought. This is painfully apparent in the street-cars. Authority winks at the overloading of the cars – authority being paid for so winking, in political influence possibly, for I cannot bring myself to think that any other species of bribery would be entertained for a moment – authority, I say, winks at this outrage, and permits one car to do the work of at least two instead of compelling the companies to double the number of their cars, and permits them, also, to cruelly over-work their horses, too, of course, in the face of the Society for the Prevention of Cruelty to Animals. The result of this over-crowding is to set the people back a long stride toward semi-civilization. What I mean by that dreadful assertion is, that the over-crowding of the cars has impelled men to adopt the rule of hanging on to a seat when they get it, though twenty beautiful women came in and stood in their midst. That is going back toward original barbarism, I take it. A car's proper cargo should be twenty-two inside and three upon each platform – twenty-eight – and no crowding. I have seen fifty-six persons on a car, here, but a large portion of them were hanging on by the teeth. Some of the men inside had to go four or five miles, and naturally enough did not like to give up their seats and stand in a packed mass of humanity all that distance. So, when a lady got in, no man offered her a seat – no man dreamt of doing such a thing. No citizen, I mean. Occasionally I have seen a man, under such circumstances, get up and give his place to a lady, but the act betrayed, like spoken words, that he was from the provinces. . .

When I am with the Romans I try to do as the Romans do. I generally succeed reasonably well. I have got so that I can sit still and let a homely old maid stand up and nurse her poodle till she is ready to drop, but the young and the blooming, alas! are too many for me. I have to get up and vacate the premises when they come. Some day, though, may be, I shall acquire a New York fortitude and be as shameless as any.

The other day an ill-bred boy in a street-car refused to give up his seat to a lady. The conductor very properly snatched him out and seated the lady. Consequence: Justice Dowling fined that *conductor* a month's wages – sixty dollars – and read him a lecture worth sixty dollars more.

The cable cars come down Broadway as the waters come down at Lodore. Years ago Father Knickerbocker had convulsions when it was proposed to lay impious rails on his sacred thoroughfare. At the present day the cars, by force of column and numbers, almost dominate the great street, and the eye of even an old New Yorker is held by these long yellow monsters which prowl intently up and down, up and down, in a mystic search.

In the gray of the morning they come out of the up-town, bearing janitors, porters, all that class which carries the keys to set alive the great downtown. Later, they shower clerks. Later still, they shower more clerks. And the thermometer which is attached to a conductor's temper is steadily rising, rising, and the blissful time arrives when everybody hangs to a strap and stands on his neighbor's toes. Ten o'clock comes, and the Broadway cars, as well as elevated cars, horse cars, and ferryboats innumerable, heave sighs of relief. They have filled lower New York with a vast army of men who will chase to and fro and amuse themselves until almost nightfall.

The cable car's pulse drops to normal. But the conductor's pulse begins now to beat in split seconds. He has come to the crisis in his day's agony. He is now to be overwhelmed with feminine shoppers. They all are going to give him two-dollar bills to change. They all are going to threaten to report him. He passes his hand across his brow and curses his beard from black to gray and from gray to black. . .

The car sweeps on its diagonal path through the Tenderloin with its hotels, its theatres, its flower shops, its 10,000,000 actors who played with Booth and Barret. It passes Madison Square and enters the gorge made by the towering walls of great shops. It sweeps around the double curve at Union Square and Fourteenth Street, and a life insurance agent falls in a fit as the car dashes over

The Broadway street cars travelled the length of Manhattan, an epic journey chronicled by novelist, poet, and journalist STEPHEN CRANE in a newspaper article published posthumously in the New York Herald in 1902.

111

the crossing, narrowly missing three old ladies, two old gentlemen, a newly-married couple, a sandwich man, a newsboy, and a dog. At Grace Church the conductor has an altercation with a brave and reckless passenger who beards him in his own car, and at Canal Street he takes dire vengeance by tumbling a drunken man on to the pavement. Meanwhile, the gripman has become involved with countless truck drivers, and inch by inch, foot by foot, he fights his way to City Hall Park. On past the Post Office the car goes, with the gripman getting advice, admonition, personal comment, an invitation to fight from the drivers, until Battery Park appears at the foot of the slope, and as the car goes sedately around the curve the burnished shield of the bay shines through the trees.

It is a great ride, full of exciting actions. Those inexperienced persons who have been merely chased by Indians know little of the dramatic quality which life may hold for them. These jungles of men and vehicles, these canyons of streets, these lofty mountains of iron and cut stone – a ride through them affords plenty of excitement. And no lone panther's howl is more serious in intention than the howl of the truck driver when the cable car bumps one of his rear wheels. . .

In his novel A Hazard of New Fortunes *(1890),* WILLIAM DEAN HOWELLS *described the experience of riding on the new 'elevated' railway line which linked one part of the city with another.*

'Not Experts – Just Sardines' – by Rollin Kirby, 1927.

At Third Avenue they took the elevated, for which she confessed an infatuation. She declared it the most ideal way of getting about in the world, and was not ashamed when he reminded her of how she used to say that nothing under the sun could induce her to travel on it. She now said that the night transit was even more interesting than the day, and that the fleeting intimacy you formed with people in second- and third-floor interiors, while all the usual street life went on underneath, had a domestic intensity mixed with a perfect repose that was the last effect of good society with all its security and exclusiveness. H said it was better than the theater, of which it reminded him, to see those people through their windows: a family party of workfolk at a late tea, some of the men in their shirt-sleeves; a woman sewing by a lamp; a mother laying her child in its cradle; a man with his head fallen on his hands upon a table; a girl and her lover leaning over the windowsill together. What suggestion! What drama! What infinite interest! At the Forty-second Street station they stopped a minute on the bridge that crosses the track to the branch road for the Central Depot, and looked up and down the long stretch of the elevated to north and south. The track that found and lost itself a thousand times in the flare and tremor of the innumerable lights; the moony sheen of the electrics mixing with the reddish points and blots of gas far and near; the architectural shapes of houses and churches and towers, rescued by the obscurity from all that was ignoble in them; and the coming and going of the trains marking the stations with vivider or fainter plumes of flame-shot steam – formed an incomparable perspective. They often talked afterward of the superb spectacle, which in a city full of painters nightly works its unrecorded miracles; and they were just to the Arachne roof spun in iron over the cross street on which they ran to the depot; but for the present they were mostly inarticulate before it. They had another moment of rich silence when they paused in the gallery that leads from the elevated station to the waiting rooms in the Central Depot and looked down upon the great night trains lying on the tracks dim under the rain of gaslights that starred without dispersing the vast darkness of the place. What forces, what fates, slept in these bulks which would soon be hurling themselves north and east and west through the night! Now they waited there like fabled monsters of Arab story ready for the magician's touch, tractable, reckless, will-less – organized lifelessness full of a strange semblance of life.

Free existence and good manners, in New York, are too much brought down to a bare rigour of marginal relation to the endless electric coil, the monstrous chain that winds round the general neck and body, the general middle and legs, very much as the boa-constrictor winds round the group of the Laocoon. It struck me that when these folds are tightened in the terrible stricture of the snow-smothered months of the year, the New York predicament leaves far behind the anguish represented in the Vatican figures.

In The American Scene *(1907) novelist* HENRY JAMES *bewailed the New Yorkers' subservience to an inhuman system of public transportation.*

New York appears to be a great city in a great hurry. The average street pace must surely be forty miles an hour. The traffic lights switch straight from red to green without any nonsense about orange, symbolising the harshness of contrast that dispenses with the intermediary things that Europeans respect. It is usually unwise to cross the road except in accordance with the green light, and even New York dogs are said to understand this symbol. Americans always know their cue, as they know when to throw in the gear just before the light goes green.

English designer and photographer CECIL BEATON *visited the city in 1938 and recorded his impressions in* Cecil Beaton's New York.

The commuter is the queerest bird of all. The suburb he inhabits has no essential vitality of its own and is a mere roost where he comes at day's end to go to sleep. Except in rare cases, the man who lives in Mamaroneck or Little Neck or Teaneck, and works in New York, discovers nothing much about the

E. B. WHITE *considered that strange but numerous breed, the New York commuter, in* 'Here is New York' *(1949).*

'House Tops' – etching by Edward Hopper, 1921.

'The commuter is the queerest bird of all' – Grand Central Station.

city except the time of arrival and departure of trains and buses, and the path to a quick lunch. He is desk-bound, and has never, idly roaming in the gloaming, stumbled suddenly on Belvedere Tower in the Park, seen the ramparts rise sheer from the water of the pond, and the boys along the shore fishing for minnows, girls stretched out negligently on the shelves of the rocks; he has never come suddenly on anything at all in New York as a loiterer, because he has had no time between trains. He has fished in Manhattan's wallet and dug out coins, but has never listened to Manhattan's breathing, never awakened to its morning, never dropped off to sleep in its night. About 400,000 men and women come charging onto the Island each week-day morning, out of the mouths of tubes and tunnels. Not many among them have ever spent a drowsy afternoon in the Public Library, with the book elevator (like an old water wheel) spewing out books onto the trays. They tend their furnaces in Westchester and in Jersey, but have never seen the furnaces of the Bowery, the fires that burn in oil drums on zero winter nights. They may work in the financial district downtown and never see the extravagant plantings of Rocke-feller Center – the daffodils and grape hyacinths and birches and the flags trimmed to the wind on a fine morning in spring. Or they may work in a mid-town office and may let a whole year swing round without sighting Governors Island from the sea wall. The commuter dies with tremendous mileage to his credit, but he is no rover. His entrances and exits are more devious than those in a prairie-dog village; and he calmly plays bridge while buried in the mud at the bottom of the East River. The Long Island Rail Road alone carried forty million commuters last year; but many of them were the same fellow retracing his steps.

The subway flatters like the dope habit,
For a nickel extending peculiar space:
You dive from the street, holing like a rabbit,
Roar up a sewer with a millionaire's face.

Squatting in the full glare of the locked express
Imprisoned, rocked, like a man by a friend's death,
O how the immense investment soothes distress,
Credit laps you like a huge religious myth.

It's a sound effect. The trouble is seeing
(So anaesthetized) a square of bare throat
Or the fold at the crotch of a clothed human being:
You'll want to nuzzle it, crop at it like a goat.

That's not in the buy. The company between stops
Offers you security, and free rides to cops.

Poet and dance critic
EDWIN DENBY *published*
'The Subway' in 1948.

The New York City taxi driver carries a variety of personalities. As he trium-phantly roars through a red light and purrs with satisfaction, 'I coulda got a ticket,' he sups of the glory of the bullfighter whose chest is stained but untorn by the close rush of the bull. 'Don't worry,' he assures you when you tell him you must make Grand Central in a few minutes: as a knight in checkered cap and old army jacket, he makes off on his crusade with jaw set and shoulders hunched, ready to do battle with time, distance and other taxis. His progress, like Sir Galahad's, is full of adventuresome delays with almost supernatural overtones, and your anxiety gnaws at you as he seems to seek out all possible hazards – the broken traffic light, the street full of holes and excavation bar-riers, the routes of parades and demonstrations. But he usually gets you there on time, even if your request was unreasonable. However, to compensate for your unreasonableness and his demanding adventure, he expects an extra tip – no extra tip, no thanks. Nevertheless, it is impossible for a taxi driver to say nothing, so he mutters, 'Big sport. How could he afford a train ride? Fancy lug-gage and no extra dime! Next time take a bus, mister, it's cheaper.'

Sometimes the cab driver is the Lord of New York, viewing it with the pride and intimate knowledge of the possessor of a suzerainty. He will talk about the 'rackets' in cryptic inside-dope terms, make veiled allusions – 'If people really knew what went on in this town's politics!' – and speak longingly of the good old days of Fiorello LaGuardia as if personally bereaved. He will give the

Writer KATE SIMON *saluted*
the New York City taxi driver
in New York, Places and Pleasures *(1971).*

'Taxi, Taxi' – painting by Eugene McEvoy.

impression that all of New York is his and its best is a little purse of secrets which he may or may not open for you, depending on his royal whim.

Haggling over price either before or after a ride, as in some foreign cities, is not part of the New York scene; our taximeters can't be argued with as they grind out their inexorable sums, except, possibly, in the group riding from John F. Kennedy International Airport. The nearest equivalent is the opening discussion of how to get where you're going. You suggest going west on 49th Street to get to a theater. Nope, impossible, 49th at this time of night is choked with cars; the way to do it is go west on 47th, over to Eighth, and cut back and around. It sounds a little irrational but you assume he is speaking from profound technical knowledge and are reluctant to question a professional's judgment in his own métier. West 47th turns out to be as clogged with cars as an old drain with rust, nothing moves but the contained winds of your impatient temper, your dinner sours, and you rush to the theater seat well immunized against the charms of the play and its actors. The taxi genie, however, drives away with the expression of one who has done his job well.

Why do I continue to ride the subways? Even the police now say they are too dangerous for a cop to patrol without a companion cop to protect his back. I can best answer with other questions.

Why does the torero confront the bull? Why does the hunter face the charging lion? Why does the bomber crew rise again to face the flak over Bremerhaven? It is not easy to feel like a hero these days, but when I head for the subway, I feel myself walking a little bit straighter, my jaw setting in a firmer line, my primitive animal reflexes becoming tauter.

In five years in the subways I have acquired skills – professionalism – of which I am proud. I am an aging man, like Willie Stargell, but there is a fine pleasure, as there must be for Stargell, in testing myself to find whether the wisdom and experience are still enough to compensate for the loss of quickness.

I feel confidence as I submerge at 42nd Street and brush past the man at the foot of the steps with his chant of 'Acid and grass, acid and grass, acid and grass.'

Inside I am cautious about avoiding eye contact, which can lead to critical encounters with roving maniacs. On the platform, I cunningly stay back from the rails pretending to notice no one, but sizing up everyone. I keep distance from men carrying paper bags which may conceal meat cleavers or .357 magnums. If someone runs, I slide discreetly behind an upright steel pillar and grasp it firmly against the possibility of being shoved onto the rails.

When the train arrives, I do not enter the cars in which the lights are out or in which too many of the doors refuse to open.

At my destination, confronting a 300-yard walk along an abandoned tunnel illuminated with a ten-watt bulb, I roll my newspaper so tightly it becomes a murderous spear and, swinging it aggressively, stride through the gloom like Bogart walking down a mean street. When I emerge whole, I feel complete and alive again and a true New Yorker.

RUSSELL BAKER's 'What A Man's Got To Do' appeared in the New York Times in 1978.

'the full glare of the locked express'

A LITTLE LOVE
IN BIG MANHATTAN

WALT WHITMAN *added the poem 'City of Orgies' to his ever-growing* Leaves of Grass *in 1867.*

City of orgies, walks and joys,
  City whom I that have lived and sung in your midst will one day make you illustrious,
Not the pageants of you, not your shifting tableaus, your spectacles, repay me,
Not the interminable rows of your houses, nor the ships at the wharves,
Nor the processions in the streets, nor the bright windows with goods in them,
Nor to converse with learn'd persons, to bear my share in the soiree or feast;
Not those, but as I pass O Manhattan, your frequent and swift flash of eyes offering me love,
Offering response to my own – these repay me,
Lovers, continual lovers, only repay me.

'Union Square' by the New York City poet – and recluse – SARA TEASDALE.

With the man I love who loves me not,
  I walked in the street-lamps' flare;
We watched the world go home that night
In a flood through Union Square.

I leaned to catch the words he said
That were light as a snowflake falling;
Ah well that he never leaned to hear
The words my heart was calling.

And on we walked and on we walked
Past the fiery lights of the picture shows –
Where the girls with thirsty eyes go by
On the errand each man knows.

And on we walked and on we walked,
At the door at last we said good-bye;
I knew by his smile he had not heard
My heart's unuttered cry.

With the man I love who loves me not
I walked in the street-lamps' flare –
But oh, the girls who ask for love
In the lights of Union Square.

'Coney Island Beach' – painting by Reginald Marsh, 1934.

About me young and careless feet
Linger along the garish street;
  Above, a hundred shouting signs
Shed down their bright fantastic glow
  Upon the merry crowd and lines
Of moving carriages below.
Oh wonderful is Broadway – only
My heart, my heart is lonely.

Desire naked, linked with Passion,
Goes strutting by in brazen fashion;
  From playhouse, cabaret and inn

Jamaican-born writer
CLAUDE McKAY *lived in
New York in the 1920s,
where he wrote his poem
'On Broadway,' (c. 1920).*

The rainbow lights of Broadway blaze
    All gay without, all glad within.
As in a dream I stand and gaze
At Broadway, shining Broadway – only
My heart, my heart is lonely.

F. SCOTT FITZGERALD, *a midwesterner resettled in the East, re-created the lonely days and nights of another midwesterner in New York in* The Great Gatsby *(1925).*

M ost of the time I worked. In the early morning the sun threw my shadow westward as I hurried down the white chasms of lower New York to the Probity Trust. I knew the other clerks and young bond-salesmen by their first names, and lunched with them in dark, crowded restaurants on little pig sausages and mashed potatoes and coffee. I even had a short affair with a girl who lived in Jersey City and worked in the accounting department, but her brother began throwing mean looks in my direction, so when she went on her vacation in July I let it blow quietly away.

I took dinner usually at the Yale Club – for some reason it was the gloomiest event of my day – and then I went upstairs to the library and studied investments and securities for a conscientious hour. There were generally a few rioters around, but they never came into the library, so it was a good place to work. After that, if the night was mellow, I strolled down Madison Avenue past the old Murray Hill Hotel, and over 33rd Street to the Pennsylvania Station.

I began to like New York, the racy, adventurous feel of it at night, and the satisfaction that the constant flicker of men and women and machines gives to the restless eye. I liked to walk up Fifth Avenue and pick out romantic women from the crowd and imagine that in a few minutes I was going to enter into their lives, and no one would ever know or disapprove. Sometimes, in my mind, I followed them to their apartments on the corners of hidden streets, and they turned and smiled back at me before they faded through a door into warm darkness. At the enchanted metropolitan twilight I felt a haunting loneliness sometimes, and felt it in others – poor young clerks in the dusk, wasting the most poignant moments of night and life.

Again at eight o'clock, when the dark lanes of the Forties were lined five deep with throbbing taxicabs, bound for the theatre district, I felt a sinking in my heart. Forms leaned together in the taxis as they waited, and voices sang, and there was laughter from unheard jokes, and lighted cigarettes made unintelligible circles inside. Imagining that I, too, was hurrying towards gaiety and sharing their initimate excitement, I wished them well.

In 'Immorality' (1927) by New York columnist and poet DON MARQUIS, *the free-versifying cockroach* archy *comments on a scene in Central Park.*

i was up to central
park yesterday watching some
kids build a snow man when
they were done and had
gone away i looked it
over they had used two
little chunks of wood for
the eyes i sat on one
of these and stared at
the bystanders along came a
prudish looking
lady from flatbush she
stopped and regarded the

'the enchanted metropolitan twilight . . .' – lithograph by Howard Cook, 1931.

snow man i stood
up on my kind legs in
the eye socket and
waved myself at her
horrors she cried even the
snow men in manhattan
are immoral officer arrest
that statue it winked
at me madam said the cop
accept the tribute
as a christmas present
and be happy my own
belief is that some
people have immorality
on the brain

archy

'Sunbathers on the Roof' – etching by John Sloan, 1941.

In his Jews Without Money *(1930) radical writer* MICHAEL GOLD *recalled how the poverty-stricken immigrants lived in the midst of the red-light district.*

The East Side of New York was then the city's red light district, a vast 606 playground under the business management of Tammany Hall. The Jews had fled from the European pogroms; with prayer, thanksgiving and solemn faith from a new Egypt into a New Promised Land.

They found awaiting them the sweatshops, the bawdy houses and Tammany Hall.

There were hundreds of prostitutes on my street. They occupied vacant stores, they crowded into flats and apartments in all the tenements. The pious Jews hated the traffic. But they were pauper strangers here; they could do nothing. They shrugged their shoulders, and murmured: 'This is America.' They tried to live.

They tried to shut their eyes. We children did not shut our eyes. We saw and knew.

On sunshiny days the whores sat on chairs along the sidewalks. They sprawled indolently, their legs taking up half the pavements. People stumbled over a gauntlet of whores' meaty legs.

The girls gossiped and chirped like a jungle of parrots. Some knitted shawls and stockings. Others hummed. Others chewed Russian sunflower seeds and monotonously spat out the shells.

The girls winked and jeered, made lascivious gestures at passing males. They pulled at coat-tails and cajoled men with fake honeyed words. They called their wares like pushcart peddlers. At five years I knew what it was they sold.

There in the shadowy, dank hall
Right alongside the ground-floor stair –
A weeping girl, attended by
A grimy hand in the mussed-up hair.
    A little love in big Manhattan.

The hair – a whiff of some cheap rinse
The hand – hard, stiff and leathery
Two equal lovers, for whom this is
As good as it'll ever be.
    A little love in big Manhattan.

It's strange to listen to two people
Standing there in the dark, unheard;
Why doesn't Sammy say a word?
Why doesn't Bessie say a word?
    A little love in big Manhattan.

They may be talking, but it's all
Blanketed by the howl, instead,
From a million iron fire escapes
And all the dark ceilings overhead.
    A little love in big Manhattan.

Ceilings on ceilings and beds over beds;
Steamy air, wrapped in smoking shrouds;
From the top floor down, a chasm falls;
From above, acres open to the clouds.
    A little love in big Manhattan.

A huge night city, such grim strangeness
Wraps you up in the darkness here!
Man and wife sleep by the million
Like drunks all bloated up with beer.
    A little love in big Manhattan.

Like monkeys in the trees, the children
Hang in their fire escapes, asleep;
Soot drifts down from above their heads,
Dropped by the moon, a chimney sweep.
    A little love in big Manhattan.

And the girl Bessie knows 'from nothing'
And Sammy, too, with his open mouth,
And Monday swims up before your eyes,
A desert of dead miles toward the south.
    A little love in big Manhattan.

And even Bessie's poor old mother
No longer asks, 'Where is that kid?'
It doesn't matter that black hair
Has all been bleached to blonde and red.
    A little love in big Manhattan.

When MOSHE LEIB HALPERN, *an immigrant from Eastern Europe, died penniless in the Bronx in 1932 his Yiddish poems, like 'Song: Weekend's Over' (here translated by John Hollander), were already treasured by the Jewish masses of New York.*

Photograph by Henri Cartier-Bresson.

It isn't that he's ill, the sad one
Who contemplates these things at night;
But sick of his own sadness only,
He lies and broods, his pipe alight.
A little love in big Manhattan.

Dance critic and poet
EDWIN DENBY*'s poem*
'Summer' was published in
1948.

I stroll on Madison in expensive clothes, sour.
Ostrich-legg'd or sweet-chested, the loping clerks
Slide me a glance nude as oh in a tiled shower
And lope on dead-pan, large male and female jerks.

Later from the open meadow in the Park
I watch a bulging pea-soup storm lie midtown;
Here the high air is clear, there buildings are murked,
Manhattan absorbs the cloud like a sage-brush plain.

In the grass sleepers sprawl without attraction:
Some large men who turned sideways, old ones on papers,
A soldier, face handkerchiefed, an erection
In his pants – only men, the women don't nap here.

Can these wide spaces suit a particular man?
They can suit whomever man's intestines can.

Novelist EDMUND WHITE
described New York's new
gay community in his
'Fantasia on the Seventies'
(1980).

For the longest time everyone kept saying the seventies hadn't started yet. There was no distinctive style for the decade, no flair, no slogans. The mistake we made was that we were all looking for something as startling as the Beatles, acid, Pop Art, hippies and radical politics. What actually set in was a painful and unexpected working-out of the terms the sixties had so blithely tossed off. Sexual permissiveness became a form of numbness, as rigidly codified as the old morality.

The characteristic face in New York these days is seasoned, wry, weathered by drama and farce. Drugs, heavy sex, and the ironic, highly concentrated experience (so like that of actors everywhere) of leading uneventful, homebodyish lives when not on stage for those two searing hours each night – this reality, or release from it, has humbled us all. It has even broken the former tyranny youth and beauty held over us. Suddenly it's okay to be thirty, forty, even fifty, to have a streak of white crazing your beard, to have a deviated septum or eyes set too close together. All the looks anyone needs can be bought – at the army-navy store, at the gym, and from the local pusher; the lisped shriek of 'Miss Thing!' has faded into the passing, over-the-shoulder offer of 'loose joints'. And we do in fact seem looser, easier in the joints, and if we must lace ourselves nightly into chaps and rough up more men than seems quite coherent with our softspoken, gentle personalities, at least we need no longer be relentlessly witty or elegant, nor need we stand around gilded pianos bawling out choruses from *Hello, Dolly*, our slender bodies embalmed in youth, bedecked with signature scarves, and soaked in eau de cologne. . .

But in the post-Stonewall decade there is a new quality to New York gay life. We don't hate ourselves so much (although I do wish everyone would stop picking on drag queens; I at least continue to see them as the Saints of

'The same old spark . . .' – photograph by Henri Cartier-Bresson.

Bleecker Street). In general, we're kinder to our friends. Discovering that a celebrity is gay does not automatically lower him now in our eyes; once it was enough to say such-and-such a conductor or pop singer was gay for him to seem to us a fake, as inauthentic as we perceived ourselves to be. The self-acceptance of the seventies might just give us the courage to experiment with new forms of love and camaraderie, including the *mariage blanc*, the three- or four-way marriage, bi- or trisexuality, a community of artists or craftsmen or citizens from which tiresome heterosexual competitiveness will be banished – a community of tested *seaworthy* New Yorkers.

I was born here,
that's no lie, he said,
right here beneath God's sky.

I wasn't born here, she said,
I come – and why?
Where I come from
folks work hard
all their lives
until they die
and never own no parts
of earth nor sky
So I come up here.
Now what've I got?
  You!

She lifted up her lips
in the dark:
The same old spark!

LANGSTON HUGHES's poem 'New Yorkers' was published in Montage of a Dream Deferred (1951).

'Lower Manhattan' – watercolour by John Marin, 1921.

TALENT

Creative people get inspiration from their immediate environment, and New York has the most immediate environment in the world.

JOSEPH PAPP

All Johnny wants to do is make music. He wants to keep everyone and everything who takes him away from his music off him. Since he can't afford human contact, he can't afford desire. Therefore he hangs around with rich zombies who never have anything to do with feelings.
This is a typical New York artisit attitude.

KATHY ACKER

In New York I first loved, and I first wrote of the things I saw with a fierce joy of creation – and knew at last that I could write. There I got the first perceptions of the life of my time. The city and its people were an open book to me; everything had its story, dramatic and full of ironic tragedy and terrible humor. There I first saw that reality transcended all the fine poetic inventions of fastidiousness and medievalism. I was never happy or well long away from New York.

JOHN REED

It is astonishing how little New York figures in current American literature. Think of the best dozen American novels of the last ten years. No matter which way your taste and prejudice carry you, you will find, I believe, that Manhattan Island is completely missing from at least ten of them, and that in the other two it is little more than a passing scene, unimportant to the main action. Perhaps the explanation is to be sought in the fact that very few authors of any capacity live in the town. It attracts all the young aspirants powerfully, and hundreds of them, lingering on, develop into very proficient hacks and quacks, and so eventually adorn the Authors' League, the Poetry Society, and the National Institute of Arts and Letters. But not many remain who have anything worth hearing to say. They may keep quarters on the island, but they do their writing somewhere else.

Primarily, I suppose, it is too expensive for them: in order to live decently they must grind through so much hack work for the cheap magazines, the movies and the Broadway theaters that there is no time left for their serious concerns. But there is also something else. The town is too full of distractions to be comfortable to artists; it is comfortable only to performers. Its machinery of dissipation is so vastly developed that no man can escape it – not even an author laboring in his lonely room, the blinds down and chewing-gum plugging his ears. He hears the swish of skirts through the key-hole; down the area-way comes the clink of ice in tall glasses; someone sends him a pair of tickets to a show which whisper promises will be the dirtiest seen since the time of the Twelve Apostles. It is a sheer impossibility in New York to escape such appeals

Critic and satirist H. L. MENCKEN *pondered the dilemma of New York's would-be writers in an essay in his* Prejudices, Sixth Series *(1927).*

to the ductless glands. They are in the very air. The town is no longer a place of work; it is a place of pleasure. Even the up-State Baptist, coming down to hear the Rev. Dr John Roach Straton tear into sin, must feel the pull of temptation. He wanders along Broadway to shiver dutifully before the Metropolitan Opera House, with its black record of lascivious music dramas and adulterous tenors, but before he knows what has struck him he is lured into a movie house even gaudier and wickeder, to sweat before a film of carnal love with the lewd music of Tschaikowsky dinning in his ears, or into a grindshop auction house to buy an ormolu clock disgraceful to a Christian, or into Childs' to debauch himself with such victuals as are seen in Herkimer county only on days of great ceremonial.

Such is the effect of organized badness, operating upon imperfect man. But what is bad is also commonly amusing, and so I continue to marvel that the authors of the Republic, and especially the novelists, do not more often reduce it to words. Is there anything more charming and instructive in the scenes that actually engage them? I presume to doubt it. There are more frauds and scoundrels, more quacks and cony-catchers, more suckers and visionaries in New York than in all the country west of the Union Hill, N. J., breweries. In other words, there are more interesting people. They pour in from all four points of the compass, and on the hard rocks of Manhattan they do their incomparable stuff, day and night, year in and year out, ever hopeful and ever hot for more.

Poet LANGSTON HUGHES *recalled the glory days of the Harlem Renaissance – when 'the Negro was in vogue' – in his autobiography* The Big Sea *(1940).*

The 1920's were the years of Manhattan's black Renaissance. It began with *Shuffle Along, Running Wild*, and the Charleston. Perhaps some people would say even with *The Emperor Jones*, Charles Gilpin, and the tom-toms at the Provincetown. But certainly it was the musical revue, *Shuffle Along*, that gave a scintillating send-off to that Negro vogue in Manhattan, which reached its peak just before the crash of 1929, the crash that sent Negroes, white folks, and all rolling down the hill toward the Works Progress Administration. . .

Put down the 1920's for the rise of Roland Hayes, who packed Carnegie Hall, the rise of Paul Robeson in New York and London, of Florence Mills over two continents, of Rose McClendon in Broadway parts that never measured up to her, the booming voice of Bessie Smith and the low moan of Clara on thousands of records, and the rise of that grand comedienne of song, Ethel Waters, singing 'Charlie's elected now! He's in right for sure!' Put down the 1920's for Louis Armstrong and Gladys Bentley and Josephine Baker.

White people began to come to Harlem in droves. For several years they packed the expensive Cotton Club on Lenox Avenue. But I was never there, because the Cotton Club was a Jim Crow club for gangsters and monied whites. They were not cordial to Negro patronage, unless you were a celebrity like Bojangles. So Harlem Negroes did not like the Cotton Club and never appreciated its Jim Crow policy in the very heart of their dark community. Nor did ordinary Negroes like the growing influx of whites toward Harlem after sundown, flooding the little cabarets and bars where formerly only colored people laughed and sang, and where now the strangers were given the best ringside tables to sit and stare at the Negro customers – like amusing animals in a zoo.

The Negroes said: 'We can't go downtown and sit and stare at you in your

The Cotton Club – Jim Crow in the heart of Harlem.

clubs. You won't even let us in your clubs.' But they didn't say it out loud – for Negroes are practically never rude to white people. So thousands of whites came to Harlem night after night, thinking the Negroes loved to have them there, and firmly believing that all Harlemites left their houses at sundown to sing and dance in cabarets, because most of the whites saw nothing but the cabarets, not the houses.

Some of the owners of Harlem clubs, delighted at the flood of white patronage, made the grievous error of barring their own race, after the manner of the famous Cotton Club. But most of these quickly lost business and folded up, because they failed to realize that a large part of the Harlem attraction for downtown New Yorkers lay in simply watching the colored customers amuse themselves. And the smaller clubs, of course, had no big floor shows or a name band like the Cotton Club, where Duke Ellington usually held forth, so, without black patronage they were not amusing at all. . .

The lindy-hoppers at the Savoy even began to practise acrobatic routines, and to do absurd things for the entertainment of the whites, that probably never would have entered their heads to attempt merely for their own effortless amusement. Some of the lindy-hoppers had cards printed with their names on them and became dance professors teaching the tourists. Then Harlem nights became show nights for the Nordics.

Some critics say that that is what happened to certain Negro writers, too — that they ceased to write to amuse themselves and began to write to amuse and entertain white people, and in so doing distorted and over-colored their material, and left out a great many things they thought would offend their American brother of a lighter complexion. Maybe — since Negroes have writer-racketeers, as has any other race. But I have known almost all of them, and most of the good ones have tried to be honest, write honestly, and express their world as they saw it.

The ordinary Negroes hadn't heard of the Negro Renaissance And if they had, it hadn't raised their wages any. As for all those white folks in the speakeasies and night clubs of Harlem — well, maybe a colored man could find *some* place to have a drink that the tourists hadn't yet discovered.

The jazz revolution known as bebop came to fruition in the small clubs on 52nd Street in the last years of the Second World War. Music critic ROSS RUSSELL recreated the era in his biography of alto sax genius Charlie Parker, Bird Lives *(1972).*

The Street was a collection of buildings, four stories high and constructed of the durable, stodgy brownstone favored by architects at the turn of the century. The brownstone buildings stood shoulder to shoulder, one wall wedged against the next, facing one another along Fifty-second Street in the block between Fifth and Sixth Avenues. Once each had housed a single, affluent New York family. Now, with corroded plumbing and wiring systems that gave cause for concern to the fire department, they provided studios for sign painters and silkscreen operators, mail-order drops, and import-export concerns run out of a hat, offices for private detectives and teachers of the piano and saxophone, and darkrooms shared by photographers who prowled Broadway night clubs with Speed Graphics and baggy pockets stuffed with flash bulbs.

By day The Street was dingier than most, a dispiriting block that lay between chic Fifth Avenue and the glitter of Broadway two blocks west. The clubs that sprang up there during the war years occupied unused basements or abandoned ground floors of the brownstone buildings. They were clustered at the west end of the block, seven in all: Jimmy Ryan's, the Onyx, Famous Door, Samoa, Downbeat, Spotlight, and Three Deuces. In front of each club the inevitable badge of the period cabaret, a marquee — its green canvas bleached by sun, stained by rain, supported by two iron poles — extended from the brownstone front to the curbstone. Some of the clubs were nothing more than damp converted basements, thirty feet wide and not much deeper, low of ceiling, with tiny checkrooms and miniature bars, furnished with a clutter of tables and chairs most likely picked up at an auction sale. . .

Customers sat at tables large enough to cover with a pocket handkerchief, and paid a cover charge of three dollars. The Street was a hustler's operation, geared to a high rate of turnover. After every thirty-minute set the clubs were cleared and the customers prodded along to the next place of entertainment. Each club displayed on its wall a printed card saying 'MAXIMUM OCCUPANCY PERMITTED ON THESE PREMISES IS 60' or whatever total had been assigned by the New York Fire Department. The limits were flagrantly violated on busy nights when the bar stood four or five deep with stags and buffs. . .

. . .The Street after dark became a place of glamour and promise. Neon lights brightened the sooty façades of the brownstones. Banners bearing the names of the featured artists inside fluttered against the awnings of the marquees, and if one were interested in the wonderful world of jazz, he might find there its principal stars in a improbable concentration.

Arriving on The Street by taxi on a warm night just after Labor Day, September, 1944, Charlie could see in a single sweeping glance the names on the banners. It was as if he had before him a chart showing, by means of its leading figures, the entire course of jazz history from the beginnings at the turn of the century in New Orleans to the present moment. At Jimmy Ryan's, the club nearest to Fifth Avenue, the legendary Sidney Bechet, the last of the master Creole clarinetists, those founding fathers of jazz reed style, headed a five-piece New Orleans band that included Zutty Singleton, a drummer who had played with the mythical Buddy Bolden, and a rhythm section of authentic New Orleans jazzmen, or 'musicianers,' as Bechet called them in his gruff patois. The old man, with his squashed face, seemingly chipped from a very hard wood, played clarinet and soprano saxophone, a curved, bell-less orphan of the reed family, blowing with a skirling vibrato that carried to the sidewalk and could be heard above the swish of taxicab tires.

At the Onyx the public was invited to hear the grand master of jazz tenor saxophone, Coleman Hawkins himself, now forty, old as jazzmen went, veteran of famous bands from 1922 to the present, still firmly in command of his improvisational powers and the earth-shaking tone that was his trademark. . .

Across the way, at the Famous Door, the matchless Art Tatum held forth, no longer as a single, but with a trio including guitarist Tiny Grimes and fleet bassist Slam Stewart. Mildred Bailey, accompanied by her husband, vibraphonist Red Norvo, and a mellow gathering of white musicians, was the attraction at the Club Downbeat. Fats Waller and a five-piece band topped the bill at the Spotlight. Advertised as 'Fifty Thousand Killer-Watts of Jive', Leo Watson and his Spirits of Rhythm led the show at the Samoa, leavening the solid musical content of the instrumental combos with maniacal scat singing and such originals as *Sweet Marihuana Brown* (set to the tune of *Sweet Georgia Brown*) and *She Ain't No Saint*, a ballad about the neighborhood call girl.

Charlie Parker at the Royal Roost, New York, 1949.

L ike most of the other clubs on Fifty-second Street, the Famous Door was on the street floor of a brownstone house and upstairs on the first floor there was a big foyer with built-in leather seats lining the walls, and beyond that were the bathrooms. After playing the first set the first night, I went upstairs to the washroom. A stately young colored girl in a white evening dress sitting alone in a corner of the deserted foyer threw me a half-timid, half-scornful look when I appeared in the doorway.

'What are you doing here all alone?' I asked her, surprised.

When she told me her name was Billie Holiday and that she was working there, too, singing with the Teddy Wilson trio, I remembered that I had seen her up in Harlem a few years before, singing and waiting on tables at the Alhambra Grill, where we used to go to hear Bobby Henderson's fine piano. The fact that I had heard her uptown made us good friends because she was a colored

Trumpet-player MAX KAMINSKY *recalled singer Billie Holiday's New York performances in his book* Jazz Band.

131

girl downtown in the white section and she felt good knowing I knew about Harlem, and when I heard her sing again I knew why I had remembered her name. She really sang in those days. Her voice *was* the blues, but she could make you feel so happy, too. In her peak years, between 1935 and 1941, her stunning sense of phrasing and tempo were still completely unself-conscious and the unaffected sweet-sadness of her voice could make you ring with joy as well as sorrow. A large, fleshy, but beautifully boned woman with a satin-smooth beige skin, she always possessed an air of hauteur, not only in her manner but in the arch of her brow, the poise of her head, and the dignity of her carriage, but her haughtiness hid a shyness so vast that she spoke in practically a whisper. When she talked to musicians, the subject was usually her mother, to whom she was devoted. There was nothing wild about her in those days; there was nothing showing then but the terrible, proud shyness; and even in her most turbulent, tortured days later on, she was always basically what she had been then – an uncompromising, devastatingly honest kind of girl, and always, in the deepest sense, a lady. Her sobriquet, Lady Day, suited her exactly. . .

Poet and art critic
FRANK O'HARA *turned*
Billie Holiday's death into a
New York City threnody in
'The Day Lady Died' (1959).

I t is 12:20 in New York a Friday
Three days after Bastille day, yes
it is 1959 and I go to get a shoeshine
because I will get off the 4:19 in Easthampton
at 7:15 and then go straight to dinner
and I don't know the people who will feed me

I walk up the muggy street beginning to sun
and have a hamburger and a malted and buy
an ugly NEW WORLD WRITING to see what the poets
in Ghana are doing these days
                              I go on to the bank
and Miss Stillwagon (first name Linda I once heard)
doesn't even look up my balance for once in her life
and in the GOLDEN GRIFFIN I get a little Verlaine
for Patsy with drawings by Bonnard although I do
think of Hesiod, trans. Richmond Lattimore or
Brendan Behan's new play or *Le Balcon* or *Les Nègres*
of Genet, but I don't, I stick with Verlaine
after practically going to sleep with quandariness

and for Mike I just stroll into the PARK LANE
Liquor Store and ask for a bottle of Strega and
then I go back where I came from to 6th Avenue
and the tobacconist in the Ziegfeld Theatre and
casually ask for a carton of Gauloises and a carton
of Picayunes, and a NEW YORK POST with her face on it

and I am sweating a lot by now and thinking of
leaning on the john door in the 5 SPOT
while she whispered a song along the keyboard
to Mal Waldron and everyone and I stopped breathing

'Her voice *was* the blues . . .' – Billy Holiday, 1943.

L unch today with M. Whatever is one to do about her? She says the money is gone finally, and unless she goes home, her family refuse absolutely to help. Cruel, I suppose, but I told her I did not see the alternative. On one level, to be sure, I do not think going home possible for her. She belongs to that sect most swiftly, irrevocably trapped by New York, the talented untalented; too acute to accept a more provincial climate, yet not quite acute enough to breathe freely within the one so desired, they go along neurotically feeding upon the fringes of the New York scene.

Only success, and that at a perilous peak, can give relief, but for artists without an art, it is always tension without release, irritation with no resulting pearl. Possibly there would be if the pressure to succeed were not so tremendous. They feel compelled to prove something, because middle-class America, from which they mostly spring, has withering words for its men of feeling, for its young of experimental intelligence, who do not show immediately that these endeavors pay off on a cash basis. But if a civilization falls, is it cash the inheritors find among the ruins? Or is it a statue, a poem, a play?

Which is not to say that the world owes M., or anyone, a living; alas, the way things are with her, she most likely could not make a poem, a good one, that is; still she is important, her values are balanced by more than the usual measure of truth, she deserves a finer destiny than to pass from belated adolescence to premature middle age with no intervening period, and nothing to show.

Writer TRUMAN CAPOTE *evoked the pathos of the city's hosts of unfulfilled artists in his essay 'New York' (1946).*

Museum of Modern Art, photograph by Henri Cartier-Bresson.

Cultural and political critic
DWIGHT MACDONALD
*paid this tribute to New
York's Museum of Modern
Art in the* New Yorker *in
1953.*

The operative word in the Museum's name is 'Modern'. The dictionary defines the adjective as meaning 'characteristic of the present and recent times; new-fashioned; not antiquated or obsolete . . .' 'Contemporary', on the other hand, is defined as 'living, occurring, or existing at the same period of time'. Herein lies the distinction between the Museum of Modern Art and the new neighbor, the Whitney Museum of American Art, whose criterion is simply chronological – anything produced since 1900. To the Museum, then, 'modern' is a value term. But what values does it represent? . . . Perhaps the most that can be said is that from the Museum's standpoint 'modern' represents a prejudice in favor of the new and against the traditional. In any event, 'modern' is a fighting word – a battle cry that has a stirring ring to some, a leaden sound to others. . .

'What is this, a three-ring circus?' a group of artists once asked in a manifesto denouncing the Museum of Modern Art. Their rhetoric was thrice too moderate. The Museum is a nine-ring circus, at least.

English critic
CYRIL CONNOLLY
*considered the delights
and difficulties of artistic
New York in his* Ideas and
Places *(1953).*

To the visiting non-competitive European all is unending delight. The shops, the bars, the women, the faces in the street, the excellent and innumerable restaurants, the glitter of Twenty-one, the old-world lethargy of the Lafayette, the hazy view of the East River or Central Park over tea in some apartment at the magic hour when the concrete icebergs suddenly flare up; the impressionist pictures in one house, the exotic trees or bamboo furniture in another, the chink of 'old-fashioneds' with their little glass pestles, the divine glories – Egyptian, Etruscan, French – of the Metropolitan Museum, the felicitous contemporary assertion of the Museum of Modern Art, the snow, the sea-breezes, the late suppers with the Partisans, the reelings-home down the black steam-spitting canyons, the Christmas trees lit up beside the liquorice ribbon of cars on Park Avenue, the Gotham Book Mart, the shabby cosiness of the Village, all go to form an unforgettable picture of what a city ought to be: that is, continuously insolent and alive, a place where one can buy a book or meet a friend at any hour of the day or night, where every language is spoken and xenophobia almost unknown, where every purse and appetite is catered for, where every street with every quarter and the people who inhabit them are fulfilling their function, not slipping back into apathy, indifference, decay. If Paris is the setting for a romance, New York is the perfect city in which to get over one, to get over anything. Here the lost *douceur de vivre* is forgotten and the intoxication of living takes its place. . .

One thing only seems to me impossible in New York — to write well. Not because the whirl and pleasurable bustle of the gregarious life built around writing is so irresistible, not because it is almost impossible to find a quiet room near a tree, or to stay in of an evening, not because intelligent conversation with a kindred spirit is hard to come by (it is not), but because this glowing, blooming and stimulating material perfection over-exites the mind, causing it to precipitate into wit and conversation those ideas which might have set into literature. Wit and wisecrack, not art, are the thorny flowers on this rocky island, this concrete Capri; they call the tune for which our proud new bass is lent us. 'Yah,' one may say instead of 'yes,' but when 'fabulous,' 'for Chris' sakes,' 'it stinks,' 'way off the beam' and 'Bourbon over ice' roar off our lips, and when we begin to notice with distaste the Europeanism of others — it's time for flight, for dripping plane-trees, misty mornings, the drizzling circle of hypercritical friends, the fecund London inertia where nothing stirs but the soul.

The Five Spot was the center for us. When Thelonious Monk came in for his historic eighteen-week stay, with John Coltrane, I was there almost every night. I was there from the beginning listening to Trane try to get around on Monk's weird charts, and gradually Trane got hold to those 'heads' and began to get inside Monk's music. Trane had just come from playing with the classic Miles Davis group that featured Cannonball, Philly Joe Jones, Paul Chambers, and Red Garland. The Club Bohemia was where I'd heard them 'max out' and make their greatest music. And that was a slick nightclub, albeit in the Village. But the Five Spot was on the East Side, on the Bowery. C.T., Cecil Taylor, had really inaugurated the playing of the Music in the place. Before that it had been one of those typical grim Bowery bars, but some of the painters who had lofts on the Bowery and in the area began to come in and drink and they used to ask Joe and Iggy to bring in some music. So the completely unorthodox Cecil was one of the first to come in. By the time Monk and Trane got there, The Five Spot was the center of the jazz world!. . .

The Five Spot gig with Monk was Trane coming into his own. After Monk, he'd play sometimes chorus after chorus, taking the music apart before our ears, splintering the chords and sounding each note, resounding it, playing it backwards and upside down trying to get to something else. And we heard our own search and travails, our own reaching for new definition. Trane was our flag.

Trane was leaping away from 'the given', and the troops of the mainstream were both shocked and sometimes scandalized, but Trane, because he had come up through the ranks, had paid all the dues, from slicksteppin on the bars of South Philly, honking rhythm and blues, through big Maybelle and Diz on up to Miles and then Monk, could not be waved aside by anybody. Though some tried and for this they were confirming their ignorance.

Poet LEROI JONES, *also known as Imamu Amiri Baraka, recalled the excitement of sax player John Coltrane's arrival on the New York jazz scene in his* Autobiography *(1984).*

In the last years of his life New York-born comedian LENNY BRUCE *was persecuted by papers, police and courts, and dogged by obscenity trials, one of which he described in his book* How To Talk Dirty and Influence People *(1965).*

New York, I'd been playing New York, concerts and night-club engagements, for eight years, but in 1964, I got busted for obscenity at the Café Au Go Go. I continued performing and got busted there again that same week.

Then I got pleurisy. My lung was filled with fluid. I couldn't breathe. I went to a doctor, but he wouldn't see me because he didn't want 'to get involved'. I finally did get a doctor – who, coincidentally, was a fan – and I ended up in a hospital, on the receiving end of a five-hour operation.

When *Newsweek* called up a friend of mine to find out how I was, he told them the surgeon cut all that *filth* out of my system too. . .

When I returned to New York, it turned out that the police didn't have complete tapes of the shows I was arrested for, so they actually had a guy in court *imitating my act* – a License Department Inspector who was formerly a CIA Agent in Vietnam – and in his courtroom impersonation of me, he was saying things that I had never said in my *life*, on stage or off. . .

'Sitting in on Lenny Bruce's current New York "obscenity" trial,' Stephanie Gervis Harrington wrote in the *Village Voice*, 'one gets the feeling of being present at an historical event – the birth of the courtroom of the absurd. Of course, if you sit through it long enough, you gradually adjust to the fact that eight grown men are actually spending weeks of their time and an unreckoned amount of the taxpayers' money in deliberation – passionate deliberation on the prosecutor's good days – over whether another grown man should be able to use four-letter words in public without going to jail.'

The ludicrousness of it all was inadvertently summed up by my attorney, Ephraim London, when he asked a witness who had been at my performance at the Café Au Go Go: 'Did you see Mr Crotch touch his Bruce?'

On reporting the incident, *The Realist* predicted, 'Henceforth and forevermore, we shall have had at that precise moment a meaningful new synonym added to our language.' And the magazine's editorial proceeded to demonstrate its use:

'Mommy, look, there's a man sitting over there with his bruce hanging out.'

'Beverly Schmidlap is a real bruceteaser, y'know?'

'Kiss my bruce, baby.'

And a cartoon by Ed Fisher had a judge saying, 'Before I pass sentence on you, Lenny Bruce, is there anything you wish to say – anything printable, that is?'

. . .What does it mean for a man to be found obscene in New York? This is the most sophisticated city in the country. This is where they play Genet's *The Balcony*. If anyone is the first person to be found obscene in New York, he must feel utterly depraved.

I was so sure I could reach those judges if they'd just let me tell them what I try to do. It was like I was on trial for rape and there I was crying, 'But, Judge, I can't rape anybody, I haven't got the wherewithal,' but nobody was listening, and my lawyers were saying, 'Don't worry, Lenny, you got a right to rape anyone you please, we'll beat 'em in the appellate court.'

New York. Five A.M.
The sidewalks empty.
Only the steam
pouring from the manhole covers seems alive,
as I amble from shop window to shop window,
sometimes stopping to stare, sometimes not.
Last week's snow is brittle now
and unrecognizable as the soft, white hair
that bearded the face of the city.
I head farther down Fifth Avenue
toward the thirties,
my mind empty
like the Buddhists tell you is possible
if only you don't try.
If only I could
turn myself into a bird
like the shaman I was meant to be,
but I can't,
I'm earthbound
and solitude is my companion,
the only one you can count on.
Don't, don't try to tell me otherwise.
I've had it all and lost it
and I never want it back,
only give me this morning to keep,
the city asleep
and there on the corner of Thirty-fourth and Fifth,
the man with the saxophone,
his fingerless gloves caked with grime,
his face also,
the layers of clothes welded to his skin.
I set down my case,
he steps backward
to let me know I'm welcome,
and we stand a few minutes
in the silence so complete
I think I must be somewhere else, not here,
not in this city, this heartland of pure noise.
Then he puts the sax to his lips again
and I raise mine.
I suck the air up from my diaphragm
and bend over into the cold, golden reed,
waiting for the notes to come,
and when they do,
for that one moment,
I'm the unencumbered bird of my imagination,
rising only to fall back
toward concrete,
each note a black flower,
opening, mercifully opening
into the unforgiving new day.

'The Man With The Saxophone' by the black woman poet known as AI *was published in her book* Sin *in 1986.*

Musicians in Washington Square.

137

'Backyards, Greenwich Village' – painting by John Sloan, 1914.

BOHEMIA

JOHN REED *was a major figure in the Greenwich Village avant-garde in the years leading up to US entry into the First World War. Reed celebrated its way of life in his long poem* The Day in Bohemia *(1913).*

In winter the water is frigid,
In summer the water is hot;
And we're forming a club for controlling the tub
For there's only one bath to the lot.
You shave in unlathering Croton,
If there's water at all, which is rare –
But the life isn't bad for a talented lad
At Forty-two Washington Square!

The dust it flies in at the window,
The smells they come in at the door,
Our trousers lie meek where we threw 'em last week
Bestrewing the maculate floor.
The gas isn't all that it should be,
It flickers – and yet I declare
There's pleasure or near it for young men of spirit
At Forty-two Washington Square!

But nobody questions your morals,
And nobody asks for the rent –
There's no one to pry if we're tight, you and I,
Or demand how our evenings are spent.
The furniture's ancient but plenty,
The linen is spotless and fair,
O life is a joy to a broth of a boy
At Forty-two Washington Square!

Up on Greenwich Avenue was the office of the *Masses*. It declared itself in its editorial manifesto to be 'a Revolutionary and Not a Reform Magazine; a Magazine with a Sense of Humour and No Respect for the Respectable, Frank; Arrogant; Impertinent; a Magazine whose Final Policy is to Do What It Pleases, and Conciliate Nobody, Not Even Its Readers.' It did not pay for contributions, because it had no money; but it was felt to be a privilege to appear in its pages. The contributions were submitted anonymously at a monthly meeting of the editors and their friends, and voted on. . .

From late in 1913, when I came to New York, I was with the magazine during the hectic years of its brief career – for it was frequently suppressed by the postal authorities, who were offended by the boldness both of its art and its opinions. Max Eastman was the acting editor; tall, handsome, sleek, and in repose as lazy looking as a hound-dog lying on the hearth, he exhibited an immense energy on the platform; he was one of the two real orators I have heard in my lifetime – and his best speech, I think, was made at the *Masses'* trial, when what were left of its editors were solemnly prosecuted for making jokes about the war for democracy. The war had scattered and divided us; friend was set against old friend and even if that had not been unhappily true, the war would inevitably have brought to an end that glorious intellectual playtime in which art and ideas, free self-expression and the passion of propaganda, were for one moment happily mated.

The Village, before America entered the war, contained two mingled currents: one of those had now disappeared. It contained two types of revolt, the individual and the social – or the aesthetic and the political, or the revolt against puritanism and the revolt against capitalism – we might tag the two of them briefly as *bohemianism* and *radicalism*. In those prewar days, however, the two currents were hard to distinguish. Bohemians read Marx and all the radicals had a touch of the bohemian: it seemed that both types were fighting in the same cause. Socialism, free love, anarchism, syndicalism, free verse – all these creeds were lumped together by the public, and all were physically dangerous to practice. . .

Writer and critic FLOYD DELL *was managing editor of The Masses, New York's leading radical magazine.*

In Exile's Return *(1934), writer* MALCOLM COWLEY *analyzed the conflict of generations in Greenwich Village after the First World War.*

But the war, and especially the Draft Law, separated the two currents. People were suddenly forced to decide what kind of rebels they were: if they were merely rebels against puritanism they could continue to exist safely in Mr Wilson's world. The political rebels had no place in it. Some of them yielded, joined the crusade for democracy, fought the Bolsheviks at Archangel, or volunteered to help the Intelligence Service by spying on their former associates and submitting typewritten reports about them to the Adjutant General's office. Others evaded the draft by fleeing to Mexico, where they were joined by a number of the former aesthetes, who had suddenly discovered that they were political rebels too. Still others stood by their opinions and went to Leavenworth Prison. Whatever course they followed, almost all the radicals of 1917 were defeated by events. The bohemian tendency triumphed in the Village, and talk about revolution gave way to talk about psychoanalysis. The *Masses*, after being suppressed, and after temporarily reappearing as the *Liberator*, gave way to magazines like the *Playboy*, the *Pagan* (their names expressed them adequately) and the *Little Review*.

After the war the Village was full of former people. There were former anarchists who had made fortunes manufacturing munitions, former Wobblies about to open speakeasies, former noblewomen divorced or widowed, former suffragists who had been arrested after picketing the White House, former conscientious objectors paroled from Leavenworth, former aviators and soldiers of fortune, former settlement workers, German spies, strike leaders, poets, city editors of Socialist dailies. But the distinguished foreign artists who had worked in the Village from 1914 till 1917, and given it a new character, had disappeared along with the active labor leaders. Nobody seemed to be doing anything now, except lamenting the time's decay. For the moment the Village was empty of young men.

But the young men were arriving from week to week, as colleges held commencement exercises or troops were demobilized...

The social centers of the Village were two saloons: the Hell Hole, on Sixth Avenue at the corner of West Fourth Street, and the Working Girls' Home, at Greenwich Avenue and Christopher Street. The Hell Hole was tough and dirty; the proprietor kept a pig in the cellar and fed it scraps from the free-lunch counter. The boys in the back room were small-time gamblers and petty thieves, but the saloon was also patronized by actors and writers from the Provincetown Playhouse, which was just around the corner. Sometimes the two groups mingled. The gangsters admired Dorothy Day because she could drink them under the table; but they felt more at home with Eugene O'Neill, who listened to their troubles and never criticized. They pitied him, too, because he was thin and shabbily dressed. One of them said to him, 'You go to any department store, Gene, and pick yourself an overcoat and tell me what size it is and I steal it for you.' The Hell Hole stayed in business during the first two or three years of prohibition, but then it was closed and I don't know where the gangsters met after that. The actors and playwrights moved on to the Working Girls' Home, where the front door was locked, but where a side door on Christopher Street still led into a room where Luke O'Connor served Old Fashioneds and the best beer and stout he could buy from the wildcat breweries.

It was in the Working Girls' Home that I first became conscious of the differ-

'Easter Eve, Washington Square' – etching by John Sloan, 1926.

ence between two generations. There were two sorts of people here: those who had lived in the Village before 1917 and those who had just arrived from France or college. For the first time I came to think of them as 'they' and 'we'.

'They' wore funny clothes: it was the first thing that struck you about them. The women had evolved a regional costume, then widely cartooned in the magazines: hair cut in a Dutch bob, hat carried in the hand, a smock of some bright fabric (often embroidered Russian linen), a skirt rather shorter than the fashion of the day, gray cotton stockings and sandals. With heels set firmly on the ground and abdomens protruding a little – since they wore no corsets and dieting hadn't become popular – they had a look of unexampled solidity; it was terrifying to be advanced upon by six of them in close formation. But this costume wasn't universal. Some women preferred tight-fitting tailored suits with Buster Brown collars; one had a five-gallon hat which she wore on all occasions, and there was a girl who always appeared in riding boots, swinging a crop, as if she had galloped down Sixth Avenue, watered her horse and tied him to a pillar of the Elevated; I called her Yoicks. The men, as a rule, were more conventional, but tweedy and unpressed. They did not let their hair grow over their collars, but they had a good deal more of it than was permitted by fashion. There were a few Russian blouses among them, a few of the authentic Windsor ties that marked the bohemians of the 1890s.

'They' tried to be individual, but there is a moment when individualism becomes a uniform in spite of itself. 'We' were accustomed to uniforms and content to wear that of the American middle classes. We dressed inconspicuously, as well as we were able.

'They' were older, and this simple fact continued to impress me long after I ceased to notice their clothes. Their ages ran from sixty down to twenty-three; at one end of the scale there was hardly any difference. But the Village had a pervading atmosphere of middle-agedness. To stay in New York during the war was a greater moral strain than to enter the army: there were more decisions to be made and uneasily justified; also there were defeats to be concealed. The Village in 1919 was like a conquered country. Its inhabitants were discouraged and drank joylessly. 'We' came among them with an unexpended store of energy: we had left our youth at home, and for two years it had been accumulating at compound interest; now we were eager to lavish it even on trivial objects.

'Sixth Avenue El' – lithograph by Stuart Davis, 1931.

'New York, The Big Store' – painting by Max Weber, 1925.

The world of the Abstract Expressionists was very macho. The painters who used to hang around the Cedar bar on University Place were all hard-driving two-fisted types who'd grab each other and say things like 'I'll knock your fucking teeth out' and 'I'll steal your girl.' In a way Jackson Pollock had to die the way he did, crashing his car up, and even Barnett Newman, who was so elegant, always in a suit and monocle, was tough enough to get into politics when he made a kind of symbolic run for mayor of New York in the thirties. The

In the fifties the group of painters known as Abstract Expressionists made New York the world centre of modern art. ANDY WARHOL *described the milieu in his book* Popism *(1980).*

143

toughness was part of a tradition, it went with their agonized, anguished art. They were always exploding and having fist fights about their work and their love lives. This went on all through the fifties when I was just new in town, doing whatever jobs I could get in advertising and spending my nights at home drawing to meet deadlines or going out with a few friends.

I often asked Larry Rivers, after we got to be friends, what it had really been like down there then. Larry's painting style was unique – it wasn't Abstract Expressionist and it wasn't Pop, it fell into the period in between. But his personality was very Pop – he rode around on a motorcycle and he had a sense of humor about himself as well as everybody else. I used to see him mostly at parties. I remember a very crowded opening at the Janis Gallery where we stood wedged in a corner at right angles to each other and I got Larry talking about the Cedar. I'd heard that when he was about to go on 'The $64,000 Question' on TV, he passed the word around that if he won, you could find him at the Cedar bar, and if he lost, he'd head straight for the Five-Spot, where he played jazz saxophone. He did win – $49,000 – and he went straight to the Cedar and bought drinks for around three hundred people.

I asked Larry about Jackson Pollock. 'Pollock? Socially, he was a real jerk,' Larry said. 'Very unpleasant to be around. Very stupid. He was always at the Cedar on Tuesdays – that was the day he came into town to see his analyst – and he always got completely drunk, and he made a point of behaving badly to everyone. I knew him a little from the Hamptons. I used to play saxophone in the taverns out there and he'd drop in occasionally. He was the kind of drunk who'd insist you play "I Can't Give You Anything but Love, Baby" or some other songs the musicians thought were way beneath them, so you'd have to see if you could play it in some way that you wouldn't be putting yourself down *too* much. . . He was a star painter all right, but that's no reason to pretend he was a pleasant person. Some people at the Cedar took him very seriously; they would announce what he was doing every single second – "There's Jackson!" or "Jackson just went to the john!"

'I'll tell you what kind of guy he was. He would go over to a black person and say, "How do you like your skin color?" or he'd ask a homosexual, "Sucked any cocks lately?" He'd walk over to me and make shooting-up gestures on his arm because he knew I was playing around with heroin then. And he could be really babyish, too. I remember he once went over to Milton Resnick and said, "You de Kooning imitator!" and Resnick said, "Step outside." Really.' Larry laughed. 'You have to have known these people to believe the things they'd fight over.' I could tell from Larry's smile that he still had a lot of affection for that whole scene.

'What about the other painters?' I asked him. 'Well,' he said, 'Franz Kline would certainly be at the Cedar every night. He was one of those people who always got there before you did and was still there after you left. While he was talking to you, he had this way of turning to someone else as you were leaving, and you got the feeling of automatic continuity – sort of, "So long . . . So this guy comes over to me and . . ." and while you may have flinched at his indiscriminate friendliness, he did have the virtue of smiling and wanting to talk all the time. There were always great discussions going on, and there was always some guy pulling out his poem and reading it to you. It was a very heavy scene.' Larry sighed. 'You wouldn't have liked it at all, Andy.'

Greenwich Village street artist.

I started walking around now after work, mostly on the West Side, Greenwich Village. Looking. Watching people. . .

. . .Coffeehouses, at that time, were very popular. The post-WWII decade of American visitors to Europe had brought back the coffeehouse as one evidence of a new reacquaintanceship with Continental cool. Certainly, for me, the coffeehouse was something totally new. Downtown New York coffee smells I associate with this period of my first permanent residence in the city. When you came up out of the subway or the PATH, the smell of coffee seemed to dominate everything.

I made the rounds of the coffeehouses, checking them and the people in them out. . . I thought everyone in those places was a writer or painter or something heavy.

Even when I got out of the service and was floating in and out of these places, I still thought for a while that all the customers were heavyweight intellectuals. Intellectual paperbacks were just coming out about that period as well. And people could be seen with the intriguingly packaged soft pocket books, folding and unfolding them out of bags and pockets. Sipping coffee and poking deeply, it seemed, ito *Moses and Monotheism* or *Seven Types of Ambiguity* or Aristophanes' comedies, mostly reissues with the slick arty covers that made merchandising moguls attribute 'genius' to the young men who conceived and orchestrated this paperback explosion.

But I was struck by the ambience of the place. People in strange clothes. (One dude I saw on the streets then dressed up like a specter from the Middle

In his Autobiography *(1984) poet and playwright* LEROI JONES, *also known as Imamu Amiri Baraka, recalled his early days in Greenwich Village in the late fifties.*

'Cityscape' by Karl Fortess, 1953.

Novelist KATHY ACKER
*evoked the late seventies
bohemian life around the
then-fashionable Mudd Club
in her short story 'New York
City in 1979'.*

Ages, like some *jongleur* wandering through the streets, complete with bells and all. In fact this dude still can be seen bouncing bowlegged through those streets, always alone. I wondered then, and still wonder, what wild shit lurks behind this creature's eyes?) The supposed freedom well advertised as the animating dream of that mixed-matched Village flock I believed as well. It was what I needed, just come out of the extreme opposite. Suddenly, I *was* free, I felt. I could do anything I could conceive of. Some days walking down the streets, with the roasted coffee bean aroma in my nose, I almost couldn't believe I had gotten out of the service and could walk down the street. . .

The streets themselves held a magic for my young self as well. Names like Minetta Lane and Jane Street and Waverly Place or Charles or Perry or Sheridan Square or Cornelia all carried with them, for me, notions of the strange, the exotic, and I dug it all, believed in it all. . .

Like it was Tim who hipped me to the dangerous state of race relations in the Village. And other of my friends did too. I found out myself from a few bad incidents. But Tim would fall back in his chair chortling and spilling the wine on his pants or shirt. 'And watch out for the Italians, Leee-Roy, they'll bop you in the head. They don't like us black boys. They'll beat you up. Especially if you with a white woman. I always carry a blackjack with me or a knife.' And he'd show you this limp-ass blackjack didn't look like it could do anything. 'Watch out for the Italians, Leee-Roy.' It'd crack Tim up.

He was right, to a certain extent. The 'local people', as folks were wont to call the largely Italian population that was intermingled with the more exotic Villagey part, apparently did not care for the wild antics and bohemian carryings-on of the permanent visitors to their neighborhood. It was like the 'townies' and the campus types. Like the 'DC boys' and those of us up on The Hill down at the Capstone. Except, with the blacks, it was, as usual, even worse. The general resentment the locals felt toward the white bohemians was quadrupled at the sight of the black species. And there were plenty people with grim stories to verify Tim's charges. Like a guy I came to know named Will Ribbon, who went with this one white woman for years and lived down below Houston Street, where it was really reputed to be dangerous for white-black liaisons. He got jumped on by a gang of the young locals and they pummeled him and called his woman names. Will goes home and gets his Beretta, and he walks up and down Thompson Street and Sullivan Street down by Broome and Prince and Spring, looking for these guys. He even goes into some of those private clubs (reputed Mafia relaxation stations) hunting for these guys. When I started working down around that area I used to carry a lead pipe in a manila envelope, the envelope under my arm like a good messenger, not intimidated but nevertheless ready.

Two rich couples drop out of a limousine. The women are wearing outfits the poor people who were in ten years ago wore ten years ago. The men are just neutral. All the poor people who're making this club fashionable so the rich want to hang out here, even though the poor still never make a buck off the rich pleasure, are sitting on cars, watching the rich people walk up to the club.

Some creeps around the club's entrance. An open-shirted skinny guy who says he's just an artist is choosing who he'll let into the club. Since it's 3:30 a.m. there aren't many creeps. The artist won't let the rich hippies into the club.

— Look at that car.

— Jesus. It's those rich hippies' car.

— Let's take it.

— That's the chauffeur over there.

— Let's kidnap him.

— Let's knock him over the head with a bottle.

— I don't want no terrorism. I wanna go for a ride.

— That's right. We've got nothing to do with terrorism. We'll just explain we want to borrow the car for an hour.

— Maybe he'll lend us the car if we explain we're terrorists-in-training. We want to use that car to try out terrorist tricks.

After 45 minutes the rich people climb back into their limousine and their chauffeur drives them away.

A girl who has gobs of brown hair like the foam on a cappuccino in Little Italy, black patent leather S&M heels, two unfashionable tits stuffed into a pale green corset, and extremely fashionable black fake leather tights heaves her large self off a car top. She's holding an empty bottle.

Diego senses there's going to be trouble. He gets off his car top. Is walking slowly towards the girl.

The bottle keeps waving. Finally the girl finds some courage heaves the bottle at the skinny entrance artist.

The girl and the artist battle it out up the street. Some of the people who are sitting on cars separate them. We see the girl throw herself back on a car top. Her tits are bouncing so hard she must want our attention and she's getting insecure, maybe violent, cause she isn't getting enough. Better give us a better show. She sticks her middle finger into the air as far as she can. She writhes around on top of the car. Her movements are so spasmatic she must be nuts.

A yellow taxi cab is slowly making its way to the club. On one side of this taxi cab's the club entrance. The other side is the girl writ(h)ing away on the black car. Three girls who are pretending to be transvestites are lifting themselves out of the cab elegantly around the big girl's body. The first body is encased into a translucent white girdle. A series of diagonal panels leads directly to her cunt. The other two dresses are tight and white. They are wriggling their way toward the club. The big girl, whom the taxi driver refused to let in his cab, wriggling because she's been rejected but not wriggling as much, is bumping into them. They're tottering away from her because she has syphilis.

It's four o'clock a.m. It's still too hot. Wet heat's squeezing this city. The air's mist. The liquid that's seeping out of human flesh pores is gonna harden into a smooth shiny shell so we're going to become reptiles.

No one wants to move anymore. No one wants to be in a body. Physical possessions can go to hell even in this night.

Now the big girl is unsuccessfully trying to climb through a private white car's window now she's running hips hooking even faster into an alleyway taxi whose driver is locking his doors and windows against her. She's offering him a blow-job. Now an ugly boy with a huge safety pin stuck through his upper lip, walking up and down the street, is shooting at us with this watergun.

The dyke sitting next to me is saying earlier in the evening she pulled at this safety pin.

Up until a few years ago Soho was an obscure district of lofts used chiefly for storage and light manufacturing. It wasn't called Soho then – it wasn't called anything because no one ever went there except the people who make Christmas tree ornaments out of styrofoam and glitter or fabric trimmings out of highly colored stretch felt. And say what you will about members of these professions, they are generally, I am sure, very nice people who not only don't make those things out of choice but also don't go around calling obscure districts of Manhattan things like Soho. Ostensibly, Soho is called Soho because it begins *So*uth of *Ho*uston Street, but if you want my opinion I wouldn't be too terribly surprised to discover that the person who thought up this name is a person whose circle of friends in 1967 included at least one too many English photographer. It was, of course, a combination of many unattractive things that led to the Soho of today, but quite definitely the paramount factor was the advent of Big Art. Before Big Art came long, painters lived, as God undoubtedly intended them to, in garrets or remodeled carriage houses, and painted paintings of a reasonable size. A painting of a reasonable size is a painting that one can easily hang over a sofa. If a painting cannot be easily hung over a sofa it is obviously a painting painted by a painter who got too big for his brushes. . . Painters, however, are not the only ones involved here. Modern sculptors . . . must bear a good part of the blame, for when clay and marble went out and demolished tractor-trailer trucks came in, Big Art was here to stay.

One day a Big Artist realized that if he took all of the sewing machines and bales of rags out of a three-thousand-square-foot loft and put in a bathroom and kitchen he would be able to live and make Big Art in the same place. He was quickly followed by other Big Artists and they by Big Lawyers, Big Boutique Owners, and Big Rich Kids. Soon there was a Soho and it was positively awash in hardwood floors, talked-to plants, indoors swings, enormous record collections, hiking boots, Conceptual Artists, video communes, Art book stores, Art grocery stores, Art restaurants, Art bars, Art galleries, and boutiques selling tie-dyed raincoats, macramé flower pots, and Art Deco salad plates.

THE COUNTRY
IN THE CITY

A *little* garden, six foot square,
A little parsly planted there,
A cabbage that shall have no head,
Nine inches long, a spinnage bed;
Some little shrubs, a little tree.
Four little sprigs of rosemary,
A little sage, a little rue,
Some heads of sallad, very few;
Three bean hills, ranging in a line,
Five little tulips – very fine;
A carrot head with scarce a root,
A gooseberry bush that bears no fruit;
All these are planted in the shade,
And in a little time shall fade –
All these do in this garden grow,
And little more we want to know
Except, that they who here would eat
Shall have a very–little–treat.

American poet PHILIP FRENEAU *published his poem 'On A Very Small Garden Belonging to a Citizen of N.Y.' in 1797.*

Returned to New York last night. Out to-day on the waters for a sail in the wide bay, southeast of Staten island – a rough, tossing ride, and a free sight – the long stretch of Sandy Hook, the highlands of Navesink, and the many vessels outward and inward bound. We came up through the midst of all, in the full sun. I especially enjoy'd the last hour or two. A moderate sea-breeze had set in; yet over the city, and the waters adjacent, was a thin haze, concealing nothing, only adding to the beauty. From my point of view, as I write amid the soft breeze, with a sea-temperature, surely nothing on earth of its kind can go beyond this show. To the left the North river with its far vista – nearer, three or four war-ships, anchor'd peacefully – the Jersey side, the banks of Weehawken, the Palisades, and the gradually receding blue, lost in the distance – to the right the East river – the mast-hemm'd shores – the grand obelisk-like towers of the bridge, one on either side, in haze, yet plainly defin'd, giant brothers twain, throwing free graceful interlinking loops high across the tumbled tumultuous current below – (the tide is just changing to its ebb) – the broad water-spread everywhere crowded – no, not crowded, but thick as stars in the sky – with all sorts and sizes of sail and steam vessels, ply-ing ferry-boats, arriving and departing coasters, great ocean Dons, iron-black, modern, magnificent in size and power, fill'd with their incalculable value of human life and precious merchandise – with here and there, above all, those daring, careening things of grace and wonder, those white and shaded swift-darting fish-birds, (I wonder if shore or sea elsewhere can outvie

WALT WHITMAN described the beauty of New York Bay in his Specimen Days, *prose jottings, published in 1882, which he called the 'most wayward, spontaneous, fragmentary book ever printed'.*

'easy undulating outlines, and picturesque, rocky scenery'

them), ever with their slanting spars, and fierce, pure, hawk-like beauty and motion – first-class New York sloop or schooner yachts, sailing, this fine day, the free sea in a good wind. And rising out of the midst, tall-topt, ship-hemm'd, modern, American, yet strangely oriental, V-shaped Manhattan, with its compact mass, its spires, its cloud-touching edifices group'd at the centre – the green of the trees, and all the white brown and gray of the architecture well blended, as I see it, under a miracle of limpid sky, delicious light of heaven above, and June haze on the surface below.

The Park throughout is a single work of art, and as such subject to the primary law of every work of art, namely, that it shall be framed upon a single, noble motive, to which the design of all its parts, in some more or less subtle way, shall be confluent and helpful. . .

It is one great purpose of the Park to supply to the hundreds of thousands of tired workers, who have no opportunity to spend their summers in the country, a specimen of God's handiwork that shall be to them, inexpensively, what a month or two in the White Mountains or the Adirondacks is, at great cost, to those in easier circumstances. The time will come when New York will be built up, when all the grading and filling will be done, and when the picturesquely-varied, rocky formations of the Island will have been converted into formations

As the city expanded northward in the nineteenth century it became apparent that if nothing was done the whole of Manhattan Island would soon be built over. A wasteland occupied by squatters' shacks was set aside for a park and a competition was held in 1858 for a design. The winning

'Late Afternoon, New York: Winter' – painting by Childe Hassam, 1900.

proposal for what was to become Central Park was submitted by FREDERICK LAW OLMSTED, *a former Staten Island farmer and travel writer, and* CALVERT VAUX, *an English architect.*

In his essay 'America and Alfred Stieglitz' (1934) social critic LEWIS MUMFORD *paid tribute to the natural beauty of a city too often thought of as utterly unnatural.*

for rows of monotonous straight streets, and piles of erect buildings. There will be no suggestion left of its present varied surface, with the single exception of the few acres contained in the Park. Then the priceless value of the present picturesque outlines of the ground will be more distinctly perceived, and its adaptability for its purpose more fully recognized. It therefore seems desirable to interfere with its easy, undulating outlines, and picturesque, rocky scenery as little as possible, and, on the other hand, to endeavor rapidly, and by every legitimate means, to increase and judiciously develop these particularly individual and characteristic sources of landscape effects.

There is, to begin with, the physical magnificence of the scene: the sweep and curve of the bay, the grand spaciousness of the river, the rhythm of the tides that encircle it, the strike of its mica-gleaming schists as they crop out in the park or the temporary excavation, and finally, the proud upthrust of the Palisades themselves. . .

Above all, there is the sky; pervading all these activities is the weather. The sharp crystalline days of early autumn, with intense blue sky and a few curls of cloud, drifting through space like the little jets of steam that were once such characteristic outlets of the older skyscrapers: the splendors of sunset on the

'Above all, there is the sky . . .' – midtown Manhattan.

waters, over the Palisades, crossing the Brooklyn Ferry, looking toward the Jersey shore from the Brooklyn Bridge; the swift, whiplike changes from heat to cold, from fog to clarity, from the sharp jeweled contours of John Bellini to the soft tones of Whistler and Fuller. Occasionally, too, the sulphurous hell of the dog days, to whip up appetite for the dank clouds in the west and the brave crackle of lightning and the drenching showers. At the other extreme the benignity and quiet of a city quenched by snow: the jingle of sleighbells in the eighteen nineties, the cold flash of electricity on the elevated tracks twenty years later. . .

And the landscape as a whole has definition, a disciplined line: the rocks run as due north and south as the points of the compass, and the very sides of the island, once scraggly, have been shaped by the hands of man into sharp lines, like the margin of a Dutch canal. No matter how great the confusion on the surface, beneath it all, in the rocks themselves is order: no matter how shifty man's top layer, the foundations are solid. If the streets are dingy, there is the dazzle of the sky itself: if the alleys and streets are foul, heavy with ancient dirt, with the effluvia of the sewers or the factories, there is the sanative taste of salt in the first wind that blows from the Atlantic. The cold sea fog in spring, sweeping inland in the midafternoon, calls one to the ocean as imperatively as the proud, deep-throated roar of the steamer, claiming the channel as she passes out to sea. So the ocean and the sky and the rivers hold the city in their grip, even while the people, like busy ants in the cracks and crevices, are unconscious of these more primal presences, save when they read a report in the morning paper, and reach for an umbrella, an overcoat, a fan.

L et me tell of a trait we boys showed: the hunger for country things.
New York is a devil's dream, the most urbanized city in the world. It is all geometry angles and stone. It is mythical, a city buried by a volcano. No grass is found in this petrified city, no big living trees, no flowers, no bird but the drab little lecherous sparrow, no soil, loam, earth; fresh earth to smell, earth to walk on, to roll on, and love like a woman.

Just stone. It is the ruins of Pompeii, except that seven million animals full of earth-love must dwell in the dead lava streets.

Each week at public school there was an hour called Nature Study. The old maid teacher fetched from a dark closet a collection of banal objects: birdnests, cornstalks, minerals, autumn leaves and other poor withered corpses. On these she lectured tediously, and bade us admire Nature.

What an insult. We twisted on our benches, and ached for the outdoors. It was as if a starving bum were offered snapshots of food, and expected to feel grateful. It was like lecturing a cage of young monkeys on the jungle joys.

'Lady, gimme a flower! Gimme a flower! Me, me, me!'

In summer, if a slummer or settlement house lady walked on our street with flowers in her hand, we attacked her, begging for the flowers. We rioted and yelled, yanked at her skirt, and frightened her to the point of hysteria.

Once Jake Gottlieb and I discovered grass struggling between the sidewalk cracks near the livery stable. We were amazed by this miracle. We guarded this treasure, allowed no one to step on it. Every hour the gang studied 'our' grass, to try to catch it growing. It died, of course, after a few days; only children are hardy enough to grow on the East Side.

Radical writer MICHAEL GOLD recalled one of the keenest deprivations felt by the youth of the old Lower East Side in his Jews Without Money *(1930).*

153

In his Old Mr Flood *(1944) journalist and veteran* New Yorker *staff member* JOSEPH MITCHELL *described the varied life of the city's surrounding waterways.*

The fish market supports a flock of four or five hundred gulls and at least two dozen of them are one-legged. 'This condition,' Mr Flood says, 'is due to the fact that sea gulls don't understand traffic lights. There's a stretch of South Street running through the market that's paved with cobblestones. And every so often during the morning rush a fish drops off a truck and is ground up by the wheels and packed down tight into the cracks between the cobbles. The gulls go wild when they see this. They wait until traffic gets halted by a red light, and then they drop out of the sky like bats out of hell and try to pull and worry the fish from between the cobbles. They're stubborn birds. They get so interested they don't notice when the light changes and all of a sudden, wham bang, the heavy truck traffic is right on top of them. Some get killed outright. Some get broken wings and flop off and hide somewhere and starve to death. Those that lose only one leg are able to keep going, but the other gulls peck them and claw them and treat them as outcasts and they have a hard, hard time.' The gimpy gulls are extremely distrustful, but Mr Flood has been able to make friends with a few. . . One or two will eat from his hands.

'Cobwebs' – etching by John Taylor Arms, 1920.

If New York were not celebrated for materialistic wonders, people would travel here to admire the splendor of the sunsets over New Jersey. They are regular events of transcendent splendor. A savage might be frightened by them, for they have the flaming grandeur of primordial catastrophe. They fill our western sky with tongues of fire. Since we understand the science of sunset colors we can admire them with equanimity. There is a commonplace practical reason for their barbaric magnificence. The industrial plants, railroad locomotives and steamships of New Jersey send up a thick cloud of sullen smoke that rolls across the Palisades, showers us with specks of grit and soot, and breaks up the light. The blue rays, which have a short wave length, are widely scattered. But the red rays, which have long wave lengths, pierce the barrier of smoke and come through to us. When the sun gets low in the western sky, the light of the sun comes to us at a long angle through the whole width of the New Jersey smoke bank, and all the color except red is diffused. Our sunsets are, therefore, abnormally red. Our days end violently – the great western arch of the sky incarnadined as if the day had taken fire.

This afternoon the sun is transmuted into an enormous orange sphere when it slips behind the smoke above the Jersey shore. I can look at it with unprotected eyes as it sinks out of sight through the smoke, gas and fumes of a huge industrial bastion. For another quarter of an hour the clouds in the west are banks of crimson. South and north of the sunset pit the clouds are washed with blue, and blue swims on the placid surface of the river. Between the celestial blue of the river and the crimson of the sky the long crag of the Palisades wall is like a deep blue band dividing the firmament from the waters. Presently the Weehawken Boulevard lights come on, the jewels on the crown of the imperial Palisades.

Tomorrow's sunset will be quite different, for the sunset pattern is infinitely varied. The western sky never repeats a design. From day to day it retains nothing but its immutable magnificence.

There is a rose in Spanish Harlem
A rare rose up in Spanish Harlem
It is a special one
It's never seen the sun
It only comes up when the moon is on the run
And all the stars are gleaming
It's growing in the street
Right up through the concrete
But soft and sweet and dreaming

Cold at my feet, the hard, dry ground at the fringes of the Ramble.
Here all the surrounding city is hidden; even in winter
When gray mists seem to condense in bare, unfocused branches,
None of the heights of buildings ringing the park is visible.
There among intricate paths, crossing themselves and twisting
Mazy configurations out of the asphalt walks,
Was the heart of the Park, with its dells and bridges over the inlet;
There was the final garden, full of the planned disorder,
    Of the garden regained, forced and sprawling.

Long-time New York Times *drama critic* BROOKS ATKINSON *praised New York's 'Savage Sunsets' in this article published in 1951.*

Singer Ben E. King was the first of many artists to record 'Spanish Harlem', written in 1960 by PHIL SPECTOR *and* JERRY LEIBER.

The Ramble is a section of Central Park from parts of which none of the surrounding city is visible. It was hymned in JOHN HOLLANDER*'s long poem* From the Ramble *(1965).*

155

Tompkins Square, 1965, photograph by Inge Morath.

Poet ROBERT LOWELL *was
born in Boston but made his
home in New York for many
years. He published 'Central
Park' in 1963.*

Scaling small rocks, exhaling smog,
gasping at game-scents like a dog,
now light as pollen, now as white
and winded as a grounded kite —
I watched the lovers occupy
every inch of earth and sky:
one figure of geometry,
multiplied to infinity,
straps down, and sunning openly. . .
each precious, public, pubic tangle
an equilateral triangle,
lost in the park, half covered by
the shade of some low stone or tree.
The stain of fear and poverty
spread through each trapped anatomy,
and darkend every mole of dust.
All wished to leave this drying crust,
borne on the delicate wings of lust
like bees,and cast their fertile drop
into the overwhelming cup.

Drugged and humbled by the smell
of zoo-straw mixed with animal,
the lion prowled his slummy cell,
serving his life-term in jail –
glaring, grinding, on his heel,
with tingling step and testicle . . .

Behind a dripping rock, I found
a one-day kitten on the ground –
deprived, weak, ignorant and blind,
squeaking, tubular, left behind –
dying with its deserter's rich
Welfare lying out of reach:
milk cartons, kidney heaped to spoil,
two plates sheathed with silver foil.

Shadows had stained the afternoon;
high in an elm, a snagged balloon
wooed the attraction of the moon.
Scurrying from the mouth of night,
a single, fluttery, paper kite
grazed Cleopatra's Needle, and sailed
where the light of the sun had failed.
Then night, the night – the jungle hour,
the rich in his slit-windowed tower . . .
Old Pharaohs starving in your foxholes,
with painted banquets on the walls,
fists knotted in your captives' hair,
tyrants with little food to spare –
all your embalming left you mortal,
glazed, black, and hideously eternal,
all your plunder and gold leaf
only served to draw the thief. . .

We beg delinquents for our life.
Behind each bush, perhaps a knife;
each landscaped crag, each flowering shrub,
hides a policeman with a club.

The leafbud straggles forth
toward the frigid light of the airshaft   this is faith
this pale extension of a day
when looking up   you know   something is changing
winter has turned   though the wind is colder
Three streets away   a roof collapses   onto people
who thought they still had time   Time out of mind

I have written so many words
wanting to live inside you
to be of use to you

*Poet and feminist
ADRIENNE RICH published
'Upper Broadway' in 1975.*

157

GEOMETRY AND ANGUISH

After 20 annual visits, I am still surprised each time I return to see this giant asparagus bed of alabaster and rose and green skyscapers.

CECIL BEATON

New York is a skyline, the most stupendous, unbelievable manmade spectacle since the hanging gardens of Babylon. Significantly, you have to be outside the city – on a bridge or the New Jersey Turnpike – to enjoy it.

JACQUES BARZUN

There were Babylon and Nineveh: they were built of brick. Athens was gold marble colums. Rome was held up on broad arches of rubble. In Constantinople the minarets flame like great candles round the Golden Horn . . . Steel, glass, tile, concrete will be the materials of the skyscrapers. Crammed on the narrow island the millionwindowed buildings will jut glittering, pyramid on pyramid like the white cloudhead above a thunderstorm.

JOHN DOS PASSOS

Returning to his native New York after an absence of twenty years novelist HENRY JAMES *was overpowered by the city's new skyline. He detailed his impressions in* The American Scene *(1907).*

Henry James (1843-1916).

The Bay had always, on other opportunities, seemed to blow its immense character straight into one's face – coming 'at' you, so to speak, bearing down on you, with the full force of a thousand prows of steamers seen exactly on the line of their longitudinal axis; but I had never before been so conscious of its boundless cool assurance or seemed to see its genius so grandly at play. This was presumably indeed because I had never before enjoyed the remarkable adventure of taking in so much of the vast bristling promontory from the water, of ascending the East River, in especial, to its upper diminishing expanses. . .

. . .So it befell, exactly, that an element of mystery and wonder entered into the impression – the interest of trying to make out, in the absence of features of the sort usually supposed indispensable, the reason of the beauty and the joy. It is indubitably a 'great' bay, a great harbour, but no one item of the romantic, or even of the picturesque, as commonly understood, contributes to its effect. The shores are low and for the most part depressingly furnished and prosaically peopled; the islands, though numerous, have not a grace to exhibit, and one thinks of the other, the real flowers of geography in this order, of Naples, of Capetown, of Sydney, of Seattle, of San Francisco, of Rio, asking how if *they* justify a reputation, New York should seem to justify one. Then, after all, we remember that there are reputations and reputations; we remember above all that the imaginative response to the conditions here presented may just happen to proceed from the intellectual extravagance of the given observer.

'The Bridge' – painting by Joseph Stella, 1922.

The Flatiron Building.

Critic LEWIS MUMFORD *described the transformation of the New York environment wrought by the skyscraper in his essay 'America and Alfred Stieglitz' (1934).*

When this personage is open to corruption by almost any large view of an intensity of life, his vibrations tend to become a matter difficult even for *him* to explain . . . There is the beauty of light and air, the great scale of space, and, seen far away to the west, the open gates of the Hudson, majestic in their degree, even at a distance, and announcing still nobler things. But the real appeal, unmistakably, is in that note of vehemence in the local life of which I have spoken, for it is the appeal of a particular type of dauntless power.

The aspect the power wears then is indescribable; it is the power of the most extravagant of cities, rejoicing, as with the voice of the morning, in its might, its fortune, its unsurpassable conditions, and imparting to a very object and element, to the motion and expression of every floating, hurrying, panting thing, to the throb of ferries and tugs, to the plash of waves and the play of winds and the glint of lights and the shrill of whistles and the quality and authority of breeze-borne cries – all, practically, a diffused, wasted clamour of *detonations* – something of its sharp free accent; in the bigness and bravery and insolence, especially, of everything that rushed and shrieked; in the air as of a great intricate frenzied dance, half merry, half desperate, or at least half defiant, performed on the huge watery floor. This appearance of the bold lacing-together, across the waters, of the scattered members of the monstrous organism – lacing as by the ceaseless play of an enormous system of steam-shuttles or electric bobbins (I scarce know what to call them), commensurate in form with their infinite work – does perhaps more than anything else to give the pitch of the vision of energy. One has the sense that the monster grows and grows, flinging abroad its loose limbs even as some unmannered young giant at his 'larks', and that the binding stitches must for ever fly further and faster and draw harder; the future complexity of the web, all under the sky and over the sea, becoming thus that of some colossal set of clockworks, some steel-souled machine-room of brandished arms and hammering fists and opening and closing jaws.

This New York produced the elevator apartment house at the end of the 'sixties, and the tall building, called the skyscraper after the topmost sail of its old clipper ships, a little later; and it used these new utilities as a means of defrauding its people of space and light and sun, turning the streets into deep chasms, and obliterating the back yards and gardens that had preserved a humaner environment even when people drank their water, not from the remote Croton River, but from the Tea-water Pump.

The spirit of pecuniary pride was reckless and indiscriminate; it annihilated whatever stood in the path of profit. It ruined the ruling classes as well as their victims. As time went on it became ever more positive in its denial of life; so that in more elegant parts of the East Side today there are splendid 'modern' mansions that are practically built back to back, even worse in some respects than the vilest slums on Cherry Street. This negative energy, this suicidal vitality, was the very essence of the new city that raised itself after the Civil War, and came to fullest bloom in the decade after the World War. Beholding it in its final manifestations, a German friend of mine wrote: *Dies ist die Hölle, und der Teufel war der Baumeister.* Men and women, if they survived in this environment, did so at the price of some sort of psychal dismemberment or paralysis. They sought to compensate themselves for their withered members by dwell-

'Delmonico Building' – lithograph by Charles Sheeler, 1927.

ing on the material satisfactions of this metropolitan life: how fresh fruits and vegetables came from California and Africa, thanks to refrigeration, how bathtubs and sanitary plumbing offset the undiminished dirt and the growing tendency toward constipation, how finally the sun lamps that were bought by the well-to-do overcame the lack of real sunlight in these misplanned domestic quarters. Mechanical apparatus, the refinements of scientific knowledge and of inventive ingenuity, would stay the process of deterioration for a time: when they failed, the jails, the asylums, the hospitals, the clinics, would be multiplied. Were not these thriving institutions too signs of progress, tokens of metropolitan intelligence and philanthropy?

I will not tell you what New York is like *from the outside*, because New York, like Moscow, those two antagonistic cities, is already the subject of countless descriptive books. Nor will I narrate a trip, but will give my lyrical reaction with all sincerity and simplicity, two qualities that come with difficulty to intellectuals, but easily to the poet. So much for modesty!

The two elements the traveler first captures in the big city are extra-human architecture and furious rhythm. Geometry and anguish. At first glance, the rhythm can seem to be gaiety, but when you look more closely at the mechanism of social life and the painful slavery of both men and machines you understand it as a typical, empty anguish that makes even crime and banditry forgivable means of evasion.

Willing neither clouds nor glory, the edges of the buildings rise to the sky. While Gothic edges rise from the hearts of the dead and buried, these ones climb coldly skyward with beauty that has no roots and no yearning, stupidly sure of themselves and utterly unable to conquer or transcend, as does spiritual architecture, the always inferior intentions of the architect. There is nothing more poetic and terrible than the skyscrapers' battle with the heavens that cover them. Snow, rain, and mist set off, wet, and hide the vast towers, but those towers, hostile to mystery, blind to any sort of play, shear off the rain's tresses and shine their three thousand swords through the soft swan of the mist.

It only takes a few days before you get the impression that that immense world has no roots, and you understand why the seer Edgar Poe had to hug mystery so close to him and let friendly intoxication boil in his veins.

When I had looked at the lights of Broadway by night, I made to my American friends an innocent remark that seemed for some reason to amuse them. I had looked, not without joy, at that long kaleidoscope of coloured lights arranged in large letters and sprawling trade-marks, advertising everything, from pork to pianos, through the agency of the two most vivid and most mystical of the gifts of God; colour and fire. I said to them, in my simplicity, 'What a glorious garden of wonder this would be, to any one who was lucky enough to be unable to read'.

Here it is but a text for a further suggestion. But let us suppose that there does walk down this flaming avenue a peasant, of the sort called scornfully an illiterate peasant;. . . that he has escaped to the land of liberty upon some general rumour and romance of the story of its liberation, but without being yet able to understand the arbitrary signs of its alphabet. The soul of such a man would surely soar higher than the sky-scrapers, and embrace a brotherhood broader than Broadway. Realising that he had arrived on an evening of exceptional festivity, worthy to be blazoned with all this burning heraldry, he would please himself by guessing what great proclamation or principle of the Republic hung in the sky like a constellation or rippled across the street like a comet. He would be shrewd enough to guess that the three festoons fringed with fiery words of somewhat similar pattern stood for 'Government of the People, For the People, By the People'; for it must obviously be that, unless it were 'Liberty, Equality, Fraternity'. His shrewdness would perhaps be a little shaken if he knew that the triad stood for 'Tang Tonic To-Day; Tang Tonic To-morrow; Tang Tonic All the Time'. He will soon identify a restless ribbon of red

'West Forty-Second Street, Night' – aquatint by John Taylor Arms, 1922.

lettering, red hot and rebellious, as the saying, 'Give me liberty or give me death'. He will fail to identify it as the equally famous saying, 'Skyoline Has Gout Beaten to a Frazzle'. Therefore it was that I desired the peasant to walk down that grove of fiery trees, under all that golden foliage and fruits like monstrous jewels, as innocent as Adam before the Fall. He would see sights almost as fine as the flaming sword or the purple and peacock plumage of the seraphim: so long as he did not go near the Tree of Knowledge.

'To Brooklyn Bridge' is the first poem in HART CRANE*'s metaphorical epic of American experience,* The Bridge *(1930).*

'Gates of the City' – aquatint by John Taylor Arms, 1922.

How many dawns, chill from his rippling rest
The seagull's wings shall dip and pivot him,
Shedding white rings of tumult, building high
Over the chained bay waters Liberty –

Then, with inviolate curve, forsake our eyes
As apparitional as sails that cross
Some page of figures to be filed away;
– Till elevators drop us from our day...

I think of cinemas, panoramic sleights
With multitudes bent toward some flashing scene
Never disclosed, but hastened to again,
Foretold to other eyes on the same screen;

And Thee, across the harbor, silver-paced
As though the sun took step of thee, yet left
Some motion ever unspent in thy stride, –
Implicitly thy freedom staying thee!

Out of some subway scuttle, cell or loft
A bedlamite speeds to thy parapets,
Tilting there momently, shrill shirt ballooning,
A jest falls from the speechless caravan.

Down Wall, from girder into street noon leaks,
A rip-tooth of the sky's acetylene;
All afternoon the cloud-flown derricks turn...
Thy cables breathe the North Atlantic still.

And obscure as that heaven of the Jews,
Thy guerdon... Accolade thou dost bestow
Of anonymity time cannot raise:
Vibrant reprieve and pardon thou dost show.

O harp and altar, of the fury fused,
(How could mere toil align thy choiring strings!)
Terrific threshold of the prophet's pledge,
Prayer of pariah, and the lover's cry, –

Again the traffic lights that skim thy swift
Unfractioned idiom, immaculate sigh of stars,
Beading thy path – condense eternity:
And we have seen night lifted in thine arms.

Under thy shadow by the piers I waited;
Only in darkness is thy shadow clear.
The City's fiery parcels all undone,
Already snow submerges an iron year...

O sleepless as the river under thee,
Vaulting the sea, the prairies' dreaming sod,
Unto us lowliest sometime sweep, descend
And of the curveship lend a myth to God.

But who, coming into New York, say, for the first time, could feel otherwise than that we were a 'great' people to have raised the frame of such a relentless commercial engine so cruelly high, and hung so much book-architecture upon it regardless, at such cost?

Such energy, too, as has poured into a common center here to pile up material resources by way of riches in labor and materials and wasted attempts at 'decoration', cramming the picturesque outlines of haphazard masses upon the bewildered eye peering from the black shadows down below? We see similar effects wherever irresistible force has broken and tilted up the earth's crust. Here is a volcanic crater of blind, confused, human forces pushing together and grinding upon each other, moved by greed in common exploitation, forcing anxiety upon all life. No noble expression of life, this. But, heedless of the meaning of it all, seen at night, the monster aggregation has myriad, haphazard beauties of silhouette and reflected or refracted light. The monster becomes rhythmical and does appeal to the love of romance and beauty. It is, then, mysterious and suggestive to the imaginative, inspiring to the ignorant. Fascinating entertainment this mysterious gloom upon which hang necklaces of light, through which shine clouds of substitutes for stars. The streets become rhythmical perspectives of glowing dotted lines, reflections hung upon them in the streets as the wisteria hangs its violet racemes on its trellis. The buildings are a shimmering verticality, a gossamer veil, a festive scene-drop hanging there against the black sky to dazzle, entertain and amaze.

The lighted interiors come through it all with a sense of life and well being. At night the city not only seems to live. It does live – as illusion lives.

And then comes the light of day. Reality. Streams of beings again pouring into the ground, 'holing in' to find their way to this or that part of it, densely packed into some roar and rush of speed to pour out somewhere else. The sordid reiteration of space for rent. The overpowering sense of the cell. The dreary emphasis of narrowness, slicing, edging, niching and crowding. Tier above tier the soulless shelf, the empty crevice, the winding ways of the windy, unhealthy canyon. The heartless grip of the selfish, grasping universal stricture. Box on box beside box. Black shadows below with artificial lights burning all day in the little caverns and squared cells. Prison cubicles. Above it all a false, cruel ambition is painting haphazard, jagged, pretentious, feudal sky-lines trying to relieve it and make it more humane by lying about its purpose. Congestion, confusion and the anxious spasmodic to and fro – stop and go. At best the all too narrow lanes, were they available, are only fifty per cent effective owing to the gridiron. In them roars a bedlam of harsh sound and a dangerous, wasteful, spasmodic movement runs in these narrow village lanes in the deep shadows. Distortion.

This man-trap of gigantic dimensions, devouring manood, denies in its affected riot of personality any individuality whatsoever. This Moloch knows no god but 'More'. Nowhere is there a clear thought or a sane feeling for good life manifest. In all, even in the libraries, museums and institutes is parasitic make-believe or fantastic abortion. But, if the citizenry is parasitic, the overgrown city itself is barbaric in the true meaning of the word. As good an example of barbarism as exists.

Architect FRANK LLOYD WRIGHT *catalogued the marvels and horrors of New York in his book* The Disappearing City *(1932).*

In When the Cathedrals
Were White (1944) Swiss
architect LE CORBUSIER
paid his ambivalent tribute to
New York.

The cardinal question asked of every traveler on his arrival is: 'What do you think of New York?' Coolly I replied: 'The skyscrapers are too small.' And I explained what I meant.

For a moment my questioners were speechless! So much the worse for them! The reasoning is clear and the supporting proofs abundant, streets full of them, a complete urban disaster.

The skyscraper is not a plume rising from the face of the city. It has been made that, and wrongly. The plume was a poison to the city. The skyscraper is an instrument. A magnificent instrument for the concentration of population, for getting rid of land congestion, for classification, for internal efficiency. A prodigious means of improving the conditions of work, a creator of economies and, through that, a dispenser of wealth. But the skyscraper as plume, multiplied over the area of Manhattan, has disregarded experience. The New York skyscrapers are out of line with the rational skyscraper which I have called: *the Cartesian skyscraper*. . .

Now we are ready to state the fundamental principle: the skyscraper *is a function of capacity* (the offices) *and the area of free ground at its base.* A skyscraper which does not fulfill this function harmoniously is a disease. That is the disease of New York.

The Cartesian skyscraper is a miracle in the urbanization of the cities of machine civilization. It makes possible extraordinary concentrations, from three to four thousand persons on each two and one half acres. It does so while taking up only 8 to 12 per cent of the ground with 88 per cent being restored, usable, available for the circulation of pedestrians and cars! These immense free areas, this whole ward in the section, will become a park. The glass skyscrapers will rise up like crystals, clean and transparent in the midst of the foliage of the trees. . .

The skyscrapers of New York are too small and there are too many of them. They are proof of the new dimensions and the new tools; the proof also that henceforth everything can be carried out on a new general plan, a symphonic plan – extent and height. . .

JEAN-PAUL SARTRE, French
philosopher, examined the
peculiar geometry of New
York in his essay
'Manhattan: the Great
American Desert' (1946).

Your streets and avenues have not the same meaning as ours. You go *through* them. New York is a city of movement. If I walk rapidly I feel at ease, but if I stop for a moment I am troubled, and I wonder: Why am I in this street rather than in one of the hundred other streets that resemble it, why near this particular drugstore, Schrafft's, or Woolworth's, rather than any other drugstore, Schrafft's, or Woolworth's from among the thousands just like it? Pure space suddenly appears. I imagine that if a triangle were to become aware of its position in space it would be frightened at seeing how accurately it was defined and yet how, at the same time, it was simply *any* triangle. In New York you never get lost; a glance suffices to show you that you are on the East Side, at the corner of Fifty-second Street and Lexington. But this spatial precision is not accompanied by any sentimental precision. In the numerical anonymity of the streets and avenues I am simply *anyone* – as defined and as indefinite as the triangle – I am anyone who is lost and conscious of being unjustifiable, without valid reason for being in one place rather than another, because one place and another look so much alike.

'New York' – lithograph by Louis Lozowick, c. 1925.

Enfranchising cable, silvered by the sea,
    of woven wire, grayed by the mist,
and Liberty dominate the Bay —
her feet as one on shattered chains,
once whole links wrought by Tyranny.

Caged Circe of steel and stone,
her parent German ingenuity.
'O catenary curve' from tower to pier,
implacable enemy of the mind's deformity,
of man's uncompunctious greed
his crass love of crass priority
    just recently
obstructing acquiescent feet
about to step ashore when darkness fell
    without a cause,
as if probity had not joined our cities
    in the sea.

'O path amid the stars
crossed by the seagull's wing!'
'O radiance that doth inherit me!'
— affirming inter-acting harmony!

Untried expedient, untried; then tried;
way out; way in; romantic passageway
first seen by the eye of the mind,
then by the eye, O steel! O stone!
Climactic ornament, a double rainbow,
as if inverted by French perspicacity,
    John Roebling's monument,
    German tenacity's also;
    composite span — an actuality.

Manhattan is the twentieth century's Rosetta Stone.
    Not only are large parts of its surface occupied by architectural mutations (Central Park, the Skyscraper), utopian fragments (Rockefeller Center, the UN Building) and irrational phenomena (Radio City Music Hall), but in addition each block is covered with several layers of phantom architecture in the form of past occupancies, aborted projects and popular fantasies that provide alternative images to the New York that exists.

Especially between 1890 and 1940 a new culture (the Machine Age?) selected Manhattan as laboratory: a mythical island where the invention and testing of a metropolitan lifestyle and its attendant architecture could be pursued as a collective experiment in which the entire city became a factory of man-made experience, where the real and the natural ceased to exist. . .

If Manhattan is still in search of a theory, then this theory, once identified, should yield a formula for an architecture that is at once ambitious and popular.

Manhattan has generated a shameless architecture that has been loved in direct proportion to its defiant lack of self-hatred, has been respected exactly to the degree that it went too far.

In spite – or perhaps because – of this, its performance and implications have been consistently ignored and even suppressed by the architectural profession.

Manhattanism is the one urbanistic ideology that has fed, from its conception, on the splendors and miseries of the metropolitan condition – hyper-density – without once losing faith in it as the basis for a desirable modern culture. *Manhattan's architecture is a paradigm for the exploitation of congestion.*

'A shameless architecture . . .'

PRAISE AND DAMNATION

WALT WHITMAN's poem 'Manhattan' appeared in the 1860 edition of Leaves of Grass.

I was asking for something specific and perfect for my city,
Whereupon lo! upsprang the aboriginal name.
Now I see what there is in a name, a word, liquid, sane, unruly,
    musical, self-sufficient,
I see that the word of my city is that word from of old,
Because I see that word nested in nests of water-bays, superb,
Rich, hemm'd thick all around with sailships and steamships, an
    island sixteen miles long, solid-founded,
Numberless crowded streets, high growths of iron, slender,
    strong, light, splendidly uprising toward clear skies,
Tides swift and ample, well-loved by me, toward sundown,
The flowing sea-currents, the little islands, larger adjoining
    islands, the heights, the villas,
The countless masts, the white shore-steamers, the lighters, the
    ferry-boats, the black sea-steamers well-model'd,
The down-town streets, the jobbers' houses of business, the
    houses of business of the ship-merchants and money-brokers,
    the river-streets.
Immigrants arriving, fifteen or twenty thousand in a week,
The carts hauling goods, the manly race of drivers of horses, the
    brown-faced sailors,
The summer air, the bright sun shining, and the sailing clouds
    aloft,
The winter snows, the sleigh-bells, the broken ice in the river,
    passing along up or down with the flood-tide or ebb-tide,
The mechanics of the city, the masters, well-form'd, beautiful-
    faced, looking you straight in the eyes,
Trottoirs throng'd, vehicles, Broadway, the women, the shops
    and shows,
A million people – manners free and superb – open voices –
    hospitality – the most courageous and friendly young men,
City of hurried and sparkling waters! city of spires and masts!
City nested in bays! my city!

Even HENRY JAMES was left speechless by the spectacle of New York in The American Scene (1907).

The ambiguity is the element in which the whole thing swims for me – so noc-turnal, so bacchanal, so hugely hatted and feathered and flounced, yet apparently so innocent, almost so patriarchal again, and matching, in its mix-ture, with nothing one had elsewhere known. It breathed its simple 'New York! New York!' at every impulse of inquiry; so that I can only echo contentedly, with analysis for once quite agreeably baffled, 'Remarkable, unspeakable New York!'

'The City from Greenwich Village' – painting by John Sloan, 1922.

When I come down to sleep death's endless night,
  The threshold of the unknown dark to cross,
What to me then will be the keenest loss,
When this bright world blurs on my fading sight?
Will it be that no more I shall see the trees
Or smell the flowers or hear the singing birds
Or watch the flashing streams or patient herds?
No, I am sure it will be none of these.

But, ah! Manhattan's sights and sounds, her smells,
Her crowds, her throbbing force, the thrill that comes
From being of her a part, her subtle spells,
Her shining towers, her avenues, her slums –
O God! the stark, unutterable pity,
To be dead, and never again behold my city!

'My City' is a sonnet by the educator, scholar, and poet JAMES WELDON JOHNSON.

Novelist THEODORE DREISER *tried to capture New York's mysterious allure in* The Color of a Great City *(1923).*

The thing that interested me then as now about New York . . . was the sharp, and at the same time immense, contrast it showed between the dull and the shrewd, the strong and the weak, the rich and the poor, the wise and the ignorant. This, perhaps, was more by reason of numbers and opportunity than anything else, for of course humanity is much the same everywhere. But the number from which to choose was so great here that the strong, or those who ultimately dominated, were so very strong, and the weak so very, very weak – and so very, very many.

I once knew a poor, half-demented, and very much shriveled little seamstress who occupied a tiny hall-bedroom in a side-street rooming-house, cooked her meals on a small alcohol stove set on a bureau, and who had about space enough outside of this to take three good steps either way.

'I would rather live in my hall-bedroom in New York than in any fifteen-room house in the country that I ever saw,' she commented once, and her poor little colorless eyes held more of sparkle and snap in them than I ever saw there, before or after. She was wont to add to her sewing income by reading fortunes in cards and tea-leaves and coffee-grounds, telling of love and prosperity to scores as lowly as herself, who would never see either. The color and noise and splendor of the city as a spectacle was sufficient to pay her for all her ills.

'Sunbath' – lithograph by Martin Lewis, c. 1935.

I often think of the vast mass of underlings, boys and girls, who, with nothing but their youth and their ambitions to commend them, are daily and hourly setting their faces New Yorkward, reconnoitering the city for what it may hold in the shape of wealth or fame, or, if not that, position and comfort in the future; and what, if anything, they will reap. Ah, their young eyes drinking in its promise! And then, again, I think of all the powerful or semi-powerful men and women throughout the world, toiling at one task or another – a store, a mine, a bank, a profession – somewhere outside of New York, whose one ambition is to reach the place where their wealth will permit them to enter and remain in New York, dominant above the mass, luxuriating in what they consider luxury.

The illusion of it, the hypnosis deep and moving that it is! How the strong and the weak, the wise and the fools, the greedy of heart and of eye, seek the nepenthe, the Lethe, of its hugeness. I always marvel at those who are willing, seemingly, to pay any price – *the* price, whatever it may be – for one sip of this poison cup. What a stinging, quivering zest they display. How beauty is willing to sell its bloom, virtue its last rag, strength an almost usurious portion of that which it controls, youth its very best years, its hope or dream of fame, fame and power their dignity and presence, age its weary hours to secure but a minor part of all this, a taste of its vibrating presence and the picture that it makes. Can you not hear them almost singing its praises?

New York is not all bricks and steel. There are hearts there, too, and if they do not break, then they at least know how to leap. It is the place where all the aspirations of the Western World meet to form one vast master aspiration, as powerful as the suction of a steam dredge. It is the icing on the pie called Christian civilization. That it may have buildings higher than any ever heard of, and gin enough to keep it gay, and bawdy shows enough, and door-openers enough, and noise and confusion enough – that these imperial ends may be achieved, uncounted millions sweat and slave on all the forlorn farms of the earth, and in all the miserable slums, including its own. It pays more for a meal than an Italian or a Pole pays for a wife, and the meal is better than the wife. It gets the best of everything, and especially of what, by all reputable ethical systems, is the worst. It has passed beyond all fear of Hell or hope of Heaven. The primary postulates of all the rest of the world are its familiar jokes. A city apart, it is breeding a race apart. Is that race American? Then so is a bashi-bazouk American. Is it decent? Then so is a street-walker decent. But I don't think that it may be reasonably denounced as dull.

In an essay in his Prejudices, Sixth Series *(1927) critic and sceptic* H. L. MENCKEN *admitted there must be something good about New York.*

Proud, cruel, everchanging and ephemeral city, to whom we came once when our hearts were high, our blood passionate and hot, our brain a particle of fire: infinite and mutable city, mercurial city, strange citadel of million-viaged time – Oh! endless river and eternal rock, in which the forms of life came, passed and changed intolerably before us, and to which we came, as every youth has come, with such enormous madness, and with so mad a hope – for what?

To eat you, branch and root and tree; to devour you, golden fruit of power and love and happiness; to consume you to your sources, river and spire and rock, down to your iron roots; to entomb within our flesh forever the huge substance of our billion-footed pavements, the intolerable web and memory of

THOMAS WOLFE *evoked the power and mystery of the city in his novel* Of Time and the River *(1935).*

dark million-visaged time.

And what is left now of all our madness, hunger, and desire? What have you given, incredible mirage of all our million shining hopes, to those who wanted to possess you wholly to your ultimate designs, your final sources, from whom you took the strength, the passion, and the innocence of youth?

What have we taken from you, protean and phantasmal shape of time? What have we remembered of your million images, of your billion weavings out of accident and number, of the mindless fury of your dateless days, the brutal stupefaction of your thousand streets and pavements? What have we seen and know that is ours forever?

Gigantic city, we have taken nothing – not even a handful of your trampled dust – we have made no image on your iron breast and left not even the print of a heel upon your stony-hearted pavements. The possession of all things, even the air we breathed, was held from us, and the river of life and time flowed through the grasp of our hands forever, and we held nothing for our hunger and desire except the proud and trembling moments, one by one. Over the trodden and forgotten words, the rust and dusty burials of yesterday, we were born again into a thousand lives and deaths, and we were left forever with only the substance of our craving flesh, and the hauntings of an accidental memory, with all its various freight of great and little things which passed and vanished instantly and could never be forgotten, and of those unbidden and unfathomed wisps and fumes of memory that share the mind with all the proud dark images of love and death.

Swiss architect LE CORBUSIER *summed up New York as a 'beautiful catastrophe' in his* When the Cathedrals Were White *(1944).*

A hundred times I have thought: New York is a catastrophe, and fifty times: it is a beautiful catastrophe.

One evening about six o'clock I had cocktails with James Johnson Sweeney – a friend who lives in an apartment house east of Central Park, over toward the East River; he is on the top floor, one hundred and sixty feet above the street; after having looked out the windows, we went outside on the balcony, and finally we climbed up on the roof.

The night was dark, the air dry and cold. The whole city was lighted up. If you have not seen it, you cannot know or imagine what it is like. You must have had it sweep over you. Then you begin to understand why Americans have become proud of themselves in the last twenty years and why they raise their voices in the world and why they are impatient when they come to our country. The sky is decked out. It is a Milky Way come down to earth; you are in it. Each window, each person, is a light in the sky. At the same time a perspective is established by the arrangement of the thousand lights of each skyscraper; it forms itself more in your mind than in the darkness perforated by illimitable fires. The stars are part of it also – the real stars – but sparkling quietly in the distance. Splendor, scintillation, promise, proof, act of faith, etc. Feeling comes into play; the action of the heart is released; crescendo, allegro, fortissimo. We are charged with feeling, we are intoxicated; legs strengthened, chests expanded, eager for action, we are filled with confidence.

That is the Manhattan of vehement silhouettes. Those are the verities of technique, which is the springboard of lyricism. The fields of water, the railroads, the planes, the stars, and the vertical city with its unimaginable diamonds. Everything is there, and it is real.

'a beautiful catastrophe . . .' Nightview, New York, photograph by Berenice Abbott, 1932.

L ove is a mischief,
Love is a brat.
Love is, admittedly, blind as a bat.
Aimless his arrows as bundles from the stork.
So I'm in love with
The City of New York

Raging by its rivers, thrusting at the sky,
Here towers Gotham, and here gape I,
Viewing with idolatry more than lenience
The City of Infinite Inconvenience.

Here on its image, harsher than a chromo,
I dote as a teen-ager dotes on Como.
As a chorine pants for the rinse peroxide,
So I for its air made of carbon monoxide.

Poet PHYLLIS McGINLEY
published 'A Kind of Love
Letter to New York' in 1948.

175

For the strap in the subway, for the empty hansom,
For the five-flight walk-up at a monarch's ransom,
For the weather omens that tell no truth
And the wait for the hotel telephone booth.

Yes, dear to my heart as to Midas his coffers
Are the noontime tables at Schrafft's and Stouffer's,
Are the maltless malteds that you go to Liggett's for,
The hit revues that you can't get tiggets for,

The smog in the winter, the neon in the dark,
The avenues and avenues with nowhere to park,
The feel of the cinder, gritty on the pane,
And the hoot of the taxi as it passes in the rain.

Too new for an empire, too big for its boots,
With cold steel cables where it might have roots,
With everything to offer and nothing to give.
It's a horrid place to visit but a fine place to live.

For there's always the linen shop Selling Out Entire,
Always the parade and the three-alarm fire,
The strike on the buses, the scandal on the docks.
The ladies on their leashes that poodles take for walks,
The morning papers that you buy the night before,
And the riveter working on a ledge next door.

Ah! some love Paris,
And some Purdue.
But love is an archer with a low I.Q.
A bold, bad bowman, and innocent of pity.
So I'm in love with
New York City.

CHRISTOPHER MORLEY's
New York One Way *was*
written for the World's Fair of
1939.

As I see that spiry outline cut against pale distance I imagine the whole human cordillera spread open in strata for my joy. I visualize publishers publishing, brokers broking, bus conductors snapping up fares with the little jingling dime-gadget, newspapers finding some sensation for this afternoon, tugboat hands in the galley at their enormous early lunch. I see elevators, taxies, subway trains careering in yellow light, people answering telephones, people thick on the broad sunny pavements at Fifth Avenue and 42nd. (There are pavements along The Avenue where by some accident of silica or quartz the sidewalk spangles beneath your feet, scintillates and sparkles.) Are all these things real and I not there to see? Principality and power are there, people and palaver; all her marvelous ridges and verticals, waiting for the smallest change of my volition. Now, as I sit here, they are only phantom: the green grape arbor, the yellow woodland, the whispering fire on the hearth, are my reality. By the miserable irony of all the arts, I deny myself the actual to summon up the dream. And New York lies back on her haunches — like the proud lions at the Public Library — just waiting to be signalled. Waiting to perform for me; waiting to thrill, dazzle, terrify, enchant; for who (it is the cry of every true lover) — who knows her as I?

In Central Park the snow had not yet melted on his favorite hill. This hill was in the center of the park, after he had left the circle of the reservoir, where he always found, outside the high wall of crossed wire, ladies, white, in fur coats, walking their great dogs, or old, white gentelmen with canes. At a point that he knew by instinct and by the shape of the buildings surrounding the park, he struck out on a steep path overgrown with trees, and climbed a short distance until he reached the clearing that led to the hill. Before him, then, the slope stretched upward, and above it the brilliant sky, and beyond it, cloudy and far away, he saw the skyline of New York. He did not know why, but there arose in him an exultation and a sense of power, and he ran up the hill like an engine, or a madman, willing to throw himself headlong into the city that glowed before him.

But when he reached the summit he paused; he stood on the crest of the hill, hands clasped beneath his chin, looking down. Then he, John, felt like a giant who might crumble this city with his anger; he felt like a tyrant who might crush this city beneath his heel; he felt like a long-awaited conquerer at whose feet flowers would be strewn, and before whom multitudes cried, Hosanna! He would be, of all, the mightiest, the most beloved, the Lord's anointed; and he would live in this shining city which his ancestors had seen with longing from far away. For it was his; the inhabitants of the city had told him it was his; he had but to run down, crying, and they would take him to their hearts and show him wonders his eyes had never seen.

And still, on the summit of that hill he paused. He remembered the people he had seen in that city, whose eyes held no love for him. And he thought of their feet so swift and brutal, and the dark gray clothes they wore, and how when they passed they did not see him, or, if they saw him, they smirked. And how their lights, unceasing, creashed on and off above him, and how he was a stranger there. Then he remembered his father and his mother, and all the arms stretched out to hold him back, to save him from this city, where, they said, his soul would find perdition.

In his novel Go Tell it On The Mountain *(1954) Harlem-born writer* JAMES BALDWIN *depicted a moment of exultation in New York's Central Park.*

How funny you are today New York
like Ginger Rogers in *Swingtime*
and St Bridget's steeple leaning a little to the left

here I have just jumped out of a bed full of V-days
(I got tired of D-days) and blue you there still
accepts me foolish and free
all I want is a room up there
and you in it
and even the traffic halt so thick is a way
for people to rub up against each other
and when their surgical appliances lock
they stay together
for the rest of the day (what a day)
I go by to check a slide and I say
that painting's not so blue

where's Lana Turner
she's out eating

FRANK O'HARA, *poet, art critic, and self-proclaimed lover of New York City, wrote his poem 'Steps' in 1961.*

and Garbo's backstage at the Met
everyone's taking their coat off
so they can show a rib-cage to the rib-watchers
and the park's full of dancers and their tights and shoes
in little bags
who are often mistaken for worker-outers at the West Side Y
why not
the Pittsburgh Pirates shout because they won
and in a sense we're all winning
we're alive

the apartment was vacated by a gay couple
who moved to the country for fun
they moved a day too soon
even the stabbings are helping the population explosion
though in the wrong country
and all those liars have left the UN
the Seagram Building's no longer rivalled in interest
not that we need liquor (we just like it)

and the little box is out on the sidewalk
next to the delicatessen
so the old man can sit on it and drink beer
and get knocked off it by his wife later in the day
while the sun is still shining

oh god it's wonderful
to get out of bed
and drink too much coffee
and smoke too many cigarettes
and love you so much

BRENDAN BEHAN'S New York *was published in 1964, the last year of the Irish dramatist's brief, sensational life.*

I am not afraid to admit that New York is the greatest city on the face of God's earth. You only have to look at it, from the air, from the river, from Father Duffy's statue. New York is easily recognizable as the greatest city in the world, view it any way and every way – back, belly and sides.

London is a wide flat pie of redbrick suburbs with the West End stuck in the middle like a currant. New York is a huge rich raisin and is the biggest city I can imagine.

A city is a place where Man lives, walks about, talks and eats and drinks in the bright light of day or electricity for twenty-four hours a day. In New York, at three o'clock in the morning, you can walk about, see crowds, read the papers and have drink – orange juice, coffee, whiskey or anything. It is the greatest show on earth, for everyone. Its fabulous beauty at night, even forty years ago, was the wonder of the world.

When I arrived home from Broadway, where my play *The Hostage* was running, my wife said to me, 'Oh isn't it great to be back. How do you feel coming home?'

'Listen Beatrice,' I said, 'It's very dark!'

And I think anybody returning home after going to New York will find their native spot pretty dark too.

We don't come to a city to be alone, and the test of a city is the ease with which you can see and talk to other people. A city is a place where you are least likely to get a bite from a wild sheep and I'd say that New York is the friendliest city I know. The young Russian poet, Yevtushenko, said that in all honesty he had to admit that New York was the most exciting place that he had ever been to in his entire life.

When it is good, New York is very, very good. Which is why New Yorkers put up with so much that is bad.

When it is good, this is a city of fantastic strength, sophistication and beauty. It is like no other city in time or place. Visitors and even natives rarely use the words 'urban character' or 'environmental style', but that is what they are reacting to with awe in the presence of massed, concentrated steel, stone, power and life. It is a quality of urban greatness that may not solve racial or social tension or the human or economic crises to which a city is prone, but it survives them.

Architecture critic of the New York Times, ADA LOUISE HUXTABLE *published her article 'Sometimes We do it Right' in 1968.*

West in Manhattan where the sun has set
The elevator rises calmly yet
In my dark tower, against the tower-dimmed sky,
Whose wide, old windows yield my narrower eye
Images no revision can defeat:
Newspapers blown along the empty street
At three a.m. (somewhere in between 'odd',
A guru told me long ago, and 'God');

Calm steam rising from manholes in the dark;
Clean asphalt of an avenue; the spark
Of gold in every mica window high
On westward faces of the peaks; the sky
Near dawn, framed in the zig-zag canyon rim
Of cross-streets; bits of distant bridge, the dim
Lustrous ropes of pale lights dipping low;
Rivers unseen beneath, sable and slow.

Gardens? Lead me not home to them: a plain
Of rooftops, gleaming after April rain
In later sunlight, shines with Ceres' gold
Sprung up, not ripped, from earth; gained as of old.
Our losses are of gardens. We create
A dense, sad city for our final state.

JOHN HOLLANDER's long poem New York *(1970) ends with the narrator calmly accepting the pleasures and the pains of life in the city.*

Besides many things, Raggles was a poet. He was called a tramp; but that was only an elliptical way of saying that he was a philosopher, an artist, a traveller, a naturalist, and a discoverer. But most of all he was a poet. In all his life he never wrote a line of verse; he lived his poetry. His Odyssey would have been a Limerick, had it been written. But, to linger with the primary proposition, Raggles was a poet.

Raggles's specialty, had he been driven to ink and paper, would have been

O. HENRY's short story 'The Making of a New Yorker' was published in his book The Trimmed Lamp *(1907).*

sonnets to the cities. He studied cities as women study their reflections in mirrors; as children study the glue and sawdust of a dislocated doll; as the men who write about wild animals study the cages in the zoo. A city to Raggles was not merely a pile of bricks and mortar, peopled by a certain number of inhabitants; it was a thing with soul characteristic and distinct; and individual conglomeration of life, with its own peculiar essence, flavor, and feeling. Two thousand miles to the north and south, east and west, Raggles wandered in poetic fervor, taking the cities to his breast. He footed it on dusty roads, or sped magnificently in freight cars, counting time as of no account. And when he had found the heart of a city and listened to its secret confession, he strayed on, restless, to another. Fickle Raggles! – but perhaps he had not met the civic corporation that could engage and hold his critical fancy. . .

One day Raggles came and laid siege to the heart of the great city of Manhattan. She was the greatest of all; and he wanted to learn her note in the scale; to taste and appraise and classify and solve and label her and arrange her with the other cities that had given him up the secret of their individuality. And here we cease to be Raggles's translator and become his chronicler.

Raggles landed from a ferry-boat one morning and walked into the core of the town with the blasé air of a cosmopolite. He was dressed with care to play the rôle of an 'unidentified man'. No country, race, class, clique, union, party clan, or bowling association could have claimed him. . . Without money – as a poet should be – but with the ardor of an astronomer discovering a new star in the chorus of the milky way, or a man who has seen ink suddenly flow from his fountain pen, Raggles wandered into the great city.

Late in the afternoon he drew out of the roar and commotion with a look of dumb terror on his countenance. He was defeated, puzzled, discomfited, frightened. Other cities had been to him as long primer to read; as country maidens quickly to fathom; as send-price-of-subscription-with-answer rebuses to solve; as oyster cocktails to swallow; but here was one as cold, glittering, serene, impossible as a four-carat diamond in a window to a lover outside fingering damply in his pocket his ribbon-counter salary.

The greetings of the other cities he had known – their homespun kindliness, their human gamut of rough charity, friendly curses, garrulous curiosity, and easily estimated credulity or indifference. This city of Manhattan gave him no clue; it was walled against him. Like a river of adamant it flowed past him in the streets. Never an eye was turned upon him; no voice spoke to him. His heart yearned for the clap of Pittsburg's sooty hand on his shoulder; for Chicago's menacing but social yawp in his ear; for the pale and eleemosynary stare through the Bostonian eyeglass – even for the precipitate but unmalicious boot-toe of Louisville or St Louis.

On Broadway Raggles, successful suitor of many cities, stood, bashful, like any country swain. For the first time he experienced the poignant humiliation of being ignored. And when he tried to reduce this brilliant, swiftly changing, ice-cold city to a formula he failed utterly. Poet though he was, it offered him no color similes, no points of comparison, no flaw in its polished facets, no handle by which he could hold it up and view its shape and structure, as he familiarly and often contemptuously had done with other towns. The houses were interminable ramparts loop-holed for defence; the people were bright but bloodless spectres passing in sinister and selfish array.

'North River Vista' – lithograph by Armin Landeck, 1932.

The thing that weighed heaviest on Raggles's soul and clogged his poet's fancy was the spirit of absolute egotism that seemed to saturate the people as toys are saturated with paint. Each one that he considered appeared a monster of abominable and insolent conceit. Humanity was gone from them; they were toddling idols of stone and varnish, worshipping themselves and greedy for though oblivious of worship from their fellow graven images. Frozen, cruel, implacable, impervious, cut to an identical pattern, they hurried on their ways like statues brought by some miracle to motion, while soul and feeling lay unaroused in the reluctant marble.

Gradually Raggles became conscious of certain types. One was an elderly gentleman with a snow-white beard, pink, unwrinkled face, and stony, sharp blue eyes, attired in the fashion of a gilded youth, who seemed to personify the city's wealth, ripeness and frigid unconcern. Another type was a woman, tall, beautiful, clear as a steel engraving, goddess-like, calm, clothed like the princesses of old, with eyes as coldly blue as the reflection of sunlight on a glacier. And another was a by-product of this town of marionettes – a broad, swaggering, grim, threateningly sedate fellow, with a jowl as large as a harvested wheat field, the complexion of a baptized infant, and the knuckles of a prize-fighter. This type leaned against cigar signs and viewed the world with frappéd contumely.

A poet is a sensitive creature, and Raggles soon shriveled in the bleak embrace of the undecipherable. The chill, sphinx-like, ironical, illegible, unnatural, ruthless expression of the city left him downcast and bewildered. Had it no heart? Better the woodpile, the scolding of vinegar-faced housewives at back doors, the kindly spleen of bartenders behind provincial free-lunch counters, the amiable truculence of rural constables, the kicks, arrests, and happy-go-lucky chances of the other vulgar, loud, crude cities than this freezing heartlessness.

Raggles summoned his courage and sought alms from the populace. Unheeding, regardless, they passed on without the wink of an eyelash to testify that they were conscious of his existence. And then he said to himself that this fair but pitiless city of Manhattan was without a soul; that its inhabitants were mannikins moved by wires and springs, and that he was alone in a great wilderness.

Raggles started to cross the street. There was a blast, a roar, a hissing and a crash as something struck him and hurled him over and over six yards from where he had been. As he was coming down like the stick of a rocket the earth and all the cities thereof turned to a fractured dream.

Raggles opened his eyes. First an odor made itself known to him – an odor of the earliet spring flowers of Paradise. And then a hand soft as a falling petal touched his brow. Bending over him was the woman clothed like the princess of old, with blue eyes, now soft and humid with human sympathy. Under his head on the pavement were silks and furs. With Raggles's hat in his hand and with his face pinker than ever from a vehement outburst of oratory against reckless driving, stood the elderly gentleman who personified the city's wealth and ripeness. From a near-by café hurried the by-product with the vast jowl and baby complexion, bearing a glass full of crimson fluid that suggested delightful possibilities.

'Drink dis, sport,' said the by-product, holding the glass to Raggles's lips.

'Park on the River' – painting by William Glackens, *c.* 1902.

Hundreds of people huddled around in a moment, their faces wearing the deepest concern. Two flattering and gorgeous policemen got into the circle and pressed back the overplus of Samaritans. An old lady in a black shawl spoke loudly of camphor; a newsboy slipped one of his papers beneath Raggles's elbow, where it lay on the muddy pavement. A brisk young man with a notebook was asking for names.

A bell clanged importantly, and the ambulance cleaned a lane through the crowd. A cool surgeon slipped into the midst of affairs.

'How do you feel, old man?' asked the surgeon, stooping easily to his task. The princess of silks and satins wiped a red drop or two from Raggles's brow with a fragrant cobweb.

'Me!' said Raggles, with a seraphic smile. 'I feel fine.'

He had found the heart of his new city.

In three days they let him leave his cot for the convalescent ward in the hospital. He had been in there an hour when the attendants heard sounds of con-

'He had found the heart of his new city . . .'

flict. Upon investigation they found that Raggles had assaulted and damaged a brother convalescent – a glowering transient whom a freight train collision had sent in to be patched up.

'What's all this about?' inquired the head nurse.

'He was runnin' down me town,' said Raggles.

'What town?' asked the nurse.

'Noo York,' said Raggles.

LIST OF CONTRIBUTORS

ACKER, Kathy
  American novelist.
AI (Florence Antony)
  American poet.
ASCH, Sholem (1880-1950)
  Yiddish novelist and story writer, born in Eastern Europe, later
  resident in the United States and Western Europe.
ATKINSON, Brooks (1894-   )
  New York Times drama critic 1925-1960.
BAKER, Russell (1925-   )
  Columnist for the *New York Times* for over thirty years.
BALDWIN, James (1924-87)
  New York-born novelist and essayist.
BARZINI, Luigi
  Italian writer.
BEATON, Cecil (1904-80)
  English photographer, designer.
BEHAN, Brendan (1926-64)
  Irish playwright and novelist.
BELLOW, Saul (1915-   )
  Canadian-born, Chicago-reared novelist.
BERGER, Meyer (1889-1959)
  Journalist on the *New York Times* and the *New Yorker*.
BERMAN, Marshal
  Radical social and literary critic, born in the Bronx.
BIERCE, Ambrose (1842-1914?)
  American journalist, satirist, short-story writer.
BRECHT, Bertolt (1898-1956)
  German poet and playwright.
BRUCE, Lenny (1926-66)
  Comedian, satirist, born in Long Island.
BRYANT, William Cullen (1794-1878)
  Poet, editor of the *New York Evening Post* for over fifty years.
CAPOTE, Truman (1924-84)
  Southern-born novelist, essayist.
CHASE, W. Parker
  Psuedonymous author of *New York the Wonder City*.
CHESTERTON, G. K. (1874-1936)
  English novelist, essayist, poet.
COBDEN, Richard (1804-65)
  English politician, economist, reformer.
CONNOLLY, Cyril (1903-74)
  English critic, editor.
COOPER, James Fennimore (1789-1851)
  Novelist, travel writer, raised in Albany, later resident in New
  York City, first American novelist to gain fame in Europe.
CORSO, Gregory (1930-   )
  New York-born poet.
COWLEY, Malcolm (1898-   )
  American critic, editor, poet.
CRANE, Hart (1899-1932)
  Ohio-born poet.
CRANE, Stephen (1871-1900)
  American journalist and novelist.
DANCKAERTS, Jasper (17th century)
  Dutch traveller.
DELL, Floyd (1887-1969)
  Novelist, editor of *The Masses*.

DENBY, Edwin (1903-83)
  Poet, dance critic, long-time New Yorker.
DICKENS, Charles (1812-70)
  English novelist, visited New York in 1842.
DOS PASSOS, John (1896-1970)
  American novelist.
DREISER, Theodore (1871-1945)
  American novelist, worked as a journalist in New York.
DYLAN, Bob (1941-   )
  Singer and song-writer.
ELLISON, Ralph (1914-   )
  American novelist.
FITZGERALD, F. Scott (1896-1940)
  American novelist and story writer.
FRENEAU, Philip (1752-1832)
  New York-born poet, champion of the American Revolution.
GINSBERG, Allen (1926-   )
  American poet, raised in New Jersey.
GOLD, Michael (pseudonym of Irwin Granich) (1893-1967)
  Writer, critic, long-time columnist for the *Daily Worker*.
GORKI, Maxim (1868-1936)
  Russian novelist, playwright, social critic.
GRAY, Spalding (1941-   )
  Actor, monologist.
GRIESINGER, Karl Theodor (19th century)
  German writer.
HALPERN, Moshe Leib (1886-1932)
  Yiddish poet, long-time New York resident.
HENRY, O. (William Sydney Porter) (1862-1910)
  American short-story writer.
HOLLANDER, John (1929-   )
  New York-born poet and critic.
HONE, Phillip (1780-1851)
  New York businessman, conservative politician, diarist.
HOWELLS, William Dean (1837-1920)
  American novelist, social critic.
HUGHES, Langston (1902-67)
  Poet, story writer, long-time Harlem resident.
HUXTABLE, Ada Louise
  Architecture critic.
IRVING, Washington (1783-1859)
  New York-born critic, satirist, story-teller.
JACOBS, Jane (1916-   )
  American social critic.
JAMES, Henry (1843-1916)
  New York-born novelist, short-story writer, travel writer.
JOHNSON, James Weldon (1871-1938)
  Poet, educator, editor.
JONES, Leroi (Imamu Amiri Baraka) (1934-   )
  Poet and playwright, raised in Newark, New Jersey.
KAMINSKY, Max (1908-   )
  Jazz trumpeter.
KELLER, Helen (1880-1968)
  American writer.
KINNELL, Galway (1927-   )
  American poet.
KOOLHAAS, Rem
  Dutch writer.

LARDNER, Ring (1885-1933)
Satirist, novelist, sports correspondent.
LE CORBUSIER (Charles-Edouard Jeanneret) (1887-1965)
Swiss-born architect.
LEIBER, Jerry
Song writer.
LEIVICK H. (1888-1962)
Yiddish poet.
LEVERTOV, Denise (1923-)
English-born poet, resident in New York.
LIEBOWITZ, Fran
American humorist.
LORCA, Federico Garcia (1896-1936)
Spanish poet and dramatist, visited New York in 1929.
LOWELL, Robert (1917-77)
American poet.
MACDONALD, Dwight (1906-82)
New York-born social, literary, movie critic and editor.
McGINLEY, Phyllis (1905-78)
Poet, frequent contributor to the New Yorker
McKAY, Claude
Jamaican-born poet, novelist.
MAGUIRE, John (1815-72)
Irish politician, journlist, Member of Parliament.
MARQUIS, Don (1878-1973)
Humorist, poet, columnist for the New York Sun and Tribune.
MARRYAT, Frederick (1792-1848)
English naval officer, author of adventure novels.
MELVILLE, Herman (1819-91)
New York-born novelist, story writer, poet.
MENCKEN, H. L. (1880-1956)
Editor, journalist, critic.
MERRILL, James (1926-)
New York-born poet.
MILLAY, Edna St Vincent (1892-1950)
American poet, for many years resident in Greenwich Village.
MILLER, Henry (1891-1980)
New York-born novelist.
MILLER, John (1666-1728)
English military chaplain in New York.
MITCHELL, Joseph (1908-)
Writer, long-time contributor to the New Yorker.
MOORE, Marianne (1887-1972)
American poet.
MORLEY, Christopher (1890-1957)
Novelist, poet, essayist, columnist.
MUMFORD, Lewis (1895-)
Born on Long Island, social and architectural critic and writer.
NASH, Ogden (1902-71)
Humorous versifier.
NEWFIELD, Jack
New York-born journalist.
NORTH, Joseph (1904-)
Left-wing journalist, editor of New Masses.
O'HARA, Frank (1926-66)
Poet, art critic, a curator at the Museum of Modern Art.
OLMSTED, Frederick Law (1822-1903)
Writer and landscape architect, designer of Central, Prospect, Riverside, and Morningside Parks in New York.
PIETRI, Pedro (1944-)
Puerto Rican-born poet.
PINERO, Miguel
American poet.

REED, John (1887-1920)
American journalist, poet, revolutionary.
RICH, Adrienne (1929-)
American poet and feminist.
RICO, Noel
New York-born poet.
ROGERS, Will (1879-1935)
American humorist.
ROOSEVELT, Theodore (1858-1919)
New York-born writer, politician, President.
ROSTEN, Leo (1908-)
Novelist, critic, humorist.
ROTH, Henry (1906-)
Polish-born, New York-reared novelist.
RUSSELL, Ross
Jazz critic.
SARTRE, Jean-Paul (1905-82)
French novelist, philosopher, critic.
SCHWARTZ, Delmore (1913-66)
Brooklyn-born poet, critic, short-story writer.
SIMON, Kate
Travel writer, memoirist.
STOLLER, Mike
Song writer.
STONE, I. F. (1907-)
Independent radical journalist.
STRONG, George Templeton
New York lawyer, diarist.
TEASDALE, Sara (1884-1933)
American poet.
THOMAS, Piri
American novelist.
THOREAU, Henry (1817-62)
American poet, essayist, social critic.
TROLLOPE, Frances (1780-1863)
English travel writer, novelist.
TROTSKY, Leon (1879-1940)
Russian-born international revolutionary.
TWAIN, Mark (Samuel Clemens) (1935-1910)
American novelist, humorist.
VEGA, Bernardo
Puerto Rican-born political activist.
VERAZZANO, Giovanni da (c.1485-c.1528)
Florentine navigator.
WARHOL, Andy (c.1930-87)
American artist, film-maker.
WHITE, E. B. (1899-1987)
Essayist, critic, children's writer, contributor to the New Yorker.
WHITE, Edmund
American novelist, critic.
WHITMAN, Walt (1819-92)
American poet, born on Long Island, raised in Brooklyn, worked as a journalist in New York for many years.
WOLFE, Thomas (1900-38)
American novelist.
WOLFE, Tom (1931-)
American journalist.
WRIGHT, Frank Lloyd (1867-1959)
American architect, designer of the Guggenheim Museum.

BIBLIOGRAPHY

ACKER, Kathy, 'New York in 1979' (New York, 1979).

AI (Florence Antony), *Sin, poems* (Boston, 1986).

ASCH, Sholem, *East River,* translated by A. H. Gross (New York, 1946).

ATKINSON, Brooks, 'Savage Sunsets', *The New York Times* (New York, 1951).

BAKER, Russell, *So This is Depravity?* (New York, 1978).

BALDWIN, James, *Go Tell it on the Mountain* (New York, 1952) and Another Country (New York, 1962).

BARZINI, Luigi, *O America: A Memoir of the 1920s* (London, 1977).

BEATON, Cecil, *Cecil Beaton's New York* (London, 1938).

BEHAN, Brendan, *Brendan Behan's New York* (Boston, 1964).

BELLOW, Saul, *Mr. Sammler's Planet* (London, 1969).

BERGER, Meyer, *The Eight Million* (New York, 1942).

BERGER, Meyer, *Meyer Berger's New York* (New York, 1960).

BERMAN, Marshal, *All That is Solid Melts in the Air* (London, 1982).

BIERCE, Ambrose, *The Devil's Dictionary* (New York, 1911).

BRECHT, Bertolt, *Poems 1913-1956* (London, 1976).

BRUCE, Lenny, *How to Talk Dirty and Influence People* (New York, 1965).

BRYANT, William Cullen, *Poems* (London, 1874).

BRYANT, William Cullen, *Orations and Addresses* (London, 1873).

CAPOTE, Truman, *Local Color* (New York, 1950).

CHASE, W. Parker, *New York, The Wonder City* (New York, 1983).

CHESTERTON, G. K., *What I Saw in America* (London, 1922).

COBDEN, Richard, *The American Diaries of Richard Cobden,* edited by Elizabeth Cawley (Princeton, 1952).

CONNOLLY, Cyril, *Ideas and Places* (London, 1953).

COOPER, James Fenimore, *Notions of the Americans* (New York, 1828).

CORSO, Gregory, *Long Live Man* (London, 1962).

COWLEY, Malcolm, *Exile's Return* (New York, 1951).

CRANE, Hart, *The Complete Poems and Selected Letters and Prose* (New York, 1966).

CRANE, Stephen, *The New York City Sketches,* edited by R. W. Stallman and E. R. Hagerman (New York, 1966).

DANCKAERTS, Jasper, *New York and its Vicinity,* translated by Henry C. Murphy (New York, 1867).

DELL, Floyd, *Love in Greenwich Village* (New York, 1926).

DENBY, Edwin, *Poems.*

DICKENS, Charles, *American Notes* (London, 1842).

DOS PASSOS, John, *Manhattan Transfer* (London, 1925).

DREISER, Theodore, *The Color of a Great City* (New York, 1923).

DYLAN, Bob, *Lyrics, 1962-1985* (London, 1987).

ELLISON, Ralph, *Invisible Man* (New York, 1952).

FITZGERALD, F. Scott, *The Great Gatsby* (London, 1925).

FRENEAU, Philip, *Poems* (New York, 1860).

GINSBERG, Allen, *Mind Breaths, Poems, 1972-1977* (San Francisco, 1977).

GOLD, Michael, *Jews Without Money* (New York, 1930).

GORKI, Maxim, *The City of the Yellow Devil* (Moscow, 1972).

GRAY, Spalding, *Sex and Death to the Age 14* (New York, 1986).

GRIESINGER, Karl Theodor, 'Kleindeutschland' (newspaper article) (Berlin, 1863).

HENRY, O., *The Complete Works* (New York, 1953).

HOLLANDER, John, *Visions from the Ramble* (New York, 1965).

HOLLANDER, John, *Town and Country Matters,* (Boston, 1972).

HONE, Philip, *The Diary of Philip Hone 1828-1851* (New York, 1889).

HOWE, Irving and GREENBERG, Eliezer (editors), *A Treasury of Yiddish Poetry* (for Leivick, Halpern) (New York, 1969).

HOWELLS, William Dean, *A Hazard of New Fortunes* (New York, 1890).

HUGHES, Langston, *The Big Sea* (New York, 1940) and *Selected Poems* (New York, 1959).

HUXTABLE, Ada Louise, *Will They Ever Finish Bruckner Boulevard?* (New York, 1970).

IRVING, Washington, *A History of New York* (New York, 1809).

JACOBS, Jane, *The Death and Life of Great American Cities* (London, 1961).

JAMES, Henry, *The American Scene* (London, 1907).

JOHNSON, James Weldon, *Black Manhattan* (New York, 1930).

JOHNSON, James Weldon, *Fifty Years and Other Poems* (New York, 1917).

JONES, Leroi, *The Autobiography of Leroi Jones/Amiri Baraka* (New York, 1984).

KAMINSKY, Max, *Jazz Band* (New York).

KELLER, Helen, *Midstream* (New York, 1929).

KINNELL, Galway, *The Avenue Bearing the Initial of Christ into the New World, Poems, 1946-1964* (Boston, 1974).
KOOLHAAS, Rem, *Delirious New York: A Retroactive Manifesto for Manhattan* (London, 1978).
LARDNER, Ring, *You Know Me Al* (New York, 1916).
LE CORBUSIER, *When the Cathedrals Were White,* translated by F. E. Hyslop (London, 1948).
LEIBER, Jerry and STOLLER, Mike, 'On Broadway', Screen Gems-EMI Music.
LEIBER, Jerry and SPECTOR, Phil, 'Spanish Harlem,' Carlin Music Corporation, London.
LEVERTOV, Denise, *With Eyes at the Backs of Our Heads* (New York, 1960).
LEIBOWITZ, Fran, *Metropolitan Life* (New York, 1983).
LORCA, Federico Garcia, *Deep Song and Other Prose* (London, 1980).
LOWELL, Robert, *Near the Ocean* (London, 1967).
McGINLEY, Phyllis, 'A Kind of Love Letter to New York', *The New Yorker,* (New York, 1948).
McKAY, Claude, *The Selected Poems of Claude McKay* (New York, 1953).
MAGUIRE, John, *The Irish in America* (London, 1868).
MARQUIS, Don, *The Lives of Archy and Mehitable* (London).
MARRYAT, Frederick, *Diary in America* (London, 1839).
MELVILLE, Herman, *Moby Dick* (New York, 1851).
MELVILLE, Herman, *Battle-Pieces* (New York, 1866).
MENCKEN, H. L., *Prejudices, Fifth Series* (London, 1926).
MENCKEN, H. L., *Prejudices, Sixth Series* (London, 1927).
MERRILL, James, *Water Street* (New York, 1962).
MILLAY, Edna St Vincent, *A Few Figs from Thistles* (New York, 1920).
MILLER, Henry, *Sexus* (New York, 1946).
MILLER, John, *New York Considered and Improved, 1695,* with introduction by V. H. Paltsias (Cleveland, 1903).
MITCHELL, Joseph, *Old Mr. Flood* (New York, 1948).
MITCHELL, Joseph, *The Bottom of the Harbor* (New York, 1959).
MOORE, Marianne, *Complete Poems* (London, 1968).
MORLEY, Christopher, *A Selection from the Writings of Christopher Morley* (New York, 1944).
MUMFORD, Lewis, *From the Ground Up* (New York, 1955).
MUMFORD, Lewis, 'America and Alfred Stieglitz' (New York, 1934).
NASH, Ogden, *Good Intentions* (New York, 1942).
NEWFIELD, Jack and OBRUL, Paul, *The Abuse of Power* (New York, 1977).
NORTH, Joseph (editor), *New Masses: An Anthology of the Rebel Thirties* (New York).
O'HARA, Frank, *The Selected Poems of Frank O'Hara* (New York, 1974).
OLMSTED, Frederick Law, jr. and KIMBALL, Theodora, *Frederick Law Olmsted: Landscape Architect* (New York, 1970).
PIETRI, Pedro, *Puerto Rican Obituary* (New York, 1973).
REED, John, *The Day in Bohemia* (New York, 1913).
REVISTA Chicano-Riquena, *A Decade of Hispanic Literature* (Houston, 1982).
RICH, Adrienne, *The Dream of a Common Language: Poems 1974-1977* (New York, 1978).
ROOSEVELT, Theodore, *New York* (New York, 1903).
ROSTEN, Leo, *The Joys of Yiddish* (New York, 1968).
ROTH, Henry, *Call it Sleep* (New York, 1934).
RUSSELL, Ross, *Bird Lives! The High Life and Hard Times of Charlie 'Yardbird' Parker* (London, 1973).
SARTRE, Jean-Paul, 'Manhattan: The Great American Desert' (1946).
SCHWARTZ, Delmore, *What Is To Be Given* (Manchester, 1976).
SIMON, Kate, *New York: Places and Pleasures* (New York, 1971).
STONE, I. F., *The Truman Era* (New York).
STRONG, George Templeton, *The Diary of George Templeton Strong, 1835-75,* edited by Allan Nevins and Milton Halsey Thomas (New York, 1952).
TEASDALE, Sara, 'Union Square' (New York).
THOMAS, Piri, *Down These Mean Streets* (New York, 1967).
THOREAU, Henry, *Letters.*
TROLLOPE, Frances, *Domestic Manners of the Americans* (London, 1832).
TROTSKY, Leon, *My Life* (New York, 1970).
TWAIN, Mark, *Mark Twain's Travels With Mr. Brown* (New York, 1867).
VEGA, Bernardo, *The Memoirs of Bernardo Vega,* edited by Cesar Andrea Iglesias (New York, 1984).
VERAZZANO, Giovanni da, 'Report to Francois I', Long Island Histrocial Society (New York, 1890).
WARHOL, Andy, *Popism: Andy Warhol's History of the Sixties* (New York, 1980).
WHITE, E. B., *Here is New York* (New York, 1949).
WHITE, Edmund, *States of Desire: Travels in Gay America.*
WHITMAN, Walt, *Leaves of Grass* (New York, 1882).
WHITMAN, Walt, *Specimen Days* (New York, 1882).
WOLFE, Thomas, *Of Time and the River* (New York, 1935).
WOLFE, Tom, *In Our Time* (New York, 1980).
WRIGHT, Frank Lloyd, *The Disappearing City* (New York, 1932).

ACKNOWLEDGMENTS

The publisher thanks the following photographers and organizations for their permission to reproduce the photographs in this book:

2 Collection of Whitney Museum of American Art. 78.17. Purchase, with funds from Mrs William A Marsteller; **4** Francisco Hidalgo; **9** Archives Snark/Milwaukee Ark Museum; **11** Musée Bartholdi, Colmar, France; **12** Philadelphia Museum of Art. Given by Carl Zigrosser; **14** Associated American Artists; **17** John Hillelson Agency; **21** The Brooklyn Museum. 97.13. Gift of the Brooklyn Institute of Arts and Sciences; **22** Mary Evans Picture Library; **23** Lauros-Giraudon (Bibliotèque Nationale); **24** Museum of the City of New York; **27** Bridgeman Art Library; **28** Popperfoto; **30** Topham Picture Library; **32** The Brooklyn Museum. 63.160.3. Dick S. Ramsay Fund; **34** Bibliotèque Nationale; **36** The Brooklyn Museum. 40.339. Gift of the Borough of Brooklyn; **38** International Museum of Photography at George Eastman House; **41** Associated American Artists; **43** Archives Snark; **44** The Keystone Collection; **46** Magnum Photos; **47** Magnum Photos; **48** courtesy Janet Marqusee Fine Arts; **51** Harper's Weekly; **54** from Thomas Nast Cartoons & Illustrations by Dover Books; **55** Associated American Artists; **56** The Butler Institute of American Art, Youngstown, Ohio. Gift of Louis Held; **59** The Bridgeman Art Library; **61** Commerce Graphics Ltd, Inc; **62, 64** Associated American Artists; **66** Magnum Photos; **69** Janine Wiedel; **71** courtesy of Marlborough Gallery; **73** Georgia Museum of Art, The University of Georgia. University Purchase GMOA 76.3449; **74** Associated American Artists; **76** Mary Evans Picture Library; **77** Dan Budnik/John Hillelson Agency; **78** James Morgan; **79** Harper's Weekly; **81** The Brooklyn Museum 67.205.1 A Augustus Healy Fund (B); **83** Popperfoto; **84** Edward Hausner/John Hillelson Agency; **87** Associated American Artists; **89** Collection of Whitney Museum of American Art 33.9; **90** Collection of Whitney Museum of American Art 69.97k; **92** Bibliotèque Nationale; **95** Frank Monaco/Rex Features; **97** Magnum Photos; **99** Worcester Art Museum, Worcester, Massachusetts; **101, 102** Archives Snark; **105** Rex Features; **106** Magnum Photos; **108** Topham Picture Library; **110** Collection of Whitney Museum of American Art. Juliana Force Purchase; **112** Museum of the City of New York; **113** Philadelphia Museum of Art: Purchased: The Harrison Fund; **114** Popperfoto, **116** courtesy Janet Marqusee Fine Arts; **117** Janine Wiedel; **119** Yale University Art Gallery. Gift of Mrs Reginald Marsh; **121** Hirschl & Adler Galleries; **122** Associated American Artists; **123** John Hillelson Agency; **125** Topham Picture Library; **126** courtesy of Kennedy Galleries Inc, New York; **129** BBC Hulton Picture Library; **131, 133** Culver Pictures Inc, **134** John Hillelson Agency; **137** Popperfoto; **138** Collection of Whitney Museum of American Art 36.153; **141** Associated American Artists; **142** Collection of Whitney Museum of American Art, New York 77.74; **143** © 1988 The Detroit Institute of Arts, Founders Society Purchase, Mr and Mrs Walter Buhl Ford, II Fund; **145** Popperfoto; **146** Associated American Artists; **150** Magnum Photos; **151** The Brooklyn Museum. 62.68. Dick S. Ramsay Fund; **152** Rex Features; **154** Associated American Artists; **156** John Hillelson Agency; **158** The Mansell Collection; **159** Collection of The Newark Museum. Purchased 1937, Felix Fuld Bequest Fund; **160** Popperfoto; **161** Hirschl & Adler Galleries; **163, 164, 167** Associated American Artists; **169** Janine Wiedel; **171** National Gallery of Art, Washington. Gift of Helen Farr Sloan; **172** Associated American Artists; **175** Commerce Graphics Ltd, Inc; **181** Associated American Artists; **183** The Brooklyn Museum 41.1085. Dick S. Ramsay Fund; **184** Francisco Hidalgo.

The publisher thanks the following for their permission to publish the extracts listed. While we have made every effort to contact all the relevant people and organizations, we regret that at the time of going to press we are unable to publish all their names. We apologize to those concerned.

11 *Call It Sleep* by Henry Roth, reprinted by permission of Penguin Books Ltd & Cooper Square, Inc; **16, 128** *The Big Sea* by Langston Hughes, reprinted by permission of Pluto Press; **17** *Invisible Man* by Ralph Ellison, reprinted by permission of Random House, Inc; **18** *In Our Time* by Tom Wolfe, reprinted by permission of Farrar Straus & Giroux, Inc; **26, 33** *Meyer Berger's New York*, reprinted by permission of Curtis Brown, Ltd; **31, 102** *What Is To Be Given* by Delmore Schwartz (1976), reprinted by permission of Carcanet Press Ltd, & New Directions, Inc; **32, 63, 102, 133** *Selected Writings* by Truman Capote, reprinted by permission of Random House, Inc; **35, 88, 113** *Here Is New York* by E. B. White, reprinted by permission of the Estate of E. B. White; **35** *Collected Earlier Poems 1940-60*. Copyright © 1958 by Denise Levertov Goodman. Reprinted by permission of New Directions Publishing Corporation; **39** *A Few Figs From Thistles* by Edna St Vincent Millay, reprinted by permission of the Estate of Edna St Vincent Millay; **41, 123** *A Treasury of Yiddish Poetry* ed Irving Howe & Eliezer Greenburg, reprinted by permission of Holt Reinhart and Winston; **44** *Black Manhattan* by James Weldon Johnson, reprinted by permission of Charles Scribner's Sons; **47, 89** *The Joys of Yiddish* by Leo Rosten, reprinted by permission of McGraw-Hill Books; **61** *Sexus* by Henry Miller, reprinted by permission of John Calder Ltd; **63** *The Bottom of the Harbor* by Joseph Mitchell, reprinted by permission of Little, Brown & Co; **64, 91** *The Eight Million* by Meyer Berger, reprinted by permission of Curtis Brown Ltd; **65** *The Death and Life of Great American Cities* by Jane Jacobs, reprinted by permission of Random House, Inc, & Jonathan Cape Ltd; **67** *Down These Mean Streets* by Piri Thomas, reprinted by permission of Random House, Inc; **74, 127, 173** *Prejudices, Sixth Series* by H. L. Mencken, reprinted by permission of Alfred A. Knopf, Inc; **77** *Poems 1913-56* by Bertolt Brecht, translated by Frank Jellinek, reprinted by permission of Methuen, London; **82** *Good Intentions* by Ogden Nash, reprinted by permission of Little, Brown & Co; **85** *Prejudices, Fifth Series* by H. L. Mencken, reprinted by permission of Alfred A. Knopf, Inc; **93** *Long Live Man* by Gregory Corso, copyright © 1962 by New

Directions Publishing Corp.; **93, 143** *Popism* by Andy Warhol, reprinted by permission of Harcourt Brace Jovanovich, Inc; **103, 125** *Montage of a Dream Deferred* by Langston Hughes, reprinted by permission of Alfred A. Knopf, Inc & David Higham Associates; **104** *Lyrics 1962-85* by Bob Dylan, reprinted by permission of Alfred A. Knopf, Inc; **106** *Collected Poems 1947-80* by Allen Ginsberg (Harper & Row, Inc, 1984; Viking Books, 1985), copyright © Allen Ginsberg, 1984, reprinted by permission of Harper & Row, Inc, & Penguin Books Ltd; **113** *Cecil Beaton's New York*, 1938, published by B T Batsford Ltd, London, quoted with the publisher's permission; **120** *The Great Gatsby* by F. Scott Fitzgerald, copyright 1925 Charles Scribner's Sons, copyright renewed 1953 Frances Scott Fitzgerald Lanahan. Reprinted by permission of Charles Scribner's Sons, an imprint of Macmillan Publishing Company, & The Bodley Head; **121** *Archy Does His Part* by Don Marquis, reprinted by permission of Faber & Faber Ltd, & Doubleday & Company,

Inc; **130** *Bird Lives* by Ross Russell, reprinted by permission of Quartet Books Ltd; **139** *Exile's Return* by Malcolm Cowley, copyright 1951, renewed © 1979 by Malcolm Cowley. All rights reserved. Reprinted by permission of Viking Penguin, Inc; **156** *Near the Ocean* by Robert Lowell, reprinted by permission of Faber & Faber Ltd, & Farrer Straus & Giroux, Inc; **168** *The Complete Poems of Marianne Moore*, by permission of Faber & Faber Ltd, & Viking Penguin Inc; **168** *Delirious New York: A Retroactive Manifesto for New York* by Rem Koolhaas, reprinted by permission of Thames & Hudson Ltd. **53, 75** *Manhattan Transfer* by John Dos Passos, by permission Elizabeth Dos Passos; **82** *All That is Solid Melts into Air* by Marshall Berman, by permission Simon & Schuster, & Verso; **103** *What a Kingdom it Was* by Galway Kinnell. Copyright © 1960 by Galway Kinnell, by permission Houghton Mifflin Company; **137** *Sin* by Ai. Copyright © 1986 by Ai, by permission Houghton Mifflin Company.

INDEX

Page numbers in *italic* refer to the illustrations